May 1988

# PRIMARY COMMODITIES
## Market Developments and Outlook
By the Commodities Division
of the Research Department

INTERNATIONAL MONETARY FUND • WASHINGTON, D.C.

# World Economic and Financial Surveys

April 1986    World Economic Outlook: A Survey by the Staff of the International Monetary Fund.

May 1986    Primary Commodities: Market Developments and Outlook, by the Commodities Division of the Research Department.

July 1986    Staff Studies for the World Economic Outlook, by the Research Department of the International Monetary Fund.

July 1986    Export Credits: Developments and Prospects, by Eduard Brau, K. Burke Dillon, Chanpen Puckahtikom, and Miranda Xafa.

October 1986    World Economic Outlook: Revised Projections, by the Staff of the International Monetary Fund.

December 1986    International Capital Markets: Developments and Prospects, by Maxwell Watson, Russell Kincaid, Caroline Atkinson, Eliot Kalter, and David Folkerts-Landau.

February 1987    Recent Experience with Multilateral Official Debt Rescheduling, by K. Burke Dillon and Gumersindo Oliveros.

April 1987    World Economic Outlook: A Survey by the Staff of the International Monetary Fund.

May 1987    Primary Commodities: Market Developments and Outlook, by the Commodities Division of the Research Department.

August 1987    Staff Studies for the World Economic Outlook, by the Research Department of the International Monetary Fund.

October 1987    World Economic Outlook: Revised Projections, by the Staff of the International Monetary Fund.

January 1988    International Capital Markets: Developments and Prospects, by Maxwell Watson, Donald Mathieson, Russell Kincaid, David Folkerts-Landau, Klaus Regling, and Caroline Atkinson.

February 1988    Officially Supported Export Credits: Developments and Prospects, by K. Burke Dillon and Luis Duran-Downing, with Miranda Xafa.

April 1988    World Economic Outlook: A Survey by the Staff of the International Monetary Fund.

May 1988    Primary Commodities: Market Developments and Outlook, by the Commodities Division of the Research Department.

WORLD ECONOMIC AND FINANCIAL SURVEYS

May 1988

# PRIMARY COMMODITIES

## Market Developments and Outlook

By the Commodities Division
of the Research Department

INTERNATIONAL MONETARY FUND • WASHINGTON, D.C.

**Cataloging-in-Publication Data**

Primary commodities: market developments and outlook/by the
Commodities Division of the Research Department.
    p.     cm. — (World economic and financial surveys,
  ISSN 0258-7440)
  "May 1988."
  ISBN 1-557-75015-7
  1. Commercial products.    2. Raw materials.
I. International Monetary Fund. Commodities Division.
II. Series.
HF1040.7.P718   1988
382′.4—dc19                                     88-15625
                                                CIP

Serial ISSN 0891-8805

Price: US$10.00
(US$6.00 university libraries, faculty members, and students)

Address orders to:
External Relations Department, Publication Services
International Monetary Fund, Washington, D.C. 20431

# Contents

|  |  | *Page* |
|---|---|---|
| **Preface** |  |  |
|  |  |  |
| **Section I.   Commodity Market Developments and Prospects** |  | **1** |
| Commodity Prices in 1987 |  | 1 |
| Commodity Price Changes and Aggregate Inflation |  | 4 |
| Export Earnings from Commodities in 1987 |  | 6 |
| Commodity Trade Negotiations and International Cooperation in 1987 |  | 7 |
| Outlook for Commodity Prices in 1988 and for the Medium Term |  | 10 |
|  |  |  |
| **Section II.   Food Commodities** |  | **12** |
| Cereals |  | 12 |
| Wheat |  | 16 |
| Maize |  | 19 |
| Rice |  | 21 |
| Vegetable Oils and Protein Meals |  | 24 |
| Soybeans and Soybean Products |  | 31 |
| Palm Oil |  | 33 |
| Coconut Oil |  | 35 |
| Groundnuts and Groundnut Oil |  | 36 |
| Rapeseed Oil |  | 37 |
| Sunflowerseed Oil |  | 39 |
| Fish Meal |  | 40 |
| Meat |  | 41 |
| Beef |  | 41 |
| Lamb |  | 42 |
| Sugar |  | 43 |
| Bananas |  | 50 |
|  |  |  |
| **Section III.   Beverages** |  | **52** |
| Coffee |  | 52 |
| Tea |  | 57 |
| Cocoa |  | 59 |
|  |  |  |
| **Section IV.   Agricultural Raw Materials** |  | **63** |
| Hardwood |  | 63 |
| Tobacco |  | 66 |
| Natural Rubber |  | 69 |
| Cotton |  | 71 |
| Wool |  | 74 |
| Jute |  | 75 |
| Sisal |  | 76 |
| Hides |  | 77 |

*Page*

**Section V. Minerals and Metals**     **78**
    Copper     81
    Aluminum     85
    Iron Ore     87
    Tin     89
    Nickel     92
    Zinc     93
    Lead     94
    Phosphate Rock     96

**Tables**

**Section**

I.
    1. Commodity Prices, 1970–88     2
    2. Movements in Commodity Prices and Related Economic Indicators, 1980–87     3
    3. Prices for Groups of Commodities, 1980–88     5
    4. Prices for Commodity Exports of Industrial Countries and of Developing Countries, 1980–88     5
    5. Export Earnings from Major Commodities, 1984–87     7
    6. Aggregate Earnings, Volumes, and Unit Values for Major Commodity Exports of Industrial Countries and of Developing Countries, 1980–87     8
    7. Developing Countries: Export Earnings by Volume and Unit Value, 1980–87     9

II.
    8. Movements in the Prices of Food Commodities and Related Economic Indicators, 1980–87     13
    9. Prices of Cereals, 1979–88     14
    10. Cereals: World Supply and Utilization, 1960/61–87/88     15
    11. Wheat: World Commodity Balance, 1981/82–87/88     16
    12. Wheat: Export Earnings, 1984–87     18
    13. Maize: World Commodity Balance, 1981/82–87/88     20
    14. Maize: Export Earnings, 1984–87     22
    15. Rice: World Commodity Balance, 1981/82–87/88     23
    16. Rice: Export Earnings, 1984–87     24
    17. Prices of Vegetable Oils and Protein Meals, 1979–88     25
    18. Major Oilseeds (Oil Equivalent): World Commodity Balance, 1981/82–87/88     26
    19. Major Oilseeds (Meal Equivalent): World Commodity Balance, 1981/82–87/88     27
    20. Soybeans: Export Earnings, 1984–87     29
    21. Soybean Oil: Export Earnings, 1984–87     29
    22. Soybean Meal: Export Earnings, 1984–87     30
    23. Palm Oil: Export Earnings, 1984–87     30
    24. Soybeans: World Commodity Balance, 1981/82–87/88     31
    25. Soybean Meal: World Commodity Balance, 1981/82–87/88     32
    26. Soybean Oil: World Commodity Balance, 1981/82–87/88     33
    27. Palm Oil: World Commodity Balance, 1981/82–87/88     34
    28. Rapeseed: World Commodity Balance, 1981/82–87/88     37
    29. Rapeseed Oil: World Commodity Balance, 1981/82–87/88     38
    30. Rapeseed Meal: World Commodity Balance, 1981/82–87/88     38
    31. Prices of Beef and Lamb, 1979–88     41
    32. Prices of Sugar, 1979–88     44
    33. Sugar: World Commodity Balance, 1981/82–87/88     45

*Page*

|  | 34. U.S. Sugar Quota Allocations by Country, 1982/83–87 | 46 |
|  | 35. European Community Sugar Quota Allocations by Country, 1981/82–87/88 | 47 |
|  | 36. Sugar: World Trade, 1984–87 | 49 |
|  | 37. Bananas: Prices in Selected Markets, 1985–87 | 51 |
| III. | 38. Prices of Beverages, 1979–88 | 53 |
|  | 39. Movements in the Prices of Beverages and Related Economic Indicators, 1980–87 | 54 |
|  | 40. Coffee: World Commodity Balance, 1981/82–87/88 | 55 |
|  | 41. Coffee: Export Earnings, 1984–87 | 58 |
|  | 42. Tea: World Commodity Balance, 1981–87 | 58 |
|  | 43. Tea: Export Earnings, 1984–87 | 60 |
|  | 44. Cocoa Beans: World Commodity Balance, 1981/82–87/88 | 62 |
|  | 45. Cocoa: Export Earnings, 1984–87 | 62 |
| IV. | 46. Prices of Agricultural Raw Materials, 1979–88 | 64 |
|  | 47. Movements in Prices of Agricultural Raw Materials and Related Economic Indicators, 1980–87 | 66 |
|  | 48. Hardwood Logs and Sawnwood: World Production, 1981–87 | 67 |
|  | 49. Hardwood Logs and Sawnwood: Export Earnings, 1984–87 | 67 |
|  | 50. Tobacco: World Leaf Production, 1981–87 | 68 |
|  | 51. Tobacco: Export Earnings, 1984–87 | 68 |
|  | 52. Natural Rubber: World Commodity Balance, 1981–87 | 71 |
|  | 53. Natural Rubber: Export Earnings, 1984–87 | 71 |
|  | 54. Cotton: World Commodity Balance, 1981/82–87/88 | 73 |
|  | 55. Cotton: Export Earnings, 1984–87 | 75 |
| V. | 56. Prices of Minerals and Metals, 1979–88 | 79 |
|  | 57. Movements in Prices of Minerals and Metals and Related Economic Indicators, 1980–87 | 80 |
|  | 58. Reported Closing World Commercial Stocks of Selected Metals, 1973–87 | 81 |
|  | 59. Copper: World Commodity Balance, 1981–87 | 82 |
|  | 60. Copper: Export Earnings, 1984–87 | 84 |
|  | 61. Aluminum: World Commodity Balance, 1981–87 | 86 |
|  | 62. Aluminum: Export Earnings, 1984–87 | 87 |
|  | 63. Iron Ore: World Commodity Balance Together with Production of Pig Iron and Steel, 1981–87 | 88 |
|  | 64. Iron Ore: Export Earnings, 1984–87 | 89 |
|  | 65. Tin: World Commodity Balance, 1981–87 | 91 |
|  | 66. Tin: Export Earnings, 1984–87 | 92 |
|  | 67. Nickel: World Commodity Balance, 1981–87 | 93 |
|  | 68. Zinc: World Commodity Balance, 1981–87 | 94 |
|  | 69. Lead: World Commodity Balance, 1981–87 | 95 |
|  | 70. Phosphate Rock and Products: World Production, Exports, and Market Prices, 1980–87 | 97 |

## Charts

**Section**

| I. | 1. Non-Fuel Primary Commodity Prices, 1980–87 | 2 |
|  | 2. Commodity Prices in Real Terms and Beginning Stocks Measured in Months of Consumption, 1980–88 | 4 |
|  | 3. Commodity Price Changes and Aggregate Inflation Trends in the Major Industrial Countries, 1980–87 | 6 |

# CONTENTS

| | | *Page* |
|---|---|---|
| **II.** | 4. Prices of Food Commodities, 1980–87 | 12 |
| **III.** | 5. Prices of Beverages, 1980–87 | 52 |
| **IV.** | 6. Prices of Agricultural Raw Materials, 1980–87 | 65 |
| **V.** | 7. Prices of Minerals and Metals, 1980–87 | 78 |

The following symbols have been used throughout this paper:

...    to indicate that data are not available;

—    to indicate that the figure is zero or less than half the final digit shown, or that the item does not exist;

–    between years or months (e.g., 1984–85 or January–June) to indicate the years or months covered, including the beginning and ending years or months;

/    between years (e.g., 1985/86) to indicate a crop or fiscal (financial) year.

"Billion" means a thousand million.

Minor discrepancies between constituent figures and totals are due to rounding.

# Preface

This study provides an analysis of recent developments relating to the major non-fuel primary commodities (hereafter referred to as commodities) traded in international markets. Particular attention is given to market price movements and the factors underlying these movements. At the beginning of 1987 the world index of non-fuel primary commodity prices stood at its lowest level since 1973. By the end of 1987, however, commodity prices had risen by nearly 30 percent from the final quarter of 1986 in U.S. dollar terms and were about 15 percent higher in SDR terms. Movements in the aggregate price index, however, masked a marked difference in the price movements for most agricultural raw materials and metals, on the one hand, and those for most food commodities and beverages, on the other. For agricultural materials and metals, large price increases were recorded during 1987, while only small increases were recorded for food commodities, and the prices of beverages fell. By early 1988 the upswing in commodity prices appeared to have lost much of its force. Nevertheless, although dollar prices of some

individual commodities are projected to decline from their end-1987 levels, the average of the aggregate price index for 1988 as a whole is expected to be about 10 percent above the 1987 average.

The study has been prepared by the staff of the Commodities Division of the Research Department under the direction of Nihad Kaibni, Division Chief. The study has benefited from comments by other Fund staff members and from the editing by David Driscoll of the Editorial Division, External Relations Department. The analyses undertaken and the projections made are those of the authors and do not necessarily represent the views of the Fund. The study is based on information available through March 1988.

It should be noted that the term "country" used in this document does not in all cases refer to a territorial entity that is a state as understood by international law and practice. The term also covers some territorial entities that are not states but for which statistical data are maintained and provided internationally on a separate and independent basis.

# I

# Commodity Market Developments and Prospects

Commodity prices experienced a strong recovery during 1987, after the steep decline of 1984–86. By December 1987 the Fund's index of non-oil commodity prices was about 15 percent above the level of a year earlier in terms of SDRs, and some 30 percent higher in terms of the depreciating U.S. dollar. All commodity groups shared in the recovery, but the greatest strength came in agricultural raw materials and metals. The surge in prices of industrial inputs can be attributed to the pick-up in economic activity in industrial countries under conditions of relatively depleted levels of stocks of these commodities, following several years of production cutbacks owing to low prices. The recovery in food prices was less marked than that of industrial inputs, in part because of historically high levels of inventories at the beginning of the year. The recovery in prices of tropical beverages, which are particularly important in the exports of many developing countries, was both relatively weak and significantly delayed, occurring only in the second half of the year.

Reflecting these various price developments, the export earnings of developing countries have begun to increase, though they have not benefited as much from the upsurge in commodity prices as have those of industrial countries. In real terms (i.e., relative to export prices of manufactures) prices of commodities exported by developing countries in December 1987 remained 20 percent below the average level of prices during 1980–84.

In the final quarter of 1987, following the global stock market crisis in mid-October, commodity prices, particularly those of industrial inputs, exhibited increased volatility and a weaker trend largely because of increased uncertainty about the sustainability of economic growth. In the early months of 1988, commodity prices held fairly steady, perhaps reflecting a better balance between demand and supply, including an expected moderation in the marked stock depletion that had continued for much of 1987. Assuming that

moderate growth continues in industrial countries, and that no major supply disruptions occur, the level of real commodity prices is projected to stabilize at about the current level and to remain roughly unchanged through the medium term. If this projection is borne out by actual developments, the recent recovery of commodity prices is unlikely to be reflected in any significant increase in underlying inflation rates.

A number of adjustments in the international trading environment in which commodity prices are determined occurred in 1987, and even more significant changes are expected in the years ahead. Some of the adjustments in the past year affected only bilateral trading arrangements, while others, such as certain initiatives undertaken in the Uruguay Round of the General Agreement on Tariffs and Trade (GATT) negotiations and those relating to some international commodity agreements were of a multilateral nature.

The remainder of this section provides an overview of these developments, while Sections II through V deal with individual commodities. Section II covers food commodities, Section III beverages, Section IV agricultural raw materials, and Section V minerals and metals. The study is based on information through February 1988.

## Commodity Prices in 1987

At the outset of 1987 the world index of prices of non-fuel primary commodities stood at its lowest level in nominal terms since the mid-1970s (Table 1). In terms of SDRs, the index was about 30 percent below the last cyclical peak in 1984 and about 20 percent below the last cyclical trough in 1982.[1] Commodity

---

[1] In this discussion the measurement of prices is given in terms of SDRs unless indicated otherwise. The SDR provides a more stable measure of value than the more commonly used measure, the U.S. dollar, particularly during periods such as the 1980s in which there have been large movements in the exchange value of

**Table 1. Commodity Prices, 1970–88**

(Indices: 1980 = 100)

| Years | Nominal Commodity Prices | | | | | | Real Commodity Prices[1] |
| | In SDRs | In U.S. dollars | In pounds sterling | In deutsche mark | In French francs | In Japanese yen | |
| --- | --- | --- | --- | --- | --- | --- | --- |
| 1970 | 48 | 37 | 36 | 75 | 49 | 59 | 106 |
| 1971 | 47 | 36 | 35 | 69 | 47 | 56 | 99 |
| 1972 | 47 | 39 | 36 | 68 | 46 | 52 | 98 |
| 1973 | 69 | 63 | 60 | 93 | 67 | 76 | 135 |
| 1974 | 83 | 76 | 76 | 109 | 87 | 98 | 137 |
| 1975 | 69 | 64 | 67 | 87 | 65 | 84 | 101 |
| 1976 | 78 | 69 | 90 | 96 | 78 | 91 | 109 |
| 1977 | 86 | 77 | 102 | 98 | 89 | 91 | 111 |
| 1978 | 81 | 78 | 94 | 86 | 83 | 72 | 98 |
| 1979 | 95 | 95 | 104 | 95 | 95 | 91 | 104 |
| 1980 | 100 | 100 | 100 | 100 | 100 | 100 | 100 |
| 1981 | 99 | 90 | 104 | 112 | 116 | 88 | 94 |
| 1982 | 95 | 81 | 107 | 108 | 125 | 89 | 86 |
| 1983 | 104 | 86 | 131 | 120 | 154 | 90 | 94 |
| 1984 | 111 | 88 | 152 | 137 | 181 | 92 | 99 |
| 1985 | 98 | 76 | 138 | 124 | 162 | 80 | 85 |
| 1986 | 81 | 73 | 116 | 88 | 120 | 55 | 69 |
| 1987 | 80 | 79 | 113 | 78 | 113 | 51 | 67 |
| 1986 I | 90 | 78 | 126 | 100 | 133 | 64 | 77 |
| II | 84 | 75 | 115 | 92 | 126 | 56 | 72 |
| III | 76 | 70 | 109 | 80 | 112 | 48 | 65 |
| IV | 76 | 70 | 115 | 78 | 110 | 50 | 64 |
| 1987 I | 74 | 72 | 108 | 73 | 104 | 49 | 62 |
| II | 76 | 76 | 107 | 75 | 108 | 48 | 64 |
| III | 82 | 80 | 115 | 81 | 116 | 52 | 68 |
| IV | 87 | 90 | 119 | 84 | 122 | 54 | 72 |
| 1988 I | 88 | 92 | 120 | 85 | 124 | 52 | 73 |

Source: Commodities Division, IMF Research Department. Data relate to a "world" index, that is, to a single basket of 34 primary commodities and do not reflect differences in the composition of the basket of primary commodities exported or imported by different countries. See Appendix I of IMF, *Primary Commodities Market Developments and Outlook 1986*, for a description of this index.

[1] Commodity prices deflated by unit values of manufactured goods exports of "developed market economies" as reported by United Nations, *Monthly Bulletin of Statistics* (New York), various issues.

prices in real terms, that is, relative to prices of manufactures, were some 35 percent below the level of 1984 and about 25 percent below their 1982 trough.

By the end of 1987, however, commodity prices had increased substantially (Chart 1). The increase in terms of SDRs from the fourth quarter of 1986 to the fourth quarter of 1987 was 15 percent. The increase in terms of dollars was more substantial (nearly 30 percent) owing to depreciation of the U.S. dollar. Despite this increase, the SDR price index in the final quarter of 1987 remained some 8 percent below the trough reached in 1982, even though the dollar index was 11 percent

the dollar. The SDR valuation basket consists of the currencies of the five members having the largest exports of goods and services during the period 1980–84, that is, the U.S. dollar, deutsche mark, French franc, Japanese yen, and pound sterling. The weights of the five currencies broadly reflect the relative importance of these currencies in international trade and finance. They are based on the value of the exports of goods and services of the members issuing the currencies and the balances of the five currencies officially held by Fund members over the five-year period 1980–84.

**Chart 1. Non-Fuel Commodity Prices, 1980–87**

(Indices: 1980 = 100)

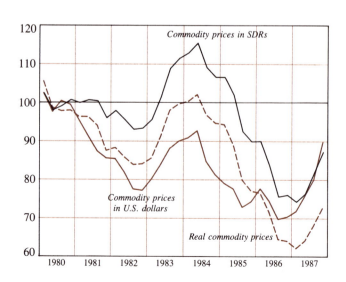

## Table 2. Movements in Commodity Prices and Related Economic Indicators, 1980–87

(Annual percentage changes)

|  | 1980 | 1981 | 1982 | 1983 | 1984 | 1985 | 1986 | 1987 |
|---|---|---|---|---|---|---|---|---|
| Commodity prices[1] |  |  |  |  |  |  |  |  |
| In SDRs | 5.1 | −0.8 | −4.3 | 9.9 | 6.4 | −12.0 | −16.8 | −1.8 |
| In U.S. dollars | 5.8 | −10.1 | −10.4 | 6.2 | 2.2 | −13.1 | −3.8 | 8.6 |
| Real[2] | −4.0 | −6.4 | −8.5 | 9.4 | 5.2 | −13.6 | −18.7 | −3.5 |
| Unit value of petroleum exports |  |  |  |  |  |  |  |  |
| In SDRs | 62.3 | 21.3 | 2.2 | −9.0 | 2.1 | −4.1 | −56.5 | 16.7 |
| In U.S. dollars | 63.5 | 9.9 | −4.3 | −11.9 | −2.1 | −5.0 | −49.8 | 28.6 |
| Unit value of manufactured exports |  |  |  |  |  |  |  |  |
| In SDRs | 9.6 | 6.0 | 4.5 | 0.4 | 1.2 | 2.1 | 2.1 | 1.7 |
| In U.S. dollars | 10.4 | −3.9 | −2.1 | −2.8 | −3.0 | 1.1 | 18.0 | 12.0 |
| Domestic prices in seven industrial countries |  |  |  |  |  |  |  |  |
| Consumer price index |  |  |  |  |  |  |  |  |
| In SDRs | 11.4 | 13.2 | 6.7 | 5.0 | 4.6 | 3.5 | 1.0 | 0.4 |
| In U.S. dollars | 12.2 | 2.6 | −0.1 | 1.7 | 0.3 | 2.5 | 16.7 | 10.7 |
| GNP deflator |  |  |  |  |  |  |  |  |
| In SDRs | 8.8 | 11.9 | 6.5 | 5.1 | 4.0 | 3.1 | 2.1 | 0.3 |
| In U.S. dollars | 9.6 | 1.4 | −0.3 | 1.8 | −0.2 | 2.2 | 18.0 | 10.6 |
| Economic activity in seven industrial countries |  |  |  |  |  |  |  |  |
| Real GNP | 1.2 | 1.7 | −0.4 | 2.8 | 5.2 | 3.2 | 2.8 | 3.1 |
| Industrial production | −0.2 | 0.6 | −3.8 | 3.8 | 8.5 | 2.8 | 1.0 | 3.3 |
| Domestic fixed investment | −2.2 | −0.2 | −5.2 | 3.9 | 9.6 | 4.5 | 2.8 | 3.3 |
| World consumption of commodities[3] |  |  |  |  |  |  |  |  |
| Index of consumption | −1.7 | 1.8 | 2.1 | 1.5 | 3.4 | 0.7 | 5.1 | 1.2 |
| World supply of commodities[3] |  |  |  |  |  |  |  |  |
| Index of production | 0.1 | 3.1 | −0.8 | −0.6 | 7.9 | 1.5 | −0.9 | 2.3 |
| Index of supply[4] | −0.4 | 3.3 | 1.3 | 1.3 | 5.1 | 2.6 | 1.4 | 0.2 |
| Index of closing stocks | 6.2 | 15.4 | 10.9 | −10.2 | 10.2 | 13.7 | −6.0 | −6.9 |

Sources: Commodities Division and Current Studies Division, IMF Research Department.

[1] Refers to IMF world index of non-fuel primary commodities. These percentages differ from those reported in IMF, *World Economic Outlook*, April 1988, which refer to the index of commodities *exported by developing countries* (given in Table 4).

[2] Index of dollar commodity prices deflated by the index of dollar unit values of manufactured exports.

[3] Overall indices constructed using the same weights for the indices of individual commodities as in overall (world) price index. Crop year data for agricultural commodities are given under the earlier calendar year, e.g., crop year 1980/81 under 1980. The commodity coverage of the indices of consumption and stocks is less comprehensive than the coverage of the indices of production and supply.

[4] Supply is defined as production plus *beginning*-of-year stocks.

higher. Real commodity prices also increased from the fourth quarter of 1986 to the fourth quarter of 1987— by 13 percent—providing some relief to the countries most dependent on exports of non-fuel primary commodities. Nevertheless, at the end of 1987 real commodity prices were still over 15 percent lower than at the trough of the 1981–82 recession.

The recovery of prices in 1987 was linked primarily to two factors: a strengthening of world economic activity through the year and lower-than-expected supplies of commodities (Table 2). High demand, especially in the United States, Japan, and the newly industrializing economies of Asia, led to a reduction of stocks of metals and, to a lesser degree, stocks of agricultural raw materials. Stocks of metals were not rebuilt quickly because much of the excess capacity that had overhung the market for metals earlier in the decade had been closed, and producers were reluctant

to reactivate this capacity in view of the excess supply that has characterized these markets for several years. In addition, labor disputes in some mining industries increased uncertainty regarding supplies. The markets for agricultural raw materials were influenced by both general and specific factors. An important general factor was the stimulation of demand for several raw materials (such as cotton, jute, and natural rubber) as a result of the recovery in world oil prices and the consequent rise in prices of petroleum-based synthetic products. Among the special factors were a weather-damaged cotton crop in 1986/87 in the United States, new demand for products made from natural rubber, implementation of conservation practices restricting exports of hardwood logs, and a surge in housing starts in Japan increasing demand for a number of building materials, notably timber.

The recovery in prices in 1987 was mirrored in an

3

inverse movement of stocks of most commodities (Chart 2).[2] Stocks of all commodities, measured in terms of months of consumption at the beginning of 1988, were considerably lower than the levels at the beginning of 1987. Stocks of agricultural raw materials and metals fell particularly sharply during 1987. Stocks of food commodities, however, although reduced, were still at relatively high levels at the beginning of 1988, and stocks of beverages actually increased during 1987, following the drawdown associated with supply scarcities in 1985–86.

Partly reflecting the changes in stocks, the largest price increases during 1987 were recorded for metals and agricultural raw materials. Exceptionally large increases were recorded from the first quarter of 1987 to the first quarter of 1988 for copper (62 percent in terms of SDRs), nickel (170 percent), hardwood logs (27 percent), aluminum (61 percent), and fine wool (80 percent). There was a 41 percent increase in the index of prices for the minerals and metals group of commodities and a 21 percent increase in the index for the agricultural raw materials group (Table 3). By contrast, the index for the group of food commodities increased by only 12 percent, while the index for beverages fell by 5 percent.

Reflecting the mix of commodity exports, the index of commodity prices weighted by industrial countries' export shares recorded a much greater increase from the first quarter of 1987 to the first quarter of 1988 (21 percent) than did the corresponding index of commodity prices for developing countries (14 percent) (Table 4). Similarly, the year-to-year increase for industrial countries' index in 1987 was 3 percent, while the 1987 index level of the developing countries was 6 percent below the 1986 level. Much of the difference in the behavior of the two price series is attributable to developments relating to the prices of beverages, in particular coffee, which has a large weight in the index for developing countries but a negligible weight in the index for industrial countries.

## Commodity Price Changes and Aggregate Inflation

There has been some concern that the recovery of commodity prices during 1987 could be a harbinger of a general rise in inflation. In view of this risk, and in response to proposals by the United States and the United Kingdom at the 1987 Annual Meetings of the Fund and the World Bank, the Fund staff has analyzed

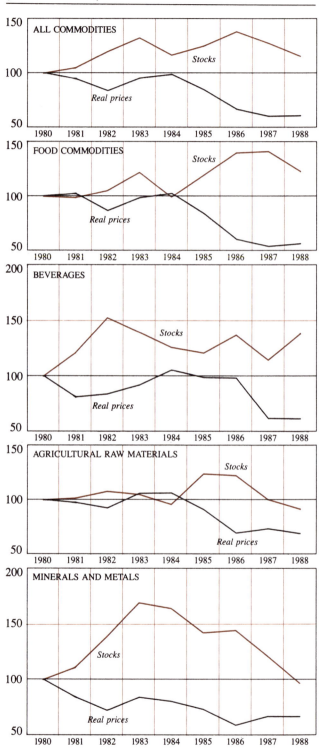

**Chart 2. Commodity Prices in Real Terms and Beginning Stocks Measured in Months of Consumption, 1980–88[1]**

(Indices: 1980 = 100)

ALL COMMODITIES — Stocks — Real prices

FOOD COMMODITIES — Stocks — Real prices

BEVERAGES — Stocks — Real prices

AGRICULTURAL RAW MATERIALS — Stocks — Real prices

MINERALS AND METALS — Stocks — Real prices

[1] Weights for commodity price indices are based on 1979–81 average export earnings; includes primary commodities for which stock data are available.

---

[2] Chart 2 shows the relationship in terms of "real prices." A similar but weaker relationship can be shown in terms of nominal prices.

**Table 3. Prices for Groups of Commodities, 1980–88**

(Indices: 1980 = 100)

| Years | In SDRs | | | | In U.S. dollars | | | |
|---|---|---|---|---|---|---|---|---|
| | Food | Beverages | Agricultural raw materials | Minerals and metals | Food | Beverages | Agricultural raw materials | Minerals and metals |
| 1980 | 100 | 100 | 100 | 100 | 100 | 100 | 100 | 100 |
| 1981 | 107 | 87 | 97 | 94 | 97 | 79 | 88 | 85 |
| 1982 | 97 | 94 | 99 | 88 | 82 | 80 | 84 | 75 |
| 1983 | 109 | 105 | 104 | 96 | 89 | 86 | 85 | 79 |
| 1984 | 112 | 127 | 116 | 94 | 89 | 100 | 91 | 74 |
| 1985 | 96 | 113 | 100 | 90 | 75 | 88 | 78 | 70 |
| 1986 | 73 | 113 | 88 | 73 | 66 | 102 | 79 | 66 |
| 1987 | 68 | 74 | 106 | 79 | 67 | 73 | 105 | 78 |
| 1986 I | 83 | 134 | 92 | 77 | 72 | 116 | 80 | 66 |
| II | 72 | 113 | 89 | 74 | 69 | 101 | 79 | 66 |
| III | 66 | 106 | 82 | 71 | 61 | 98 | 76 | 65 |
| IV | 66 | 99 | 87 | 71 | 61 | 92 | 80 | 66 |
| 1987 I | 66 | 78 | 92 | 70 | 64 | 76 | 89 | 68 |
| II | 68 | 72 | 97 | 73 | 68 | 72 | 96 | 73 |
| III | 67 | 71 | 113 | 82 | 66 | 70 | 111 | 81 |
| IV | 70 | 74 | 122 | 90 | 72 | 76 | 126 | 93 |
| 1988 I | 74 | 74 | 111 | 99 | 78 | 77 | 117 | 104 |

Source: Commodities Division, IMF Research Department.

**Table 4. Prices for Commodity Exports of Industrial Countries and of Developing Countries, 1980–88**

(Indices: 1980 = 100)

| Years | Nominal Commodity Prices[1] | | | | Real Commodity Prices[1,2] | |
|---|---|---|---|---|---|---|
| | In SDRs | | In U.S. dollars | | | |
| | Industrial countries | Developing countries | Industrial countries | Developing countries | Industrial countries | Developing countries |
| 1980 | 100 | 100 | 100 | 100 | 100 | 100 |
| 1981 | 102 | 96 | 93 | 87 | 97 | 90 |
| 1982 | 98 | 92 | 83 | 78 | 88 | 83 |
| 1983 | 107 | 101 | 88 | 83 | 96 | 91 |
| 1984 | 112 | 110 | 88 | 87 | 99 | 98 |
| 1985 | 98 | 97 | 76 | 76 | 86 | 85 |
| 1986 | 80 | 83 | 72 | 75 | 68 | 71 |
| 1987 | 82 | 78 | 81 | 77 | 69 | 65 |
| 1986 I | 88 | 93 | 76 | 80 | 75 | 79 |
| II | 83 | 84 | 74 | 75 | 71 | 72 |
| III | 74 | 78 | 68 | 72 | 63 | 67 |
| IV | 75 | 78 | 69 | 72 | 63 | 66 |
| 1987 I | 75 | 74 | 73 | 71 | 63 | 62 |
| II | 79 | 74 | 78 | 73 | 66 | 62 |
| III | 84 | 79 | 83 | 77 | 70 | 66 |
| IV | 89 | 85 | 92 | 87 | 74 | 70 |
| 1988 I | 91 | 84 | 96 | 89 | 76 | 70 |

Source: Commodities Division, IMF Research Department.

[1] See Appendix I of IMF, *Primary Commodities Market Developments and Outlook 1986*, for commodity weights in these indices.

[2] Commodity prices deflated by unit values of manufactured goods exports of "developed market economies" as reported by United Nations, *Monthly Bulletin of Statistics* (New York), various issues.

the link between commodity prices and general trends in consumer prices in industrial countries. Although preliminary, the results confirm that commodity prices can sometimes serve as a leading indicator of general inflation trends.

Chart 3 shows the relationship between developments in the price index of a broad basket of commodities—including oil and gold as well as the commodities included in the Fund's traditional index of non-oil commodity prices—and movements in consumer prices in the major industrial countries. Following a marked decline in the commodity price index in the first half of 1986, which reflected a sharp drop in oil prices and excess supply conditions in most other commodity markets, consumer price increases decelerated to only 1 percent toward the end of 1986 as compared with price increases of 3–4 percent during the previous two years. The recovery in commodity prices began in the middle of 1986; about six months later consumer prices in industrial countries also picked up, accelerating to some 3 percent by the end of 1987. By comparison, the average rate of increase in the GNP deflator, which is often regarded as indicative of underlying inflation trends, has remained comparatively stable at some 3 percent a year in the major countries as a group since 1985. On this basis, the firming of consumer price increases during 1987 appears to suggest that the underlying inflation trend has simply reasserted itself following a period of exceptionally low inflation attributable to weak commodity prices.

Whether the recent upward trend in consumer price inflation continues will depend partly on the behavior of commodity prices. It will, however, also depend importantly on conditions in labor markets as well as on the behavior of exchange rates and monetary policy.

## Export Earnings from Commodities in 1987

Despite the rise in commodity prices, earnings from exports of commodities remained depressed in 1987, and developing countries fared less well than industrial countries. In terms of SDRs, estimated aggregate earnings from exports of 19 leading commodities declined by 3 percent compared with 1986 (Table 5). When measured in terms of U.S. dollars, however, there was an increase of 7 percent. In 1987, estimated earnings from coffee exports fell sharply—by 36 percent in terms of SDRs—as did earnings from maize exports—by 35 percent. Large increases, however, are estimated for export earnings from cotton (49 percent), aluminum (27 percent), and copper (21 percent). Industrial countries benefited from the increase in commodity prices to a much greater extent than

**Chart 3. Commodity Price Changes and Aggregate Inflation Trends in the Major Industrial Countries, 1980–87[1]**

(Percent a year)[2]

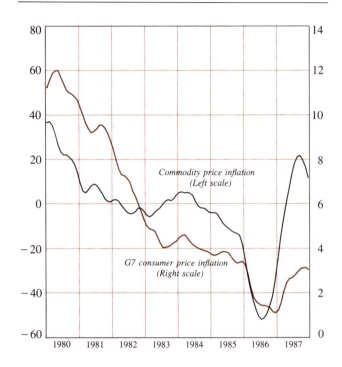

[1] Composite inflation is an average of percentage changes for individual countries weighted by the average U.S. dollar value of their respective GNPs over the preceding three years. Commodity price index is a world export-weighted basket of commodities that includes oil and gold as well as the commodities included in the Fund's published index of non-oil commodity prices, converted into the average exchange rate of the major industrial countries where the weights are the same as those used for the composite inflation index.

[2] Centered three-month moving average of percentage changes over the same month of preceding year.

developing countries because the product mix of their exports gives greater weight to commodities for which the price increases were larger. To the extent that the rise in commodity prices during 1987 is reflected in export earnings with a lag, some additional strength in export earnings from commodities is expected to materialize in 1988, with the developing countries benefiting relatively more, reflecting the delayed increase in coffee prices.

During much of the 1980s, commodity export volumes have tended to expand significantly faster in developing countries than in the industrial countries (Table 6). The depressed prices of commodities have nevertheless been of greater proportionate importance to developing countries because primary commodities account for a greater share of total exports in these countries. Similarly, important differences exist among

**Table 5. Export Earnings from Major Commodities, 1984–87**

| | 1984 | 1985 | 1986 | 1987 | 1984 | 1985 | 1986 | 1987 |
|---|---|---|---|---|---|---|---|---|
| | *(In billions of SDRs)* | | | | *(In billions of U.S. dollars)* | | | |
| **Total 19 commodities** | **114** | **103** | **87** | **84** | **117** | **105** | **102** | **109** |
| Industrial countries[1] | 52 | 43 | 34 | 36 | 53 | 44 | 40 | 46 |
| Developing countries | 58 | 56 | 49 | 44 | 59 | 57 | 57 | 57 |
| U.S.S.R. and Eastern European countries | 5 | 4 | 4 | 4 | 5 | 4 | 5 | 6 |
| Cereals | | | | | | | | |
| Wheat | 17.8 | 15.1 | 11.1 | 10.6 | 18.2 | 15.3 | 13.0 | 13.7 |
| Maize | 10.0 | 8.6 | 5.8 | 3.8 | 10.3 | 8.8 | 6.8 | 4.9 |
| Rice | 3.7 | 3.1 | 2.5 | 2.5 | 3.8 | 3.1 | 3.0 | 3.2 |
| Vegetable oils and protein meals | | | | | | | | |
| Soybeans | 7.0 | 5.5 | 4.8 | 4.7 | 7.2 | 5.5 | 5.6 | 6.0 |
| Soybean meal | 4.2 | 3.5 | 3.5 | 4.2 | 4.3 | 3.6 | 4.1 | 5.4 |
| Soybean oil | 2.8 | 2.2 | 1.0 | 1.2 | 2.9 | 2.3 | 1.2 | 1.6 |
| Palm oil | 2.8 | 2.6 | 1.6 | 1.7 | 2.9 | 2.6 | 1.8 | 2.3 |
| Sugar | 9.8 | 8.8 | 8.1 | 7.6 | 10.1 | 8.9 | 9.4 | 9.8 |
| Beverages | | | | | | | | |
| Coffee | 10.4 | 10.7 | 12.1 | 7.8 | 10.6 | 10.9 | 14.2 | 10.1 |
| Tea | 2.5 | 2.0 | 1.5 | 1.2 | 2.5 | 2.1 | 1.7 | 1.5 |
| Cocoa[2] | 3.4 | 3.6 | 3.2 | 2.8 | 3.5 | 3.6 | 3.7 | 3.6 |
| Agricultural raw materials | | | | | | | | |
| Hardwood | 4.5 | 4.3 | 3.8 | 3.7 | 4.6 | 4.4 | 4.5 | 4.8 |
| Tobacco | 4.0 | 4.0 | 3.3 | 3.0 | 4.1 | 4.1 | 3.9 | 3.9 |
| Natural rubber | 3.4 | 2.7 | 2.5 | 2.8 | 3.5 | 2.7 | 2.9 | 3.6 |
| Cotton | 6.9 | 6.0 | 4.5 | 6.7 | 7.1 | 6.1 | 5.2 | 8.6 |
| Metals | | | | | | | | |
| Copper | 4.4 | 4.5 | 3.9 | 4.7 | 4.5 | 4.5 | 4.6 | 6.1 |
| Aluminum | 7.8 | 7.4 | 7.3 | 9.3 | 8.0 | 7.5 | 8.5 | 12.0 |
| Iron ore | 6.8 | 6.9 | 5.9 | 5.3 | 7.0 | 7.0 | 6.9 | 6.9 |
| Tin | 1.7 | 1.9 | 0.8 | 0.8 | 1.7 | 1.9 | 0.9 | 1.0 |

Sources: See tables on individual commodities in Sections II to V.
[1] Covers 21 countries as defined in the IMF, *International Financial Statistics*.
[2] Exports of countries producing cocoa beans.

the developing countries themselves. For the 73 developing countries that export mainly non-fuel primary commodities,[3] aggregate export earnings in terms of SDRs in 1987 increased by only 1 percent (Table 7). For nine developing countries that export mainly manufactured goods, however, aggregate export earnings increased by 12 percent in 1987. Aggregate earnings of the non-fuel primary commodity exporters in 1987 were only 5 percent above the level of 1980, with an increase in volume of exports of over 30 percent outweighing a sharp fall of over 20 percent in unit values. By contrast, aggregate earnings of the exporters of manufactures in 1987 were nearly 85 percent above the level of 1980; the increase was mainly accounted for by a corresponding rise in export volumes, although unit values for manufactured exports have been less sluggish than those for primary product exports. For the 20 countries that export mainly fuel commodities,

an increase of 10 percent in aggregate earnings in SDRs is estimated for 1987, largely as a result of a modest price increase for petroleum. This increase, however, followed a sharp decline of over 40 percent in aggregate earnings for these countries in 1986.

## Commodity Trade Negotiations and International Cooperation in 1987

During 1987 there were some important modifications in the international environment in which commodity trade occurs. Many of the modifications were the result of changes in bilateral arrangements between countries. Those changes that involved multilateral action have for the most part not yet affected commodity trade, but are expected to have an impact in the years ahead. They include the multilateral trade negotiations within the context of the Uruguay Round of the GATT and negotiations regarding some inter-

[3] Based on export shares in 1980.

**Table 6.   Aggregate Earnings, Volumes, and Unit Values for Major Commodity Exports of Industrial and Developing Countries, 1980–87**

(Indices: 1980 = 100)

|  | 1980 | 1981 | 1982 | 1983 | 1984 | 1985 | 1986 | 1987 |
|---|---|---|---|---|---|---|---|---|
| **Earnings** | | | | | | | | |
| In terms of SDRs | | | | | | | | |
| World[1] | 100 | 104 | 97 | 104 | 112 | 102 | 86 | 83 |
| Industrial countries | 100 | 110 | 100 | 104 | 111 | 92 | 74 | 77 |
| Developing countries | 100 | 98 | 94 | 104 | 115 | 112 | 97 | 89 |
| In terms of U.S. dollars | | | | | | | | |
| World[1] | 100 | 94 | 83 | 86 | 89 | 80 | 78 | 83 |
| Industrial countries | 100 | 100 | 85 | 85 | 87 | 72 | 67 | 76 |
| Developing countries | 100 | 89 | 80 | 86 | 91 | 87 | 87 | 88 |
| **Volumes** | | | | | | | | |
| World[1] | 100 | 100 | 100 | 102 | 103 | 103 | 101 | 106 |
| Industrial countries | 100 | 98 | 97 | 97 | 98 | 91 | 88 | 96 |
| Developing countries | 100 | 101 | 102 | 107 | 108 | 115 | 113 | 115 |
| **Unit values** | | | | | | | | |
| In terms of SDRs | | | | | | | | |
| World[1] | 100 | 104 | 97 | 102 | 109 | 99 | 85 | 78 |
| Industrial countries | 100 | 112 | 103 | 107 | 113 | 101 | 84 | 80 |
| Developing countries | 100 | 97 | 92 | 97 | 106 | 97 | 86 | 77 |
| In terms of U.S. dollars | | | | | | | | |
| World[1] | 100 | 95 | 83 | 84 | 86 | 77 | 77 | 78 |
| Industrial countries | 100 | 102 | 88 | 88 | 89 | 79 | 76 | 79 |
| Developing countries | 100 | 89 | 78 | 80 | 84 | 76 | 77 | 77 |
| In real terms | | | | | | | | |
| World[1] | 100 | 99 | 88 | 92 | 97 | 86 | 73 | 66 |
| Industrial countries | 100 | 106 | 94 | 96 | 100 | 88 | 72 | 67 |
| Developing countries | 100 | 93 | 83 | 88 | 95 | 85 | 73 | 65 |
| **Market prices** | | | | | | | | |
| In terms of SDRs | | | | | | | | |
| World[1] | 100 | 97 | 92 | 103 | 108 | 95 | 78 | 74 |
| Industrial countries | 100 | 103 | 95 | 108 | 109 | 94 | 73 | 70 |
| Developing countries | 100 | 92 | 89 | 97 | 105 | 93 | 82 | 74 |
| In terms of U.S. dollars | | | | | | | | |
| World[1] | 100 | 88 | 79 | 85 | 85 | 74 | 71 | 73 |
| Industrial countries | 100 | 93 | 81 | 89 | 86 | 73 | 66 | 70 |
| Developing countries | 100 | 83 | 75 | 80 | 82 | 72 | 74 | 74 |
| In real terms | | | | | | | | |
| World[1] | 100 | 92 | 84 | 93 | 96 | 82 | 67 | 62 |
| Industrial countries | 100 | 97 | 86 | 97 | 96 | 82 | 62 | 59 |
| Developing countries | 100 | 88 | 82 | 89 | 96 | 83 | 71 | 64 |

Sources: See tables on individual commodities in Sections II to V. Indices for individual commodities aggregated in accordance with earnings share in total for 19 commodities in 1980 for world, industrial countries, and developing countries.

[1] Includes U.S.S.R. and Eastern European countries.

national commodity agreements. A final factor affecting commodity trade in 1987 was the increase in compensatory financing of export earnings shortfalls of individual countries by multilateral agencies.

The Uruguay Round of GATT negotiations began in early 1987. The present round, the eighth in a series of GATT negotiations held since 1947, involves two elements that are of particular relevance to international trade in commodities. First, in response to the global excess stocks of some agricultural commodities, particularly food crops, which have arisen in part because of the distortionary effects of agricultural policies in the major industrial countries, GATT ne-

gotiations to liberalize national policies and agricultural trade are being held for the first time. Second, also for the first time, many developing countries are participating actively in the GATT negotiations, including the negotiations covering trade in tropical and natural resource-based products, manufactures, and services as well as agricultural trade. Through observance of the most-favored-nation principle, a cornerstone of the GATT, these negotiations offer the prospect of wider access to national commodity markets by all commodity exporting countries. As of the early months of 1988, the first phase of the negotiations, which was devoted to adopting procedural modalities

**Table 7. Developing Countries: Export Earnings by Volume and Unit Value, 1980–87**

(Annual percentage changes)

| | 1980 | 1981 | 1982 | 1983 | 1984 | 1985 | 1986 | 1987 |
|---|---|---|---|---|---|---|---|---|
| **Values** | | | | | | | | |
| In terms of SDRs | 30.9 | 8.5 | − 5.9 | − 1.6 | 11.3 | − 3.2 | − 19.6 | 8.5 |
| Fuel exporters | 40.5 | 4.6 | − 13.5 | − 11.9 | 3.4 | − 9.1 | − 43.5 | 10.4 |
| Primary product exporters | 21.7 | 4.1 | − 3.6 | 6.7 | 14.6 | − 3.4 | − 12.3 | 1.0 |
| *Agricultural exporters* | *17.0* | *11.4* | *− 2.7* | *7.3* | *20.3* | *− 3.7* | *− 14.2* | *0.7* |
| *Mineral exporters* | *31.1* | *− 8.6* | *− 5.4* | *5.4* | *1.9* | *− 2.7* | *− 7.3* | *1.7* |
| Exporters of manufactures | 21.6 | 20.5 | 6.0 | 8.1 | 19.1 | 2.6 | − 2.5 | 12.0 |
| Service and remittance countries | 23.1 | 12.1 | 1.0 | 2.5 | 11.6 | 2.4 | − 5.1 | 3.2 |
| In terms of U.S. dollars | 31.8 | − 1.7 | − 11.9 | − 4.7 | 6.8 | − 4.1 | − 7.1 | 19.6 |
| Fuel exporters | 41.5 | − 5.3 | − 19.0 | − 14.7 | − 0.9 | − 9.9 | − 34.7 | 21.7 |
| Primary product exporters | 22.6 | − 5.7 | − 9.7 | 3.3 | 9.9 | − 4.3 | 1.3 | 11.4 |
| *Agricultural exporters* | *17.8* | *0.9* | *− 8.9* | *3.9* | *15.4* | *− 4.6* | *− 0.9* | *11.0* |
| *Mineral exporters* | *32.0* | *− 17.2* | *− 11.5* | *2.1* | *− 2.3* | *− 3.6* | *7.2* | *12.1* |
| Exporters of manufactures | 22.5 | 9.2 | − 0.7 | 4.6 | 14.2 | 1.6 | 12.6 | 23.5 |
| Service and remittance countries | 24.0 | 1.6 | − 5.4 | − 0.7 | 7.0 | 1.4 | 9.7 | 13.8 |
| **Volumes** | − 4.1 | − 5.9 | − 7.7 | 3.0 | 7.1 | 0.8 | 5.5 | 7.3 |
| Fuel exporters | − 13.3 | − 14.9 | − 16.3 | − 3.6 | 0.7 | − 5.7 | 13.7 | 0.1 |
| Primary product exporters | 6.7 | 1.4 | 0.1 | 5.7 | 8.1 | 5.5 | 2.9 | 4.4 |
| *Agricultural exporters* | *5.7* | *6.9* | *0.7* | *6.7* | *10.6* | *5.0* | *3.2* | *6.6* |
| *Mineral exporters* | *8.6* | *− 8.6* | *− 1.2* | *3.6* | *1.9* | *7.1* | *2.1* | *− 0.4* |
| Exporters of manufactures | 10.4 | 8.8 | 2.0 | 10.1 | 14.0 | 4.2 | 12.1 | 14.0 |
| Service and remittance countries | 3.5 | 2.5 | 0.9 | 7.2 | 9.3 | 7.6 | 9.0 | 0.4 |
| **Unit values** | | | | | | | | |
| In terms of SDRs | 36.5 | 15.3 | 2.0 | − 4.5 | 4.0 | − 4.0 | − 23.8 | 1.1 |
| Fuel exporters | 62.0 | 22.9 | 3.3 | − 8.6 | 2.7 | − 3.5 | − 50.3 | 10.3 |
| Primary product exporters | 14.1 | 2.7 | − 3.7 | 0.9 | 6.1 | − 8.5 | − 14.8 | − 3.2 |
| *Agricultural exporters* | *10.7* | *4.3* | *− 3.4* | *0.5* | *8.8* | *− 8.2* | *− 16.9* | *− 5.5* |
| *Mineral exporters* | *20.7* | *− 0.1* | *− 4.3* | *1.8* | *0.1* | *− 9.1* | *− 9.2* | *2.1* |
| Exporters of manufactures | 10.2 | 10.7 | 3.9 | − 1.9 | 4.4 | − 1.5 | − 13.1 | − 1.7 |
| Service and remittance countries | 19.0 | 9.4 | 0.1 | − 4.4 | 2.1 | − 4.9 | − 12.9 | 2.8 |
| In terms of U.S. dollars | 37.5 | 4.5 | − 4.5 | − 7.5 | − 0.3 | − 4.9 | − 11.9 | 11.5 |
| Fuel exporters | 63.2 | 11.3 | − 3.3 | − 11.5 | − 1.6 | − 4.5 | − 42.6 | 21.5 |
| Primary product exporters | 14.9 | − 7.0 | − 9.8 | − 2.3 | 1.7 | − 9.3 | − 1.5 | 6.7 |
| *Agricultural exporters* | *11.5* | *− 5.5* | *− 9.6* | *− 2.6* | *4.3* | *− 9.1* | *− 4.0* | *4.2* |
| *Mineral exporters* | *21.6* | *− 9.5* | *− 10.4* | *− 1.5* | *− 4.1* | *− 9.9* | *5.0* | *12.5* |
| Exporters of manufactures | 11.0 | 0.3 | − 2.7 | − 5.0 | 0.1 | − 2.4 | 0.4 | 8.3 |
| Service and remittance countries | 19.8 | − 0.9 | − 6.3 | − 7.4 | − 2.1 | − 5.8 | 0.7 | 13.3 |

Source: IMF, *World Economic Outlook*, April 1988.

and to considering country proposals for the multi-faceted negotiations, was drawing to a close. The negotiations themselves are expected to extend over the next 2–3 years. There is, however, wide sentiment among the negotiators that, in view of the persistent threat of protectionism, the negotiations should progress and, if possible, should attempt to yield an "early harvest" of agreements on some measures to liberalize trade, including possibly agricultural trade, before the end of 1988.

As in recent years, international commodity agreements with market intervention mechanisms played a relatively minor role in international commodity trade in 1987. Nevertheless, after a series of lengthy negotiations starting in mid-1985, countries invited to a United Nations Conference on Natural Rubber finally reached accord on the text of a new agreement in March 1987. The new agreement, which is expected to become operative in late 1988, is described in Section IV of this paper. Important decisions were also taken during 1987 by the International Coffee Council and the International Cocoa Council that were designed to make operations under the 1983 International Coffee Agreement and the 1986 Cocoa Agreement more effective. Export quotas were reintroduced for coffee exporting countries in October, and provisions were agreed to enable buffer stock purchases of cocoa in April–May 1987 and again in January–February 1988. These developments are discussed in Section III.

Although only small changes were made in 1987 in the various multilateral schemes that exist to compensate countries for export earnings shortfalls, a significant increase in such financing in 1987 had the effect of stabilizing many developing countries' export earnings, thereby maintaining their capacity to import and buoying world trade. Drawings under the Fund's compensatory financing facility (CFF) rose from SDR 0.6 billion in 1986 to SDR 1.2 billion in 1987, reflecting the drop in earnings associated with the downturn in commodity prices that occurred in 1986. In addition to use of the CFF, many primary producing countries have benefited from access to the European Community's (EC) STABEX and COMPEX facilities. STABEX transfers (which are made only to the African, Caribbean, and Pacific (ACP) countries associated with the EC under the Lomé Conventions), increased sharply from SDR 112 million in 1986 to SDR 202 million in 1987. In early 1987, the EC adopted the COMPEX system, which is designed to compensate the least developed non-ACP countries for shortfalls in earnings from agricultural commodities. COMPEX transfers in 1987, on account of export earnings shortfalls in 1986, amounted to SDR 5.6 million.

## Outlook for Commodity Prices in 1988 and for the Medium Term

Commodity price forecasting is always difficult, but the risks become particularly acute in the wake of major turning points in prices, such as the one that occurred in 1987. Forecasting in the current context requires basic judgments to be made about the nature and causes of the previous sharp decline in prices and of the recent recovery before a view can be taken on the outlook. In particular, the occurrence of a recession-like decline in commodity prices in 1984–86 during an upswing of the business cycle raised concerns that the decline might be more closely related to long-term structural factors (such as "downsizing" and other materials-saving practices in automobile production) that reduce the demand for primary commodities, rather than to short-term reversible factors (such as changes in the level of economic activity in industrial countries or commodity supply shocks). Recent analysis suggests that the 1984–86 decline was largely cyclical and not the beginning of a structural decline in prices.[4] The fairly strong recovery in prices that

began in 1987, including its moderation in recent months, is consistent with this interpretation.

The projections are predicated on the usual assumptions of fixed real effective exchange rates (at the levels prevailing during March 1988), constant interest rates (at the levels of March 1988), and no changes in government policies; it is also assumed that world oil prices would average $16.50 per barrel in 1988 and remain unchanged in real terms over the medium term; and that economic growth in the industrial countries will slow somewhat in 1988 from its 1987 level, but will return to a range of 2¾ percent to 3.0 percent per year (i.e., about the rate of increase expected in productive potential) in 1989–92. On this basis, an increase of about 5 percent in the world index of commodity prices in SDR terms is projected in the baseline projections, compared with a decline of over 1 percent in 1987.[5] In 1989, and over the medium term, prices are forecast to increase by 2.5–4.0 percent a year, reflecting the recovery in economic activity and some medium-term supply response, through reductions in productive capacity in response to the low levels of prices in 1985–86. These projections in nominal terms correspond to roughly a 1 percent rise in commodity prices in real terms in 1988 and to constant real prices during 1989–92. The changes forecast for the developing country index of commodity prices are quite similar.

Projected movements in the baseline projections for the four major component groups of the non-oil primary commodities show somewhat greater variability. Prices of industrial inputs, including agricultural raw materials and metals, are determined in markets where demand factors tend to play an important role in short-term movements. These prices are projected to rise at a slower pace during 1988 than during 1987, and over the medium term to grow at 3–4 percent a year in dollar terms during 1989–92, which is equivalent to unchanged prices in real terms. Food prices, after a brief recovery in 1988 related in part to weather in South Asia, are expected to remain weak in real terms through the medium term, largely reflecting the spillover effects of excess supplies originating in the protected domestic sectors of industrial countries. Prices of tropical beverages are expected to continue the recovery begun in mid-1987 through 1988, partly reflecting a new export quota agreement that will limit traded world supplies of coffee.

Movements in the overall commodity price and

---

[4] Thomas K. Morrison and Michael Wattleworth, "The 1984–86 Commodity Recession: An Analysis of the Underlying Causes," *Staff Papers*, International Monetary Fund (Washington), Vol. 35 (June 1988).

[5] Year-on-year changes mask a considerable part of the movement of commodity prices. In this case, commodity prices fell *during* 1986 and rose *during* 1987 (see Table 1). During 1988 the prices of most commodities are expected to remain close to their end-1987 levels, although some are expected to fall. This outcome, however, implies an increase of some 5 percent over the average for 1987.

indices for groups of commodities disguise the much greater variability in prices for individual commodities. In the near and medium term a considerable number of sharp price increases are likely, although such increases will probably be sustained only for short periods and are likely to be followed by sharp declines. The lower the level of stocks, the more vulnerable the individual commodity market will be to disruptions caused by weather and inadequate supply, and, in fewer cases, to unexpectedly strong demand. Price prospects for individual commodities are examined in the following sections.

The baseline projections are, of course, based on assumptions that may not be fully consistent with one another. In particular, the assumptions imply that the existing large external imbalances among the major countries will be smoothly financed through the necessary shifts in portfolio preferences without any corresponding changes in exchange rates, interest rates, or changes in policies among countries. Since such an outcome may not materialize, and given that several of the foreseeable adjustment mechanisms involve some slowdown in economic activity in industrial countries, the balance of risk in the commodity price forecast must be seen to be primarily on the downside. The downside risks would probably be greater, however, if adjustments are left entirely to private markets because such adjustments might well also involve higher interest rates, particularly in the United States. Such a shift would reduce residual demand for commodity stocks and would be likely to lead to a more vulnerable stock situation, such as the one that existed for some commodities in early 1987. Moreover, any scenario involving a more rapid adjustment of external imbalances would require changes in the composition of demand among the major countries that could well involve a net reduction in world demand for raw material imports, resulting in a weakening of commodity prices. Finally, if oil prices weakened significantly from those assumed, substitution on the demand side toward petroleum-based synthetic products and away from natural primary commodities could be expected, resulting in a further weakening of commodity prices.

# II

# Food Commodities

The prices of most food commodities bottomed out in the second half of 1986 and the first half of 1987 and then increased by modest amounts. This turn-around followed a three-year period beginning mid-1984 during which the group price index fell by about 40 percent (Chart 4). The upturn, however, was small in comparison with the increases in the prices of many other commodities during the second half of 1987. The change in the direction of the movement in prices of food commodities was largely a result of changes in supply. Production of food commodities is expected to show a modest decrease in crop year 1987/88, in contrast to an exceptionally large increase in 1984/85 and the substantial increases of the two following years (Table 8). The supply situation has also been altered somewhat on account of a very large increase in 1986/87 in consumption of food commodities, in particular of cereals, principally because of greater use of these commodities in animal feed. The group index of closing stocks of food commodities is expected to fall by over 10 percent in the crop year 1987/88, although stocks of most food commodities are expected to remain at high levels. With reference to individual food com-modities, the prices of both cereals and vegetable oils and protein meals in 1986–87 were far below the levels of 1983–84, while the sugar price has been at a low level since 1981. The reasons for these price patterns are discussed in this section.

## Cereals

The prices of all cereals have fallen sharply during the 1980s, except for a temporary increase in the price of feed grains in 1983/84 associated with drought in many countries and acreage reductions in the United States. In 1987, the prices of wheat, maize, and rice expressed in both SDRs and U.S. dollars were, re-spectively, 33 percent, 37 percent, and 40 percent below their average prices in 1979–80 (Table 9). The price collapse reflects excess supply throughout the 1980s. With the exception of 1983/84, total cereal

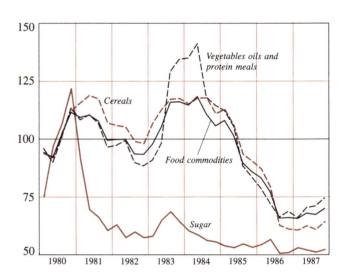

**Chart 4. Prices of Food Commodities, 1980–87**

(In SDRs; indices: 1980 = 100)

output exceeded utilization in every crop year from 1981/82 onward, resulting in a buildup of stocks at end-1986/87 to the equivalent of 23 percent of annual utilization—a level not realized since the early 1960s (Table 10). The collapse of prices also reflects a shrinking volume of world trade in cereals, from an average of 208 tons a year between 1980/81 and 1984/85 to 181 tons in 1985/86 and 188 tons in 1986/87. Commercial import demand declined mainly because former large importers, such as China, India, and Indonesia, achieved a high degree of self-sufficiency in the production of major cereals, because financial difficulties in many countries limited the demand for cereals, and because the ready availability of food aid reduced the need for commercial cereal imports.[6]

---

[6] The U.S.S.R. and Japan are the world's largest cereal importers, each accounting for about 15 percent of global grain imports. Japanese imports (mainly of coarse grains) are fairly stable, so prospects for U.S.S.R. grain output and utilization have a major impact on short-term fluctuations in world wheat and coarse grain prices.

**Table 8. Movements in the Prices of Food Commodities and Related Economic Indicators, 1980–87**

(Annual percentage changes)

| | 1980 | 1981 | 1982 | 1983 | 1984 | 1985 | 1986 | 1987 |
|---|---|---|---|---|---|---|---|---|
| Prices of food commodities[1] | | | | | | | | |
| In SDRs | 7.9 | 6.7 | −9.4 | 12.5 | 3.3 | −14.3 | −24.0 | −7.3 |
| In U.S. dollars | 8.6 | −3.2 | −15.2 | 8.7 | −0.7 | −15.5 | −12.2 | 2.5 |
| Real[2] | −1.7 | 0.9 | −13.4 | 12.0 | 2.1 | −15.9 | −25.7 | −8.9 |
| Domestic prices in seven industrial countries | | | | | | | | |
| Consumer price index | | | | | | | | |
| In SDRs | 11.4 | 13.2 | 6.7 | 5.0 | 4.6 | 3.5 | 1.0 | 0.4 |
| In U.S. dollars | 12.2 | 2.6 | −0.1 | 1.7 | 0.3 | 2.5 | 16.7 | 10.7 |
| GNP deflator | | | | | | | | |
| In SDRs | 8.8 | 11.9 | 6.5 | 5.1 | 4.0 | 3.1 | 2.1 | 0.3 |
| In U.S. dollars | 9.6 | 1.4 | −0.3 | 1.8 | −0.2 | 2.2 | 18.0 | 10.6 |
| Real GNP in seven industrial countries | 1.2 | 1.7 | −0.4 | 2.8 | 5.2 | 3.2 | 2.8 | 3.1 |
| World consumption of food commodities[3] | | | | | | | | |
| Index of consumption | −2.4 | 3.7 | 4.0 | 0.9 | 2.2 | 0.7 | 7.1 | 1.3 |
| World supply of food commodities[3] | | | | | | | | |
| Index of production | −0.1 | 4.3 | 4.9 | −3.7 | 8.0 | 2.0 | 2.9 | −1.4 |
| Index of supply[4] | −0.8 | 4.2 | 5.4 | −1.1 | 4.7 | 4.1 | 5.6 | −1.0 |
| Index of closing stocks | 2.6 | 10.3 | 17.0 | −16.6 | 21.4 | 24.9 | 1.1 | −11.3 |

Sources: Commodities Division and Current Studies Division, IMF Research Department.

[1] Refers to IMF world index of food commodities. These percentages differ from those reported in the *World Economic Outlook*, April 1988, which refer to the index of commodities *exported by developing countries*.

[2] Index of dollar prices of food commodities deflated by the index of dollar unit values of manufactured exports.

[3] Overall indices constructed using the same weights for the indices of individual commodities as in overall (world) price index. Crop year data for agricultural commodities are given under the earlier calendar year, e.g., crop year 1980/81 under 1980. The commodity coverage of the indices of consumption and stocks is less comprehensive than the coverage of indices of production and supply.

[4] Supply is defined as production plus *beginning*-of-year stocks.

The growth in world grain output during the 1980s mainly reflected higher yields. While the average yield for all cereals in the 1980s was 21 percent higher than in the 1970s, the area harvested increased by only 2 percent. Improvements in yield reflected the use of high-yielding varieties accompanied by complementary measures, such as greater use of fertilizer, irrigation, and pesticides; also, generally favorable weather conditions have prevailed since 1981/82. In addition, beginning about 1985, policies in industrial countries aimed at reducing excessive stocks, and policies in the U.S.S.R. intended to raise productivity resulted in the idling of the least productive land, thereby raising the average yield of the land remaining in use. Over the past two years, favorable weather conditions have increased the output of cereals and improved the availability of food in developing countries, especially in the low-income food deficit countries of sub-Saharan Africa, which experienced severe food shortages in 1984–85.

Government price support policies in the first half of the 1980s were a major reason slowing adjustment of harvested area to lower world market prices. Until 1985/86, price support policies in effect in the United States, the EC, and Japan, prevented declining world market prices from being reflected in returns to producers. Moreover, the strengthening of the U.S. dollar between 1981 and 1985 offset much of the decline in the dollar-denominated prices for non-U.S. exporters so that there was little incentive for them to reduce production.

In the United States, up to 1986/87 price support loan rates provided a floor to U.S. producer and export prices, but were set at levels high enough to allow less efficient producers in other countries to compete effectively in world markets. As a result, the U.S. share in world grain markets declined from over 50 percent in 1980/81 to 37 percent in 1985/86, and at the end of the 1985/86 crop year, the United States held about 56 percent of global wheat and coarse grain stocks and about 10 percent of global rice stocks. The U.S. 1985 farm bill (officially called the Food Security Act of 1985) had the objective of making agricultural policy more market oriented in order to reduce the budgetary costs of farm income support and storage of government-owned stocks, and to enable U.S. exporters to

**Table 9.    Prices of Cereals, 1979–88**

| Years | Index of Prices of Cereals[1] | Wheat[2] | Maize[3] | Rice[4] |
|---|---|---|---|---|
| | (1980 = 100) | | (In SDRs a ton) | |
| 1979 | 90.7 | 125 | 91 | 259 |
| 1980 | 100.0 | 133 | 97 | 333 |
| 1981 | 114.4 | 148 | 111 | 409 |
| 1982 | 101.8 | 145 | 98 | 266 |
| 1983 | 113.4 | 147 | 127 | 259 |
| 1984 | 115.1 | 149 | 133 | 246 |
| 1985 | 100.4 | 134 | 111 | 214 |
| 1986 | 72.3 | 98 | 75 | 179 |
| 1987 | 61.9 | 87 | 59 | 177 |
| 1986 I | 86.9 | 117 | 93 | 203 |
| II | 79.0 | 103 | 90 | 174 |
| III | 62.4 | 85 | 62 | 174 |
| IV | 60.9 | 88 | 57 | 167 |
| 1987 I | 60.4 | 89 | 55 | 162 |
| II | 62.3 | 88 | 61 | 164 |
| III | 60.6 | 85 | 58 | 178 |
| IV | 64.1 | 88 | 61 | 204 |
| 1988 I | 68.5 | 94 | 65 | 220 |
| | (1980 = 100) | | (In U.S. dollars a ton) | |
| 1979 | 90.1 | 160 | 116 | 334 |
| 1980 | 100.0 | 173 | 126 | 434 |
| 1981 | 103.8 | 175 | 131 | 483 |
| 1982 | 86.5 | 160 | 108 | 293 |
| 1983 | 93.1 | 157 | 136 | 277 |
| 1984 | 90.8 | 152 | 136 | 252 |
| 1985 | 78.1 | 136 | 112 | 217 |
| 1986 | 64.9 | 115 | 88 | 210 |
| 1987 | 61.5 | 114 | 75 | 230 |
| 1986 I | 75.1 | 132 | 104 | 229 |
| II | 70.5 | 119 | 104 | 202 |
| III | 57.7 | 103 | 75 | 209 |
| IV | 56.4 | 106 | 68 | 201 |
| 1987 I | 58.5 | 112 | 69 | 205 |
| II | 62.0 | 114 | 78 | 213 |
| III | 59.5 | 108 | 73 | 228 |
| IV | 66.1 | 118 | 81 | 274 |
| 1988 I | 72.0 | 128 | 88 | 301 |

Source: Commodities Division, IMF Research Department.

[1] The weights in the index are as follows: wheat, 48 percent; maize, 36 percent; rice, 16 percent.

[2] U.S. No. 1 hard winter wheat, ordinary protein, f.o.b. Gulf of Mexico ports.

[3] U.S. No. 2 yellow corn, f.o.b. Gulf of Mexico ports.

[4] Thai white milled rice, 5 percent broken, f.o.b. Bangkok.

regain market shares.[7] The main feature of the farm bill is the linkage of price-support loan rates to past market prices; loan rates were reduced substantially for the 1986/87 crop year. Acreage reduction programs (a prerequisite for producers to qualify for income support) are mandatory when stocks exceed certain specified levels. Up to 50 percent of income support

payments may be made in the form of negotiable generic certificates, which may be redeemed for government-owned commodities. This scheme provides substantial budgetary savings over cash payments,[8] and, in the case of maize, the use of certificates has allowed the government to influence market prices to maintain export competitiveness. For wheat, certificates have been issued as payment-in-kind subsidies to exporters to enable them to bridge the gap between domestic prices and prevailing world market prices under the export enhancement program (EEP) provisions of the farm bill.[9] For rice a "marketing loan" is in effect, whereby price support loans may be repaid by producers at rates below the loan rate and equivalent to the prevailing world market price. The implementation of the 1985 farm bill, while it promoted more market competition, had the effect of reducing world cereal prices in 1986–87 to levels consistent with the large supply imbalances.

The increasing budgetary cost to the EC of price support policies under the Common Agricultural Policy also led to revisions in the regime for 1986/87 designed to restrain production and link producer returns more closely with market prices.[10] A tax on producers, or "co-responsibility levy," of 3 percent of the intervention price was introduced, thereby lowering net producer prices. Intervention prices in ECU terms for feed wheat and barley were reduced by 5 percent, and there were changes in quality standards which had the effect of lowering support prices. For 1987/88, effective intervention prices in ECU terms were reduced by 6 percent for all grains. In both years, however, adjustments of agricultural exchange rates ("green" rates) partly offset the lowering of ECU intervention prices on prices received by producers in many EC countries so that the impact on cereal output was marginal. For 1988/89 and the three succeeding years, a threshold level for production of all grains of 160 million tons has been established, and if this is exceeded, intervention prices will be reduced by 3 percent in the following year. An additional 3 percent co-responsi-

[7] The cost of farm programs (for all commodities including grains) rose from $4 billion in fiscal year 1981 (year ending September) to over $15 billion a year in 1983–85.

[8] Programs under the 1985 farm bill were originally expected to cost $17.5 billion in fiscal 1986, but a higher-than-expected producer participation rate and weaker-than-expected export sales raised expenditure to $25.8 billion. Expenditure declined to $23.1 billion in fiscal 1987, partly because of increased use of generic certificates, and because a cap was imposed on payments to individual producers.

[9] Other provisions of the 1985 farm bill designed to increase cereal exports include short-term export credit guarantees, direct export credits (in cash or in-kind), and intermediate loan guarantees.

[10] The EC Commission estimates that the cost of supporting grain within the EC increased from ECU 1.7 billion in 1984 to ECU 5 billion in 1987 and may rise to ECU 6 billion in 1988. This reflects both increased export subsidies needed to bridge the gap between high domestic prices and declining world market prices, and the appreciation of the ECU against the U.S. dollar since March 1985 which further reduced world market prices in ECU terms.

**Table 10.    Cereals: World Supply and Utilization, 1960/61–87/88**

| Crop Years | Area Harvested | Yield | Production | Utilization[1] | Closing Stocks[2] | Stocks/ Utilization Ratio[3] |
|---|---|---|---|---|---|---|
| | (In millions of hectares) | (In tons a hectare) | (In millions of tons) | | | (In percent) |
| 1960/61 | 647 | 1.31 | 846 | 832 | 199 | 24 |
| 1961/62 | 642 | 1.26 | 806 | 833 | 172 | 21 |
| 1962/63 | 647 | 1.34 | 867 | 865 | 174 | 20 |
| 1963/64 | 653 | 1.33 | 870 | 870 | 175 | 20 |
| 1964/65 | 663 | 1.39 | 924 | 920 | 179 | 19 |
| 1965/66 | 660 | 1.40 | 921 | 955 | 142 | 15 |
| 1966/67 | 660 | 1.52 | 1,006 | 980 | 169 | 17 |
| 1967/68 | 673 | 1.54 | 1,038 | 1,017 | 189 | 19 |
| 1968/69 | 678 | 1.59 | 1,079 | 1,047 | 222 | 21 |
| 1969/70 | 680 | 1.60 | 1,087 | 1,102 | 207 | 19 |
| 1970/71 | 671 | 1.64 | 1,103 | 1,144 | 165 | 14 |
| 1971/72 | 680 | 1.76 | 1,197 | 1,179 | 183 | 16 |
| 1972/73 | 670 | 1.73 | 1,161 | 1,201 | 143 | 12 |
| 1973/74 | 698 | 1.82 | 1,273 | 1,266 | 149 | 12 |
| 1974/75 | 700 | 1.74 | 1,218 | 1,223 | 141 | 12 |
| 1975/76 | 717 | 1.74 | 1,247 | 1,236 | 150 | 12 |
| 1976/77 | 719 | 1.90 | 1,363 | 1,309 | 204 | 16 |
| 1977/78 | 717 | 1.87 | 1,337 | 1,338 | 202 | 15 |
| 1978/79 | 717 | 2.05 | 1,466 | 1,436 | 232 | 16 |
| 1979/80 | 713 | 2.00 | 1,428 | 1,451 | 210 | 14 |
| 1980/81 | 724 | 2.00 | 1,447 | 1,461 | 196 | 13 |
| 1981/82 | 734 | 2.04 | 1,498 | 1,464 | 229 | 16 |
| 1982/83 | 717 | 2.16 | 1,548 | 1,505 | 272 | 18 |
| 1983/84 | 708 | 2.10 | 1,485 | 1,553 | 204 | 13 |
| 1984/85 | 709 | 2.32 | 1,645 | 1,592 | 256 | 16 |
| 1985/86 | 714 | 2.33 | 1,665 | 1,575 | 346 | 22 |
| 1986/87 | 710 | 2.36 | 1,679 | 1,641 | 385 | 23 |
| 1987/88[4] | 688 | 2.32 | 1,600 | 1,648 | 337 | 20 |

Source: U.S. Department of Agriculture, *World Grain Situation and Outlook*, December 1987 and earlier issues.

[1] For countries where stocks data are not available, utilization estimates represent "apparent" utilization, that is, they include annual stock level adjustments.

[2] Stocks data are based on an aggregate of differing local marketing years and should not be construed as representing world stock levels at a fixed point in time. World stock levels have been adjusted for estimated year-to-year changes in the U.S.S.R. grain stocks, but do not purport to include the absolute level of U.S.S.R. grain stocks. Data do not include stocks in China, in some countries in Eastern Europe, and in some other countries for which stocks data are not available.

[3] Ratio of marketing year ending stocks to utilization.

[4] U.S. Department of Agriculture estimate.

bility levy will be charged at the beginning of each year, but will be reimbursed if the threshold is not exceeded; it will be partially reimbursed if the threshold is exceeded by less than 3 percent. A paid set-aside (acreage reduction) program will be implemented whereby producers taking at least 20 percent of arable land out of production for at least five years will receive an annual payment of between ECU 100 and ECU 600 a hectare, depending on the quality of the land.[11] Finally, a ceiling on agricultural spending of ECU 27.5 billion was established for 1988/89.

In Japan both producer and consumer prices of rice are several times higher than world market prices, and few imports are permitted. For these reasons, the

reduction of producer prices for rice by almost 6 percent in 1987, the first reduction since 1956, had little impact on the world rice market. Nonetheless, proposals for more fundamental reforms of agricultural policies are under review by the government.

As a result of the acreage reduction programs in the United States, lower returns to producers in countries where agriculture is less subsidized, especially Australia and Argentina, and the idling of marginal land in the U.S.S.R., the total area planted to cereals declined by 1 percent in 1986/87 and is estimated to have fallen by an additional 3 percent in 1987/88. Owing in part to less favorable weather conditions, global production of cereals is expected to decline by 5 percent in 1987/88 to 1.6 billion tons. Utilization is projected to exceed production for the first time since 1983/84, and global stocks at the end of the 1987/88

[11] The proposed set-aside would apply to cereals, oilseeds, sugar beet, and potatoes.

15

**Table 11.   Wheat: World Commodity Balance, 1981/82–87/88**

(In millions of tons, unless otherwise indicated)

| | July/June Crop Years | | | | | | |
|---|---|---|---|---|---|---|---|
| | 1981/82 | 1982/83 | 1983/84 | 1984/85 | 1985/86 | 1986/87 | 1987/88[1] |
| **Production** | **450** | **477** | **489** | **512** | **499** | **529** | **501** |
| China | 60 | 68 | 81 | 88 | 86 | 90 | 87 |
| European Community | 58 | 65 | 64 | 83 | 72 | 72 | 72 |
| India | 36 | 38 | 43 | 45 | 44 | 47 | 46 |
| United States | 76 | 75 | 66 | 71 | 66 | 57 | 57 |
| U.S.S.R. | 81 | 84 | 77 | 69 | 78 | 92 | 81 |
| Other countries | 139 | 147 | 158 | 156 | 153 | 171 | 158 |
| **Utilization** | **444** | **462** | **482** | **496** | **487** | **519** | **521** |
| China | 73 | 81 | 91 | 95 | 92 | 99 | 99 |
| United States | 23 | 25 | 30 | 31 | 29 | 33 | 33 |
| U.S.S.R. | 102 | 101 | 93 | 91 | 92 | 102 | 96 |
| Other countries | 246 | 255 | 268 | 279 | 274 | 285 | 293 |
| **Closing stocks** | **87** | **102** | **109** | **125** | **137** | **147** | **127** |
| United States | 32 | 41 | 38 | 39 | 52 | 50 | 35 |
| Other countries | 55 | 61 | 71 | 86 | 85 | 97 | 92 |
| Stocks/utilization ratio (*in percent*) | 20 | 22 | 23 | 25 | 29 | 28 | 24 |

Source: U.S. Department of Agriculture, *Foreign Agriculture Circular: World Grain Situation and Outlook* (Washington), various issues.
[1] Estimate.

crop year are expected to fall to the equivalent of 20 percent of annual utilization.

## Wheat

After successive record harvests between 1980/81 and 1984/85 (crop years ended June), global wheat production fell by 2.5 percent in 1985/86 and then recovered by 6 percent in 1986/87 to a new record of almost 530 million tons (Table 11). These fluctuations in output reflect variations in yield, as area harvested declined slightly. The growth of global wheat consumption lagged behind that of production in the first half of the 1980s resulting in a sharp buildup of stocks, which reached one quarter of annual utilization in 1984/85. Global consumption fell by 1.8 percent in 1985/86 as other grains were substituted for wheat in animal feed, but increased by 7 percent in 1986/87 as this substitution was reversed. The ratio of stocks to utilization rose further to 28 percent in 1985/86 and stabilized at this level in 1986/87. Reflecting the rapid buildup of global stocks during the 1980s, wheat export prices in the United States declined from an average of $178 a ton in 1980/81 to $108 a ton in 1986/87.[12]

At the beginning of the 1985/86 crop year, export prices fell to their lowest level since 1978, averaging $126 a ton in the third quarter of 1985. Factors contributing to the price weakness were the large carryover stock from 1984/85 and the prospect of a rebound in wheat production in the U.S.S.R., the world's largest importer. In the United States, farm prices fell below the loan rate of $121.25 a ton for 1985, which induced producers to place a record volume of wheat under government loan. The resulting tightening of supplies available to the market had the effect of raising prices to an average of $132 a ton in the final quarter of 1985 and the first quarter of 1986. Despite a reduction in the loan rate for 1986 to $88.18 a ton, international prices in this period were supported by lower crops in Argentina, Canada, and Europe, owing to adverse weather.

Following a brief surge in prices in May 1986 associated with the nuclear accident at Chernobyl in the U.S.S.R., prices declined under the influence of a favorable outlook for production in the United States and the U.S.S.R., and the announcement in the United States of a reduction in the loan rate for the 1987 crop to $83.76 a ton, the minimum permitted under the 1985 Farm Bill. In the third quarter of 1986, export prices averaged $103 a ton, the lowest level reached since 1977/78. Prices then rose modestly through the next two quarters, being influenced by a tightening of free supplies to the U.S. market owing to strong participation of producers in the price support program, the possibility of weather damage to the winter wheat crops in the United States and the U.S.S.R., and an improved U.S. export performance under the EEP with sales to Egypt and China and expectations of a resumption of sales to the U.S.S.R. Export prices rose

[12] Price quotations refer to U.S. No. 1 hard red winter wheat, ordinary protein, f.o.b. Gulf of Mexico ports. They exceed spot prices in midwest markets by about $10 a ton.

sharply in May 1987, averaging $119 a ton, mainly in response to the announcement at the end of April of the sale of 4 million tons of wheat to the U.S.S.R. under the EEP.[13] Also influencing wheat prices at this time were a period of hot, dry weather in the midwest region of the United States and the perception among traders that the recent period of low prices might be at an end, as evidenced by a rise in many other commodity prices.

Export prices weakened again, averaging $107 a ton in June and July, after timely rainfall ensured good yields in the United States. Prices then rallied to $115 a ton by November under the influence of stepped-up export sales to a number of countries, a spillover of high rice prices to the wheat market, and optimism that drought-induced production shortfalls in China, India, and Pakistan would further increase import demand and reduce stocks significantly by the end of the 1987/88 crop year. The upswing, however, was tempered by increased farmer selling to take advantage of higher prices in the light of negative underlying influences including the announcement of a new loan rate for the 1988 crop of $79.74 a ton, the minimum permitted,[14] excellent sowing conditions for the 1987/88 crop, and the temporary weakness in commodity prices induced by the stock market collapse in October 1987.

In December 1987 prices rose sharply, averaging $125 a ton owing to strong foreign demand; U.S. export sales exceeded 1 million tons a week for five consecutive weeks with the assistance of EEP subsidies. To ensure that export sales did not tighten the domestic market excessively and thereby raise the rate of EEP subsidy, a weekly auction of government-owned wheat of up to 25 million bushels (0.68 million tons) a week commenced in November.

Global wheat production rose by 6 percent to a record 529 million tons in 1986/87. Output rose in all major producing countries except in the United States, where area harvested declined by 6 percent as a result of the acreage reduction provisions of the price support program.[15] Yield in the United States was also reduced by winter damage and spring dryness, and production declined by 14 percent to 57 million tons. Low prices

influenced production decisions in Australia and Argentina, where market intervention is relatively small, and area harvested fell by about 4 percent in each country. Improved weather conditions raised yields, however, and output in each country was marginally higher than in 1985/86 at 16.2 and 9 million tons, respectively. By contrast, in Canada and the EC, domestic subsidies (albeit at lower levels than in previous years) insulated producers from low international prices so that area harvested for the 1986/87 crop increased. Income support to farmers in Canada reached a record level in 1986/87,[16] and a special assistance program to help offset the impact of subsidies granted by other countries was also introduced in December 1986. Area harvested rose by 3.6 percent, and with a record yield production rose by 29 percent to a record 31.4 million tons. EC intervention prices for the 1986/87 crop were reduced in ECU terms by 5 percent for feed wheat but remained unchanged for breadmaking wheat. Despite the introduction of the 3 percent co-responsibility levy, producer prices in France and the United Kingdom (the major producing countries) remained approximately unchanged because of adjustments to their "green" rates of exchange. For the twelve members of the EC as a whole, the area harvested to wheat rose by 2.6 percent but the yield declined so that output rose marginally to 72 million tons. The area harvested in the U.S.S.R. declined by 3 percent as marginal lands were taken out of production, and, aided by favorable weather and improved distribution of fertilizer, the yield reached a new record as output rose by 18 percent to 92 million tons. Output in Eastern Europe rose by 4 percent to 39 million tons, reflecting both larger area planted and better yield, while favorable weather in China and India together with higher procurement prices were mainly responsible for increases in output of 5 percent and 6 percent, respectively.

After declining by 2 percent in 1985–86 because of lower output in China and lower feed use in the United States, global utilization of wheat rose by 7 percent in 1986/87 to a record 519 million tons. This mainly reflected a sharp increase in feed wheat usage, which rose by 17 percent compared with an annual average growth rate of 5 percent in previous years. The Republic of Korea and Mexico took advantage of low prices for weather-damaged Australian wheat, while increased usage in Canada, the EC, and the U.S.S.R. was made possible by higher domestic production. Although utilization rebounded in 1986/87, it was insufficient to prevent a further buildup of stocks by

---

[13] Net prices paid by importers under the EEP ranged from $25 to $30 a ton below U.S. export prices, the difference being paid by subsidies in-kind.

[14] The loan rate for the 1988 crop was raised subsequently to $81.20 a ton under the budget agreement between the President and Congress in December 1987 (the Omnibus Budget Reconciliation Act).

[15] To be eligible for price support loans and deficiency payments in 1987, farmers were required to reduce their area planted to wheat by 27.5 percent of their base acreage (the average of individual acreage in the five previous seasons), compared with a 25 percent reduction in 1986. A 27.5 percent average reduction is again in effect for 1988.

[16] Under the Western Grains Stabilization Scheme, net cash flow to producers is guaranteed to at least equal the average realized in the last five years.

**Table 12. Wheat: Export Earnings, 1984–87**

| | 1984 | 1985 | 1986 | 1987[1] | 1984 | 1985 | 1986 | 1987[1] |
|---|---|---|---|---|---|---|---|---|
| | *(Values in SDRs)* | | | | *(Values in U.S. dollars)* | | | |
| **Earnings** *(in billions)* | **17.8** | **15.1** | **11.1** | **10.6** | **18.2** | **15.3** | **13.0** | **13.7** |
| Industrial countries | 15.7 | 12.9 | 10.1 | 9.7 | 16.1 | 13.1 | 11.9 | 12.5 |
| Developing countries | 1.5 | 1.5 | 0.6 | 0.5 | 1.5 | 1.6 | 0.7 | 0.7 |
| U.S.S.R. and Eastern European countries | 0.6 | 0.7 | 0.4 | 0.4 | 0.6 | 0.7 | 0.5 | 0.5 |
| **Volumes** *(in millions of tons)* | **116.4** | **105.3** | **95.7** | **102.9** | **116.4** | **105.3** | **95.7** | **102.9** |
| Industrial countries | 101.9 | 88.5 | 86.4 | 92.6 | 101.9 | 88.5 | 86.4 | 92.6 |
| *Australia* | *10.6* | *15.8* | *16.2* | *13.6* | *10.6* | *15.8* | *16.2* | *13.6* |
| *Canada* | *21.6* | *17.4* | *16.4* | *16.7* | *21.6* | *17.4* | *16.4* | *16.7* |
| *France* | *15.8* | *19.0* | *15.4* | *13.5* | *15.8* | *19.0* | *15.4* | *13.5* |
| *United States* | *43.6* | *26.1* | *26.4* | *37.2* | *43.6* | *26.1* | *26.4* | *37.2* |
| *Other* | *10.3* | *10.2* | *12.0* | *11.6* | *10.3* | *10.2* | *12.0* | *11.6* |
| Developing countries | 10.8 | 12.0 | 5.4 | 5.7 | 10.8 | 12.0 | 5.4 | 5.7 |
| *Argentina* | *7.4* | *9.7* | *4.1* | *4.3* | *7.4* | *9.7* | *4.1* | *4.3* |
| *Other* | *3.4* | *2.3* | *1.3* | *1.4* | *3.4* | *2.3* | *1.3* | *1.4* |
| U.S.S.R. and Eastern European countries | 3.7 | 4.8 | 3.9 | 4.6 | 3.7 | 4.8 | 3.9 | 4.6 |
| **Unit values** *(a ton)* | **153** | **143** | **116** | **104** | **157** | **145** | **136** | **134** |
| Industrial countries | 154 | 145 | 117 | 104 | 158 | 147 | 137 | 135 |
| Developing countries | 139 | 128 | 104 | 92 | 143 | 130 | 122 | 119 |
| U.S.S.R. and Eastern European countries | 153 | 140 | 103 | 94 | 157 | 142 | 121 | 122 |
| **Market prices** *(a ton)*[2] | **149** | **134** | **98** | **87** | **152** | **136** | **115** | **113** |

Sources: UN Food and Agriculture Organization, *1986 FAO Trade Yearbook* (Rome) for exports; Commodities Division, IMF Research Department for prices.

[1] Data on exports are estimates of Commodities Division, IMF Research Department.

[2] U.S. No. 1 hard red winter wheat, ordinary protein, f.o.b. Gulf of Mexico ports.

10 million tons to a record 147 million tons. Nevertheless, the ratio of ending stocks to total utilization at the end of the 1986/87 crop year remained virtually unchanged at 28 percent.

Higher wheat production in both China and the U.S.S.R., the major importing countries, reduced their need to import wheat in 1986, and the volume of world trade in wheat fell by 9 percent to 96 million tons (Table 12). Among exporting countries, EC countries and Argentina experienced a fall in export volume because of adverse weather, while exports from Australia, Canada, and the United States increased.[17] The decline in export volume in 1986 coincided with a 6 percent decline in unit values, and global earnings from wheat exports fell by 15 percent to $13 billion. The intention of China and the U.S.S.R. to improve nutrition and livestock standards and to increase stocks, together with low prices offered by the United States under the EEP, is expected to result in an upswing in the volume of world trade in 1987 to 103 million tons.

---

[17] The main importers of U.S. wheat in 1986/87 were Algeria, Egypt, Iraq, Japan, and Morocco. China and the U.S.S.R. were not offered equivalent subsidized prices under export enhancement until late in the year; they are expected to become the largest purchasers of U.S. wheat in 1987/88.

Although unit values have declined further there is expected to be a small increase in earnings to $13.7 billion.

In the 1987/88 crop year, global wheat production is expected to decline by 5 percent to 501 million tons under the influence of reduced price support and less favorable weather conditions in a number of countries compared with 1986/87. Wet weather in the U.S.S.R. hampered the harvest of the 1987 spring wheat crop and seeding of the 1988 winter wheat crop. As a result, the 1987/88 crop is expected to fall by 12 percent to 81 million tons and to be of lower quality than in 1986/87. The expected reduction of 11 million tons in U.S.S.R. output accounts for over two fifths of the projected decline in global production of 28 million tons. Wheat yield in the EC will also be depressed by the heavy rainfall which occurred in the first quarter of the crop year. Intervention prices were set unchanged in terms of ECUs for 1987/88, but intervention purchases will only be made at 94 percent of the intervention price. The impact of this 6 percent reduction in nominal price support on planting decisions, however, could be offset by devaluations of the green exchange rates. Output is projected to rise marginally, entirely reflecting a small increase in area harvested. In the United States, the target price was reduced by

3 percent for 1988 to $155.43 a ton after being held constant since 1984 at $160.94 a ton,[18] and the required acreage reduction was set at 27.5 percent of base acreage, the same reduction as in 1986/87. In addition, deficiency payments provided in advance of the harvest will decline by 27 percent to $56 a ton. Consequently, area harvested is expected to fall by 8 percent, but with a higher yield resulting from the most productive land remaining in use, output is expected to remain at 57 million tons. Initial price support payments in Canada were reduced by 15 percent for the 1988 crop, and a 5 percent reduction in area harvested is expected. Assuming a return to normal yield after the 1986/87 record, output is projected to decline by 16 percent to 26 million tons. In Argentina, area harvested in 1988 is expected to decline only marginally, as wheat farmers have few production alternatives.[19] If weather conditions return to normal after two successive adverse years, output is expected to rise by about 1 million tons. Guaranteed minimum prices (GMPs) for wheat in Australia declined by $A 10 a ton in 1986/87 and are expected to fall by a further $A 14–20 a ton in 1987/88.[20] As a result, area harvested is expected to be reduced by 20 percent to the lowest level in a decade. Output may decline by nearly 4 million tons (23 percent) to 13 million tons as the extremely favorable weather conditions of 1986/87 are not expected to be repeated.

Global utilization of wheat is expected to rise marginally in 1987/88 to 521 million tons. This mainly reflects higher food use in developing countries where high rice prices will lead to increased consumption of wheat. Utilization in the U.S.S.R. is expected to decline by 6 percent due to lower stockbuilding; although production is expected to fall, both food and feed use should increase, assisted by a substantial rise in imports. Utilization in China and the United States is expected to be largely unchanged from that in 1986/87. With the sharp drop in global production, end-period stocks are projected to fall by 20 million tons (14 percent), and the ratio of stocks to utilization is expected to decline for the first time since 1980/81 to 24 percent.

## Maize

The United States has a predominant position in world maize production and trade, accounting for about 45 percent of global output and two thirds of global exports. Consequently, year-to-year variations in supplies in the United States caused by climatic conditions and the U.S. Government's price support programs have a major influence on international maize market conditions. Owing to the recovery of U.S. production from the effects of drought in 1983/84 (crop years ended September), world output rose by 32 percent in 1984/85 and by a further 5 percent in 1985/86 to a record 480 million tons (Table 13). World maize utilization recovered more slowly than production in 1984/85 (by 6 percent), and then fell by 4 percent in 1985/86 as higher output of other coarse grains in the U.S.S.R. reduced consumption and import requirements for maize. As a result of these developments, the ratio of world stocks to utilization increased from 9 percent in 1983/84 to 14 percent in 1984/85 and to 29 percent in 1985/86, and export prices declined sharply, from an average of $143 a ton in 1983/84 to $97 a ton in 1985/86.[21] In 1986/87, global output declined slightly owing to acreage reduction in the United States, and utilization increased by 8 percent as the cattle cycle in many countries entered the rebuilding phase. The ratio of stocks to utilization rose further to 33 percent at year-end, however, and prices continued to decline, averaging $72 a ton, which was the lowest price recorded since 1971/72.

In the first quarter of the 1985/86 crop year (the final quarter of 1985) export prices averaged $104 per ton, or 11 percent lower than a year earlier. The price weakness reflected a record U.S. maize harvest of over 225 million tons on top of already ample supplies. Farm prices in the United States fell below the loan rate for the 1985 crop of $100.39 a ton, and, as a result, a high proportion of the crop was placed under loan. By reducing the "free" supplies available, this lent some support to the market through the first half of 1986 when export prices averaged $104 a ton, or well above the loan rate for the 1986 crop of $75.59 a ton.[22]

---

[18] The target price determines the gross remuneration to producers because deficiency payments make up the difference between the loan rate and the target price.

[19] Some relief from low prices will be afforded by the elimination of a 5 percent export tax in July 1987.

[20] The GMP is the level at which the government will support wheat prices. It is determined as 95 percent of the estimated average of net returns to farmers in the current crop year and the two lowest returns of the previous three years. Actual prices fell so far below estimated prices in the 1986/87 crop year that the government was required to subsidize growers for the first time.

[21] Price quotations refer to U.S. No. 2 yellow corn, f.o.b. Gulf of Mexico ports. They exceed spot prices in midwest markets by about $8 a ton.

[22] The provisions of the 1986 program for maize, in addition to the sharp cut in the loan rate to $75.59 a ton, were an unchanged target price of $119.29 a ton (resulting in a deficiency payment of $43.70 a ton); a mandatory acreage reduction of 17.5 percent of base acreage; and an optional paid (in-kind) land diversion of 2.5 percent. Maize, along with wheat, other feed grains, cotton, and rice, was also subject to an optional "50/92" provision, whereby producers could plant between 50 and 92 percent of their permitted acreage (after the mandatory reduction) and still receive deficiency payments on 92 percent of total permitted acreage.

**Table 13. Maize: World Commodity Balance, 1981/82–87/88**

(In millions of tons, unless otherwise indicated)

| | October/September Crop Years | | | | | | |
|---|---|---|---|---|---|---|---|
| | 1981/82 | 1982/83 | 1983/84 | 1984/85 | 1985/86 | 1986/87 | 1987/88[1] |
| **Production** | **439** | **440** | **347** | **459** | **480** | **474** | **446** |
| China | 59 | 60 | 68 | 73 | 64 | 69 | 78 |
| United States | 206 | 209 | 106 | 195 | 225 | 210 | 182 |
| Other countries | 174 | 171 | 173 | 191 | 191 | 195 | 186 |
| **Utilization** | **413** | **419** | **414** | **437** | **418** | **450** | **463** |
| China | 60 | 63 | 68 | 68 | 58 | 67 | 77 |
| United States | 127 | 138 | 122 | 131 | 133 | 150 | 153 |
| Other countries | 226 | 218 | 224 | 238 | 227 | 233 | 233 |
| **Closing stocks** | **85** | **106** | **39** | **61** | **123** | **147** | **130** |
| United States | 64 | 90 | 26 | 42 | 103 | 124 | 110 |
| Others | 21 | 16 | 13 | 19 | 20 | 23 | 20 |
| Stocks/utilization ratio (*in percent*) | 21 | 25 | 9 | 14 | 29 | 33 | 28 |

Source: U.S. Department of Agriculture, *Foreign Agriculture Circular: World Grain Situation and Outlook* (Washington).
[1] Estimate.

In the third quarter of 1986, however, export prices fell sharply to an average of $75 a ton because of expectations of another large domestic crop for 1986/87, lower than anticipated domestic feed use as cattle and hog numbers continued to decline, and the announcement of a 5 percent reduction in the loan rate for the 1987 crop to $71.65 a ton.[23] Export prices fell further to $68 a ton in the final quarter of 1986 (the first quarter of the 1986/87 crop year) as a record stock carryover of 103 million tons and current production of 210 million tons (a decline of only 7 percent from 1985/86 despite heavy participation in the price support program) raised aggregate supply to a new record. Also, export prospects were dimmed by upward revisions to estimates of grain output in the U.S.S.R. Export prices improved marginally in the first quarter of 1987 as the placement of large supplies under loan tightened the supply available to the market. Prices rose to $78 a ton in the second quarter in response to a resumption of purchases by the U.S.S.R., a pickup in U.S. exports to other countries because of smaller-than-expected maize crops in Argentina and South Africa, and an upturn in U.S. feed use of maize. Generally favorable weather conditions during the planting and growing seasons for the 1987/88 crop caused export prices to decline to an average of $74 a ton in the third quarter; prices received by farmers ranged between $63 and $67 a ton. In the final quarter

of 1987 (the first quarter of the 1987/88 crop year) prices recovered to $81 a ton despite a stock carry-in even larger than in 1986/87 (124 million tons) and a reduction in the loan rate for the 1988 crop by 4 percent to $68.50 a ton.[24] The price recovery reflected the perception that market conditions could tighten considerably by the end of the crop year; 1987/88 production is expected to decline to 182 million tons, the lowest since the drought-affected 1983/84 crop, and there was a surge in exports to the U.S.S.R. and Asian countries owing, in part, to weather-related production shortfalls in other exporting countries, notably Argentina and Thailand.

Farm prices throughout 1986 and 1987 were lower than the export prices quoted above by a differential related to transportation costs to port and were at all times below the respective loan rates. The excess supply situation in the U.S. market, whereby stocks have risen to about 60 percent of annual utilization, was mainly responsible for producer prices falling below the loan rate, which previously had acted as a price floor. An additional factor depressing prices was the widespread use by producers of generic certificates to redeem maize placed previously under loan. Generic certificates have been issued by the government from April 1986 onward as part of advance deficiency and

[23] Under the 1987 maize program, the target price was unchanged at $119.29 a ton so that the deficiency payment increased (by the amount by which the loan rate was lowered) to $47.64 a ton. The acreage reduction requirement and the paid land diversion were raised to 20 percent and 15 percent of base acreage, respectively, and the "50/92" provision remained in effect.

[24] The loan rate for 1988 was raised subsequently to $69.68 a ton under the December 1987 Omnibus Budget Reconciliation Act. In addition, the target price was reduced by 3 percent to $115.35 a ton, and deficiency payments were lowered by 9 percent to $43.31 a ton. The acreage reaction requirement of 20 percent of base acreage remained in effect, but the optional paid land diversion was reduced to 10 percent. There will also be a "0/92" provision which is similar to the "50/92" provision in effect in 1987 except that diversion payment will still be made even if no land is planted.

diversion payments to producers participating in the farm support reduction program. They have a fixed face value so that when prices fall, the amount of a commodity for which certificates can be exchanged increases. Since the price at which the exchange takes place (the posted county price) is determined by the government and is related to local market prices, a producer is assured of a profit whenever the market price is below the loan rate.[25] The redemption has the effect of channeling maize which otherwise would have remained in government storage into the market, and thereby exerts downward pressure on prices. By adjusting the posted country price, the government can influence the rate of use of certificates, and through them market prices, so that the U.S. maize remains competitive in export markets.

Although maize prices declined sharply over the past two crop years, the response of producers in countries other than the United States was limited. Output in China, the world's second largest producer, increased by 8 percent in 1986/87 and is expected to rise by a further 13 percent to 78 million tons in 1987/88 in response to improved producer-price incentives, which aim at supplying the domestic livestock industry. In the EC, intervention prices were effectively reduced by 6 percent in terms of ECUs for the 1987/88 crop, but adjustments in green rates meant that national currency intervention prices in France and the United Kingdom were reduced by only 1 percent and 2 percent, respectively. Area planted to maize in 1987/88 is expected to decline by a total of 5 percent for the EC countries as a whole, and a decline in production of about 1 million tons is expected. Production in Brazil, the third largest producer, reached a record 26.5 million tons in 1986/87 because of higher area planted, but is expected to fall by 2.5 million tons in 1987/88. Drought is expected to reduce Thailand's production by 1.5 million tons in 1987/88. Production in Argentina, however, should rebound by 1 million tons in 1987/88 after weather damage to the 1986/87 crop. Total non-U.S. production is projected to remain stable in 1987/88 after increasing by 10 million tons the previous year.

World maize utilization increased by 32 million tons (8 percent) in 1986/87. Utilization in China rose by 9 million tons (16 percent) while consumption in the U.S.S.R. fell by 4 million tons (16 percent), both changes reflecting developments in domestic production. Utilization in the United States increased by 17 million tons (13 percent) as both the cattle and hog cycles started their rebuilding phase. Continued strong growth of feed consumption of maize is expected in the United States and China in 1987/88, but this may be offset in part by the ready availability of domestic feed-quality wheat and a slowdown in the growth of the livestock sector in the U.S.S.R. Globally, maize utilization is projected to increase by 13 million tons (3 percent) in 1987/88.

After peaking at $10.3 billion in 1984, the value of world maize exports declined to $8.8 billion in 1985 entirely on account of lower unit values (Table 14). The continuing decline in prices together with an 18 percent fall in export volume reduced global earnings to $6.8 billion in 1986. The reduction in volume mainly reflected a 10 million ton drop in imports by the U.S.S.R. owing to increased domestic output of maize and other coarse grains. It is estimated that a small recovery in the volume of world maize exports occurred in 1987. Although import demand by the U.S.S.R. continued to decline, this was offset by increased imports by China, Japan, and the Republic of Korea to support their livestock industries. A further drop in unit values, however, reduced export earnings to an estimated $4.9 billion. The decline in aggregate earnings from maize exports in terms of SDRs since 1984 has been even larger than the decline in terms of dollars.

Prices are likely to rise modestly in 1988 because global utilization is projected to exceed supply for the first time since 1984. Nevertheless, farm prices in the United States may not rise to the level of the loan rate ($69.68 a ton) because it is the policy of the government to maximize maize exports through competitive pricing. As noted, the government has considerable flexibility to influence the use of generic certificates to maintain prices below the loan rate and this would consequently restrain the upward movement of world prices.

## Rice

Since about 90 percent of world rice production and consumption are concentrated in Asia and since production is highly dependent on monsoon conditions, periods of heavy import demand tend to coincide with periods of reduced export availability. Most of the crop is consumed in the countries where it is produced, and only 4 percent of global production enters international trade.[26] Therefore, production shortfalls in only a few countries can result in a rapid and significant tightening of market conditions.

---

[25] In addition to repaying loans at less than face value, producers benefit because interest charges which accrue when a loan is repaid in cash are foregone, and storage charges are eliminated if the maize so acquired is sold immediately.

[26] The United States produces less than 2 percent of world output, but is the second largest exporter after Thailand, accounting for about 18 percent of the volume of global exports.

21

**Table 14.  Maize: Export Earnings, 1984–87**

| | 1984 | 1985 | 1986 | 1987 | 1984 | 1985 | 1986 | 1987[1] |
|---|---|---|---|---|---|---|---|---|
| | (Values in SDRs) | | | | (Values in U.S. dollars) | | | |
| **Earnings** (*in billions*) | **10.0** | **8.6** | **5.8** | **3.8** | **10.3** | **8.8** | **6.8** | **4.9** |
| Industrial countries | 8.3 | 6.4 | 3.7 | 2.8 | 8.5 | 6.5 | 4.4 | 3.7 |
| Developing countries | 1.6 | 2.1 | 2.0 | 0.9 | 1.6 | 2.1 | 2.3 | 1.1 |
| U.S.S.R. and Eastern | | | | | | | | |
| European countries | 0.1 | 0.1 | 0.1 | 0.1 | 0.2 | 0.2 | 0.1 | 0.1 |
| **Volumes** (*in millions of tons*) | **68.8** | **69.7** | **57.5** | **57.8** | **68.8** | **69.7** | **57.5** | **57.8** |
| Industrial countries | 56.7 | 50.4 | 34.5 | 42.1 | 56.7 | 50.4 | 34.5 | 42.1 |
| *United States* | *49.1* | *44.0* | *27.1* | *33.3* | *49.1* | *44.0* | *27.1* | *33.3* |
| *Other countries* | *7.6* | *6.4* | *7.4* | *6.8* | *7.6* | *6.4* | *7.4* | *6.8* |
| Developing countries | 11.4 | 18.3 | 21.0 | 15.0 | 11.4 | 18.3 | 22.2 | 15.0 |
| U.S.S.R. and Eastern | | | | | | | | |
| European countries | 0.7 | 1.0 | 0.8 | 0.7 | 0.7 | 1.0 | 0.8 | 0.7 |
| **Unit values** (*a ton*) | **145** | **123** | **101** | **66** | **149** | **125** | **118** | **85** |
| Industrial countries | 146 | 127 | 107 | 67 | 150 | 129 | 126 | 87 |
| Developing countries | 138 | 113 | 90 | 60 | 141 | 115 | 105 | 77 |
| U.S.S.R. and Eastern | | | | | | | | |
| European countries | 196 | 175 | 136 | 93 | 201 | 178 | 159 | 120 |
| **Market prices** (*a ton*)[2] | **133** | **111** | **75** | **58** | **136** | **112** | **88** | **76** |

Sources: UN Food and Agriculture Organization, *1986 FAO Trade Yearbook* (Rome) for exports; Commodities Division, IMF Research Department for prices.

[1] Data on exports are estimates of Commodities Division, IMF Research Department.

[2] U.S. No. 2 yellow corn, f.o.b. Gulf of Mexico ports.

Production shortfalls and higher import demand in India in 1980 and in the Republic of Korea in 1981 led to a 45 percent increase in export prices in both years, when prices peaked at $483 a ton on average.[27] As production recovered in 1982, prices declined to $259 a ton in the final quarter of that year. Market conditions tightened again in 1983 in response to weather-induced production shortfalls in Brazil, India, Indonesia, the Islamic Republic of Iran, and Iraq, and prices rose to $282 a ton in the final quarter. During the next three years, market conditions eased considerably. Increased output in 1984 in Bangladesh, China, and Pakistan enabled the global production of milled rice to increase by 8 percent in the 1983/84 crop year. Further, albeit much smaller, increases in production occurred in 1984/85 and 1985/86, and with production exceeding utilization, global stocks rose from the equivalent of 6 percent of annual utilization in 1983/84 to 8 percent in 1985/86 (Table 15). Import demand also weakened because former large importers, such as China, India, Indonesia, and Korea, became self-sufficient. Prices declined to an average of $215 a ton in the final quarter of 1985.

Large-scale imports by Brazil, which anticipated a significant shortfall of its 1985/86 crop below domestic needs, were mainly responsible for a strengthening of world prices to an average of $229 a ton in the first

quarter of 1986. But from the second quarter of 1986 onward, the major influence on prices was the start of the U.S. rice support program under the 1985 Farm Bill. The key feature of the program (which is not a part of the wheat or feed grains programs) is the marketing loan whereby producers can repay their loans at the higher of the world market price or 50 percent of the loan rate. This allowed domestic prices to fall below the loan rate[28] and enabled U.S. exporters to reduce prices to the extent necessary to regain market shares. As competition between the United States and other major exporters intensified, prices fell to $202 a ton in the second quarter of 1986 and averaged $205 a ton in the second half year.

In the 1986/87 crop year,[29] global production declined by 1 percent to 317 million tons (milled basis). Low prices resulted in a smaller area planted in Indonesia and Thailand while yields in India and Thailand were reduced by dry weather. Output in China, however, increased by 2 percent and Brazilian production recovered, increasing by 5 percent. Global utilization

---

[27] Price quotations refer to Thai milled white rice, 5 percent broken, f.o.b. Bangkok.

[28] For 1986, the loan rate (average of all types, unmilled) was reduced by 10 percent to $158.73 a ton, while the target price remained unchanged from 1985 at $262.35 a ton. A mandatory acreage reduction of 35 percent of base acreage was also in effect. For 1987, the loan rate was reduced by 5 percent to $150.80 a ton, and the target price was lowered by 2 percent to $257.06 a ton. The required acreage reduction remained at 35 percent.

[29] The crop year covers rice harvested over a 6–8 month period from the first Northern Hemisphere harvest in October to the last Southern Hemisphere harvest in April.

**Table 15.  Rice: World Commodity Balance, 1981/82–1987/88**

(In millions of tons)

| | Crop Years[1] | | | | | | |
|---|---|---|---|---|---|---|---|
| | 1981/82 | 1982/83 | 1983/84 | 1984/85 | 1985/86 | 1986/87 | 1987/88[2] |
| **Production (unmilled basis)** | **413** | **420** | **454** | **469** | **470** | **465** | **442** |
| China | 144 | 161 | 169 | 178 | 169 | 172 | 175 |
| India | 80 | 71 | 90 | 88 | 96 | 90 | 72 |
| Indonesia | 33 | 34 | 35 | 38 | 39 | 39 | 39 |
| Bangladesh | 21 | 21 | 22 | 22 | 23 | 23 | 22 |
| Thailand | 18 | 17 | 20 | 20 | 20 | 18 | 15 |
| United States | 8 | 7 | 5 | 6 | 6 | 6 | 6 |
| Other countries | 109 | 109 | 113 | 117 | 117 | 117 | 113 |
| **Production (milled basis)** | **281** | **286** | **309** | **319** | **320** | **317** | **302** |
| **Utilization (milled basis)** | **282** | **290** | **309** | **314** | **316** | **319** | **309** |
| China | 101 | 112 | 117 | 124 | 117 | 120 | 121 |
| India | 54 | 49 | 58 | 57 | 62 | 60 | 52 |
| Indonesia | 22 | 24 | 25 | 25 | 26 | 27 | 27 |
| Bangladesh | 14 | 15 | 15 | 15 | 15 | 16 | 15 |
| Other countries | 91 | 90 | 94 | 93 | 96 | 96 | 94 |
| **Closing stocks (milled basis)** | **21** | **17** | **17** | **22** | **26** | **24** | **17** |
| India | 5 | 3 | 6 | 7 | 9 | 9 | 5 |
| Indonesia | 2 | 2 | 2 | 3 | 3 | 2 | 2 |
| United States | 2 | 2 | 1 | 2 | 2 | 2 | 1 |
| Others | 12 | 10 | 8 | 10 | 12 | 11 | 9 |
| Stocks/utilization ratio *(in percent)* | 7 | 6 | 6 | 7 | 8 | 7 | 6 |

Source: U.S. Department of Agriculture, *World Grain Situation and Outlook* (Washington, D.C.), various issues.

[1] Rice is harvested over a 6–8 month period; thus crop year 1981/82 represents crops harvested in late 1981 and early 1982 in the Northern Hemisphere and in early 1981 in the Southern Hemisphere.

[2] U.S. Department of Agriculture estimates.

continued to rise, reaching 319 million tons, because the rise in China's output made increased domestic consumption possible, and low import prices allowed the substitution of rice for coarse grains in the diet of many countries, particularly in Africa. Global stocks were reduced by 2 million tons, and this reduction lent some support to market prices in the first half of 1987 when prices averaged $209 a ton.

In the second half of 1987, prices rose sharply on account of a long delay in the onset of the monsoon in South and Southeast Asia, which reduced the prospects for the 1987/88 crop in India and Thailand. Indian production is now expected to fall by 20 percent, compared with 1986/87 and Thai production by 17 percent. In addition, output in Bangladesh was affected by floods accompanying the delayed arrival of the monsoon in September, and is expected to decline by 4 percent. As a consequence, despite an expected 2 percent increase in China's production, global output of milled rice is projected to fall by 5 percent to 302 million tons in 1987/88. Although the shortfall in Indian production is expected to be met by reducing consumption and using stocks of rice and wheat rather than by importing, the anticipated lower availability of Thai rice for export (especially in 1988) tightened

the market considerably in the final quarter of 1987 and prices averaged $274 a ton or almost 50 percent higher than in the corresponding quarter of 1986. Any further upward movement in prices in 1988 may, however, be constrained by the substitution of wheat for rice imports in African and Middle Eastern countries.

For 1987 as a whole, the global volume of trade in rice is estimated to have declined by 2 percent (Table 16). This reflects not only a small reduction in Thai exports, but also reduced availability in Australia, where low prices led to a reduction in planted area, and in Indonesia where the yield was affected by pest infestation. U.S. rice exports are also expected to decline slightly after rising by 26 percent in 1986. On the import side, the reduced volume of trade in 1987 mainly reflects the virtual absence of Brazil from the market after record imports in 1986. Despite the decline in volume, the value of world trade in rice is expected to increase by 7 percent to $3.2 billion in 1987, which would be the first increase recorded since 1984. The value in 1987 in terms of SDRs, however, is expected to be marginally lower than in 1986. In 1988, the volume of Thai exports is projected to be more than 50 percent below 1987 volume, and the United States is likely to become the world's largest exporter.

23

**Table 16.   Rice: Export Earnings, 1984–87**

| | 1984 | 1985 | 1986 | 1987[1] | 1984 | 1985 | 1986 | 1987[1] |
|---|---|---|---|---|---|---|---|---|
| | *(Values in SDRs)* | | | | *(Values in U.S. dollars)* | | | |
| **Earnings** *(in billions)* | **3.7** | **3.1** | **2.5** | **2.5** | **3.8** | **3.1** | **3.0** | **3.2** |
| Industrial countries | 1.4 | 1.3 | 1.1 | 1.1 | 1.4 | 1.3 | 1.3 | 1.4 |
| Developing countries | 2.3 | 1.8 | 1.4 | 1.4 | 2.4 | 1.8 | 1.7 | 1.8 |
| **Volumes** *(in millions of tons)* | **12.7** | **11.1** | **12.2** | **12.0** | **12.7** | **11.1** | **12.2** | **12.0** |
| Industrial countries | 3.5 | 3.5 | 3.8 | 3.6 | 3.5 | 3.5 | 3.8 | 3.6 |
| *United States* | *2.1* | *1.9* | *2.4* | *2.3* | *2.1* | *1.9* | *2.4* | *2.3* |
| *Other countries* | *1.3* | *1.5* | *1.4* | *1.3* | *1.3* | *1.5* | *1.4* | *1.3* |
| Developing countries | 9.2 | 7.6 | 8.4 | 8.4 | 9.2 | 7.6 | 8.4 | 8.4 |
| *Thailand* | *4.6* | *4.1* | *4.5* | *4.2* | *4.6* | *4.1* | *4.5* | *4.2* |
| *Other countries* | *4.6* | *3.5* | *3.9* | *4.2* | *4.6* | *3.5* | *3.9* | *4.2* |
| **Unit values** *(a ton)* | **290** | **280** | **210** | **210** | **300** | **280** | **240** | **270** |
| Industrial countries | 410 | 380 | 290 | 290 | 420 | 380 | 340 | 380 |
| Developing countries | 250 | 230 | 170 | 170 | 260 | 230 | 200 | 220 |
| **Market prices** *(a ton)[2]* | **246** | **214** | **179** | **178** | **252** | **217** | **210** | **230** |

Sources: UN Food and Agriculture Organization, *1986 FAO Trade Yearbook* (Rome) for exports; Commodities Division, IMF Research Department for prices.

[1] Data on exports are estimates of Commodities Division, IMF Research Department.

[2] Thai milled white rice, 5 percent broken, f.o.b. Bangkok.

## Vegetable Oils and Protein Meals

The index of prices for vegetable oils and protein meals in 1987 was 9 percent higher than in 1986 in terms of U.S. dollars, but was nearly 2 percent lower in terms of SDRs (Table 17). In both years prices were far below the level of 1984—about one third lower in terms of dollars and about 44 percent lower in terms of SDRs—and prices were lower than in any other year since 1972. The downward pressure on the prices of vegetable oils and protein meals is mainly attributable to the strong recovery and continued expansion of production since 1983/84, when several largely coincidental factors markedly reduced output and stocks.[30] Production and stocks reached unprecedented levels in 1985/86 and remained at those levels in 1986/87. Prospects are for a further increase in output in 1987/88 (Tables 18 and 19) but increased consumption is expected to leave accumulated stocks slightly below the previous year's level.

Vegetable oils and protein meals are derived mainly from oilseeds, most of which are not consumed directly but rather are processed to expel their oil content and to produce meal. The demand for vegetable oils is derived mainly from the food and soap or detergent manufacturing industries, and the demand for meals, which are mainly used to produce animal feed, is derived from the demand for livestock products. In both of these markets, products are highly substitutable. For technical reasons or because of consumer preferences, however, some products may be preferred over others in particular end uses. The preferences for specific vegetable oils have been weakened in recent years as a result of technological improvements in processing that have increased the interchangeability of vegetable oils in a variety of uses and consequently have made price a more important criterion in the choice of oil by purchasers. Similarly, as a wide variety of materials can be used to manufacture animal feeds—including oilseed meals, grains, grain by-products, cassava, and citrus and beet pulp—price also is an important determinant of use among these various feedstuffs.

On the supply side, the market is considerably more heterogeneous and complex. One important characteristic is that some oilseeds are produced as annual crops (mainly soybeans, sunflowerseed, cottonseed, groundnut, and rapeseed) while others are perennial tree crops (mainly coconut, oil palm, and olives). Consequently, the supply response to changes in price prospects and the stability of supply from these two types of crops varies. Most producers of annual oilseed crops can adjust supply rapidly to a changing world price outlook, generally within a year. Tree crop producers have considerably less flexibility to increase

---

[30] These consisted of the marked reduction in the U.S. soybean crop as a result of the payment-in-kind program as well as unfavorable weather conditions; the decline in Malaysian palm oil production as a result of tree stress following introduction of biological pollination, reduced fertilizer use in response to low 1982 prices for palm oil, and drought in 1983; and lower copra production in the Philippines as a result of drought conditions and typhoon damage.

**Table 17. Prices of Vegetable Oils and Protein Meals, 1979–88**

| Year | Index of Prices of Vegetable Oils and Protein Meals [1] | Soybean Oil [2] | Palm Oil [3] | Sunflowerseed Oil [4] | Rapeseed Oil [5] | Coconut Oil [6] | Groundnut Oil [7] | Soybean Meal [8] | Groundnut Meal [9] | Fish Meal [10] |
|---|---|---|---|---|---|---|---|---|---|---|
| | *(1980 = 100)* | | | | | *(In SDRs a ton)* | | | | |
| 1979 | 103.6 | 512 | 506 | 590 | 492 | 762 | 688 | 188 | 184 | 306 |
| 1980 | 100.0 | 460 | 448 | 486 | 439 | 517 | 660 | 199 | 209 | 388 |
| 1981 | 105.5 | 430 | 483 | 542 | 410 | 483 | 884 | 214 | 228 | 396 |
| 1982 | 93.8 | 405 | 402 | 479 | 378 | 422 | 530 | 197 | 189 | 320 |
| 1983 | 113.2 | 493 | 471 | 522 | 467 | 686 | 668 | 222 | 215 | 423 |
| 1984 | 127.2 | 707 | 709 | 748 | 670 | 1,126 | 990 | 192 | 183 | 364 |
| 1985 | 97.5 | 567 | 498 | 593 | 532 | 588 | 894 | 155 | 144 | 276 |
| 1986 | 71.6 | 292 | 220 | 312 | 262 | 253 | 487 | 157 | 142 | 273 |
| 1987 | 70.5 | 258 | 264 | 279 | 236 | 341 | 387 | 157 | 125 | 296 |
| 1986 I | 78.8 | 362 | 258 | 375 | 318 | 294 | 541 | 167 | 150 | 268 |
| II | 72.3 | 300 | 208 | 330 | 276 | 216 | 493 | 158 | 140 | 278 |
| III | 66.4 | 245 | 173 | 264 | 210 | 189 | 455 | 155 | 139 | 273 |
| IV | 68.8 | 266 | 240 | 283 | 248 | 313 | 457 | 150 | 137 | 274 |
| 1987 I | 66.1 | 245 | 263 | 264 | 234 | 310 | 398 | 143 | 126 | 257 |
| II | 70.4 | 267 | 263 | 304 | 240 | 321 | 398 | 155 | 131 | 280 |
| III | 71.1 | 253 | 246 | 274 | 223 | 366 | 375 | 158 | 106 | 318 |
| IV | 74.4 | 268 | 286 | 272 | 247 | 370 | 376 | 172 | 137 | 329 |
| 1988 I | 78.0 | 301 | 309 | 304 | 284 | 393 | 376 | 163 | 130 | 349 |
| | *(1980 = 100)* | | | | | *(In U.S. dollars a ton)* | | | | |
| 1979 | 102.8 | 662 | 654 | 762 | 636 | 985 | 889 | 243 | 238 | 395 |
| 1980 | 100.0 | 598 | 583 | 633 | 571 | 673 | 859 | 259 | 272 | 504 |
| 1981 | 95.8 | 507 | 571 | 639 | 483 | 570 | 1,043 | 253 | 269 | 468 |
| 1982 | 79.6 | 447 | 445 | 529 | 417 | 467 | 585 | 218 | 208 | 354 |
| 1983 | 92.8 | 527 | 501 | 558 | 499 | 730 | 711 | 238 | 229 | 453 |
| 1984 | 100.4 | 725 | 729 | 767 | 687 | 1,155 | 1,017 | 197 | 188 | 373 |
| 1985 | 75.7 | 576 | 501 | 602 | 540 | 590 | 905 | 157 | 146 | 280 |
| 1986 | 64.4 | 342 | 257 | 366 | 307 | 296 | 569 | 185 | 166 | 321 |
| 1987 | 70.2 | 334 | 343 | 360 | 305 | 442 | 500 | 203 | 162 | 383 |
| 1986 I | 68.0 | 407 | 289 | 422 | 358 | 330 | 607 | 188 | 169 | 302 |
| II | 64.5 | 348 | 241 | 382 | 320 | 251 | 572 | 184 | 163 | 322 |
| III | 61.4 | 294 | 208 | 318 | 252 | 227 | 548 | 187 | 167 | 328 |
| IV | 63.8 | 320 | 289 | 341 | 299 | 378 | 551 | 180 | 165 | 330 |
| 1987 I | 64.0 | 309 | 331 | 333 | 295 | 391 | 501 | 180 | 159 | 324 |
| II | 70.0 | 345 | 341 | 393 | 310 | 415 | 515 | 200 | 170 | 363 |
| III | 69.8 | 323 | 314 | 350 | 284 | 467 | 478 | 202 | 135 | 405 |
| IV | 76.8 | 360 | 384 | 365 | 331 | 496 | 504 | 231 | 184 | 442 |
| 1988 I | 82.0 | 412 | 423 | 416 | 388 | 537 | 515 | 223 | 178 | 478 |

Source: Commodities Division, IMF Research Department.

[1] The weights in the index are as follows: soybeans, 41 percent; soybean meal, 24 percent; soybean oil, 11 percent; palm oil, 10 percent; coconut oil, 6 percent; fish meal, 5 percent; groundnut oil, 2 percent; groundnut meal, 1 percent; sunflowerseed oil and rapeseed oil are not included in the index.

[2] Dutch, f.o.b. ex-mill Rotterdam.

[3] Sumatra/Malaysian oil, c.i.f. Northwest European ports.

[4] Any origin, ex-tank Rotterdam.

[5] Dutch, f.o.b. ex-mill.

[6] Philippine/Indonesian oil, in bulk, c.i.f. Rotterdam.

[7] Any origin, c.i.f. Rotterdam.

[8] U.S. origin, c.i.f. Rotterdam.

[9] Argentine meal, in bulk, c.i.f. Rotterdam.

[10] Any origin, c.i.f. Hamburg.

supply in the short term because of long gestation periods, lengthy economic life spans, and relatively low variable costs of cultivation and harvest.[31]

[31] For example, the economic life span of an oil palm tree is about 30 years. The first crop is produced in about the third year after planting and output peaks between the eighth and tenth years.

The complexity of the market emanates from the fact that while different market forces govern the demand for oils and the demand for meals, most oils are produced as a joint product with meal in the processing of oilseeds, and the relative importance of each component varies considerably among oilseeds.

25

**Table 18.    Major Oilseeds (Oil Equivalent): World Commodity Balance, 1981/82–87/88**

| | October/September Crop Years | | | | | | |
| | 1981/82 | 1982/83 | 1983/84 | 1984/85 | 1985/86 | 1986/87[1] | 1987/88[2] |
|---|---|---|---|---|---|---|---|
| | *(In millions of tons; oil equivalent)*[3] | | | | | | |
| **Production** | **45.1** | **47.3** | **45.2** | **51.5** | **54.4** | **54.0** | **56.6** |
| Soybeans | 15.1 | 16.7 | 15.0 | 16.8 | 17.3 | 17.4 | 18.1 |
| Palm oil | 6.0 | 5.9 | 6.3 | 6.9 | 8.1 | 8.0 | 8.5 |
| Sunflowerseed | 5.8 | 6.6 | 6.2 | 7.0 | 7.7 | 7.6 | 8.2 |
| Rapeseed | 4.5 | 5.3 | 5.2 | 6.2 | 6.8 | 7.2 | 8.1 |
| Groundnuts | 5.8 | 5.2 | 5.4 | 5.7 | 5.6 | 5.8 | 5.4 |
| Cottonseed | 4.1 | 3.9 | 3.8 | 5.0 | 4.4 | 3.9 | 4.3 |
| Copra | 3.0 | 2.9 | 2.4 | 2.9 | 3.3 | 2.9 | 2.8 |
| Palm kernels | 0.8 | 0.8 | 0.9 | 1.0 | 1.2 | 1.2 | 1.2 |
| **Noncrush use** | **7.3** | **7.3** | **7.6** | **7.7** | **7.9** | **8.3** | **8.9** |
| Soybeans | 2.7 | 2.6 | 2.9 | 2.7 | 2.5 | 3.0 | 3.0 |
| Groundnuts | 2.4 | 2.3 | 2.5 | 2.6 | 2.7 | 2.8 | 3.1 |
| Other | 2.2 | 2.4 | 2.2 | 2.4 | 2.7 | 2.5 | 2.8 |
| **Crushings/oil production** | **38.3** | **39.8** | **38.5** | **42.5** | **45.6** | **46.3** | **47.8** |
| Soybean oil | 12.7 | 13.6 | 12.8 | 13.3 | 13.8 | 15.0 | 15.5 |
| Palm oil | 6.0 | 5.9 | 6.3 | 6.9 | 8.1 | 8.0 | 8.5 |
| Sunflowerseed oil | 5.0 | 5.7 | 5.5 | 6.2 | 6.6 | 6.5 | 7.0 |
| Rapeseed oil | 4.4 | 5.0 | 4.9 | 5.6 | 6.2 | 6.7 | 7.0 |
| Groundnut oil | 3.3 | 2.9 | 2.9 | 3.0 | 3.0 | 3.0 | 2.7 |
| Cottonseed oil | 3.3 | 3.1 | 3.0 | 3.9 | 3.5 | 3.1 | 3.3 |
| Coconut oil | 2.9 | 2.8 | 2.3 | 2.6 | 3.3 | 2.9 | 2.7 |
| Palm kernel oil | 0.7 | 0.8 | 0.8 | 1.0 | 1.1 | 1.1 | 1.1 |
| **Oil consumption** | **38.6** | **39.8** | **38.4** | **41.9** | **44.6** | **46.0** | **47.9** |
| Soybean oil | 13.1 | 13.5 | 13.0 | 13.2 | 13.5 | 14.8 | 15.6 |
| Palm oil | 5.7 | 6.2 | 6.0 | 6.7 | 7.8 | 7.9 | 8.5 |
| Sunflowerseed oil | 5.1 | 5.6 | 5.5 | 6.0 | 6.5 | 6.5 | 6.9 |
| Rapeseed oil | 4.5 | 4.9 | 4.9 | 5.6 | 6.1 | 6.6 | 7.0 |
| Groundnut oil | 3.3 | 2.9 | 2.9 | 3.0 | 3.0 | 3.1 | 2.7 |
| Cottonseed oil | 3.2 | 3.1 | 3.1 | 3.8 | 3.5 | 3.2 | 3.3 |
| Coconut oil | 3.0 | 2.8 | 2.2 | 2.7 | 3.2 | 2.8 | 2.8 |
| Palm kernel oil | 0.7 | 0.8 | 0.8 | 0.9 | 1.0 | 1.1 | 1.1 |
| **Closing stocks** | **6.7** | **6.9** | **6.1** | **8.0** | **9.9** | **9.9** | **9.4** |
| As oilseeds[4] | 3.8 | 4.0 | 3.1 | 4.4 | 5.3 | 4.7 | 4.6 |
| *Soybeans* | *2.6* | *3.1* | *2.4* | *3.2* | *4.2* | *3.6* | *3.2* |
| *Other* | *1.2* | *0.9* | *0.7* | *1.2* | *1.1* | *1.1* | *1.4* |
| As oil[5] | 2.9 | 2.9 | 3.0 | 3.6 | 4.6 | 4.9 | 4.8 |
| *Soybean oil* | *1.4* | *1.5* | *1.3* | *1.4* | *1.7* | *1.9* | *1.8* |
| *Palm oil* | *0.8* | *0.5* | *0.8* | *1.0* | *1.3* | *1.4* | *1.4* |
| *Other* | *0.7* | *0.9* | *0.9* | *1.2* | *1.6* | *1.6* | *1.6* |

Source: U.S. Department of Agriculture, *Foreign Agriculture Survey: Oilseeds and Products* (Washington), various issues.
[1] Preliminary.
[2] U.S. Department of Agriculture forecast.
[3] Derived from oilseed data using standard conversion factors.
[4] Change in oilseed stocks equals production less noncrush use less crushings.
[5] Change in oil stocks equals oil production less oil consumption.

For example, soybeans are 80 percent meal and 18 percent oil by weight, while copra is only 36 percent meal but 62 percent oil by weight. Soybeans are crushed mainly in response to meal demand. Hence the supply of soybean oil tends to be determined by the demand for meal, rather than the direct demand for soybean oil. Consequently, strong demand for meal has resulted in expanding soybean oil supplies, with little reference to the prevailing market prices for soybean oil. This factor is of particular importance because the soybean complex dominates prices in both the oil and meal markets. Soybean oil is by far the most important vegetable oil produced in terms of volume and strongly influences the prices of other oils, although its leadership has been narrowed in recent years by the expansion of palm oil production. As a consequence of these relationships, while protein meal prices have been relatively stable because of substitution with other feeds, the supply structure for soybean oil helps to make vegetable oil prices highly unstable.

Despite the depressed level of market prices of oilseeds and their products in recent years, world oilseed production has continued to expand and to add

**Table 19.  Major Oilseeds (Meal Equivalent): World Commodity Balance, 1981/82–87/88**

| | 1981/82 | 1982/83 | 1983/84 | 1984/85 | 1985/86 | 1986/87[1] | 1987/88[2] |
|---|---|---|---|---|---|---|---|
| | | | October/September Crop Years | | | | |
| | | | *(In millions of tons; meal equivalent)*[3] | | | | |
| **Production** | **106.0** | **113.0** | **102.7** | **119.2** | **122.2** | **121.4** | **127.4** |
| Soybeans | 68.2 | 74.2 | 64.9 | 73.4 | 76.4 | 77.0 | 80.0 |
| Cottonseed | 12.9 | 12.2 | 11.8 | 16.1 | 14.2 | 12.5 | 14.0 |
| Rapeseed | 7.6 | 9.0 | 8.7 | 10.4 | 11.2 | 11.8 | 13.4 |
| Sunflowerseed | 6.8 | 7.9 | 7.2 | 8.4 | 9.0 | 8.7 | 9.3 |
| Groundnuts | 8.0 | 7.1 | 7.7 | 8.1 | 8.1 | 8.3 | 7.7 |
| Copra | 1.6 | 1.6 | 1.3 | 1.6 | 1.9 | 1.7 | 1.6 |
| Palm kernels | 0.9 | 1.0 | 1.1 | 1.2 | 1.4 | 1.4 | 1.4 |
| **Noncrush use** | **19.5** | **19.7** | **20.6** | **20.6** | **20.8** | **22.1** | **23.1** |
| **Crushings/meal production** | **87.6** | **91.8** | **85.7** | **94.5** | **97.0** | **101.8** | **105.6** |
| Soybean meal | 57.3 | 60.5 | 55.3 | 58.2 | 60.6 | 66.3 | 68.5 |
| Cottonseed meal | 10.2 | 9.9 | 9.6 | 12.6 | 11.1 | 9.8 | 10.7 |
| Rapeseed meal | 7.3 | 8.4 | 8.1 | 9.4 | 10.2 | 11.0 | 11.6 |
| Sunflowerseed meal | 5.9 | 6.7 | 6.4 | 7.3 | 7.7 | 7.4 | 8.0 |
| Groundnut meal | 4.5 | 3.9 | 4.1 | 4.3 | 4.2 | 4.3 | 3.8 |
| Copra meal | 1.6 | 1.5 | 1.3 | 1.5 | 1.9 | 1.7 | 1.6 |
| Palm kernel meal | 0.8 | 0.9 | 0.9 | 1.2 | 1.3 | 1.3 | 1.4 |
| **Meal consumption** | **88.1** | **91.4** | **84.8** | **94.7** | **96.9** | **101.6** | **105.7** |
| Soybean meal | 57.8 | 59.8 | 54.8 | 58.5 | 60.5 | 66.0 | 68.5 |
| Cottonseed meal | 10.2 | 10.1 | 9.6 | 12.4 | 11.1 | 10.0 | 10.7 |
| Rapeseed meal | 7.3 | 8.4 | 8.0 | 9.5 | 10.1 | 10.9 | 11.7 |
| Sunflowerseed meal | 5.9 | 6.7 | 6.4 | 7.2 | 7.6 | 7.4 | 8.0 |
| Groundnut meal | 4.5 | 3.9 | 4.1 | 4.3 | 4.4 | 4.3 | 3.9 |
| Copra meal | 1.6 | 1.5 | 1.1 | 1.6 | 1.9 | 1.7 | 1.6 |
| Palm kernel meal | 0.8 | 1.0 | 0.8 | 1.2 | 1.3 | 1.3 | 1.3 |
| **Closing stocks** | **16.2** | **18.1** | **15.4** | **19.3** | **23.8** | **21.5** | **20.1** |
| As oilseeds[4] | 13.5 | 15.0 | 11.4 | 15.5 | 19.9 | 17.4 | 16.1 |
| *Soybeans* | *11.8* | *13.7* | *10.4* | *13.8* | *18.3* | *15.9* | *13.9* |
| *Rapeseeds* | *0.6* | *0.5* | *0.4* | *0.7* | *0.8* | *0.7* | *1.3* |
| *Other* | *1.1* | *0.8* | *0.6* | *1.0* | *0.8* | *0.8* | *0.9* |
| As meal[5] | 2.7 | 3.1 | 4.0 | 3.8 | 3.9 | 4.1 | 4.0 |
| *Soybean meal* | *1.9* | *2.6* | *3.1* | *2.8* | *2.9* | *3.2* | *3.2* |
| *Other* | *0.8* | *0.5* | *0.9* | *1.0* | *1.0* | *0.9* | *0.8* |

Source: U.S. Department of Agriculture, *Foreign Agriculture Survey: Oilseeds and Products* (Washington), various issues.

[1] Preliminary.
[2] U.S. Department of Agriculture forecast.
[3] Derived from oilseed data using standard conversion factors.
[4] Change in oilseed stocks equals production less noncrush use less crushings.
[5] Change in meal stocks equals meal production less meal consumption.

to the already abundant level of accumulated stocks. This upward spiral of production is a continuation of a long-term trend that began in the early 1970s and reflects world market conditions as well as domestic government policies. As a result, the relative importance of the various products and the relative share of the countries or regions that produce them in world production and exports have changed markedly. These structural changes on the supply side have been accompanied by important changes on the demand side, again as a result of both market forces and government policies.

In the 1970s world oilseed production expanded rapidly in response to the strong demand growth for both oilseed meals used in animal feeds and for vegetable oils. The steep price increases recorded early in the decade[32] encouraged the expansion of oilseed production and processing in many parts of the world. In the ten years ending 1979/80, production of the eight commodities listed in Table 18, in terms of oil equivalent, increased by 73 percent, or by an annual rate of 5.6 percent. Of the overall increase in the 1970s, 88 percent is attributable to four commodities: soybeans (49 percent), palm oil (17 percent), and rapeseed and sunflowerseed (11 percent each).

World oilseed production, in terms of oil equivalent, continued to grow rapidly in the 1980s, increasing from 44.1 million tons in 1979/80 to 54.4 million tons in

---

[32] For example, between 1969 and 1973 the price of soybeans increased by 182 percent, the price of soybean oil by 121 percent, and the price of soybean meal by 219 percent.

1985/86, or at an annual rate of 3.5 percent. After declining in 1983/84, world production recovered sharply with two consecutive years of surplus production. Consequently, stocks increased rapidly in 1984/85 and 1985/86, and this caused prices to fall sharply. After declining from the equivalent of 20 percent of oil consumption in 1980/81 to less than 16 percent in 1983/84, stocks of oilseeds and oils, in terms of oil equivalent, increased to 19 percent in 1984/85 and 22 percent in 1985/86. Nevertheless, the growth of production was temporarily halted in 1986/87 and stocks remained near the previous year's level. Reflecting this, prices began to recover in the second half of 1986.

Competition among exporting countries and among oilseeds and their products has intensified in recent years because of abundant supplies and limited consumption growth. Protein meal consumption in industrial countries probably has approached the saturation point. This has been reinforced by slow economic growth in developing countries. Furthermore, in the EC, which accounts for over one half of world soybean meal imports, demand for imported oilseeds was curtailed by abundant supplies of low-priced competing feedstuffs, such as nonfat dried milk, field peas and beans, and increased supplies of domestically produced rapeseed and sunflowerseed meals. Slower growth of consumption has been accompanied by strong competition among exporters, and since 1984 dominance of the relatively stagnant export market for soybean meal has shifted from industrial to developing countries.

Competition between palm oil, soybean oil, and rapeseed oil has intensified in recent years. India, a large vegetable oil importer, now imports mainly palm oil and increased quantities of lower priced rapeseed oil, whereas formerly most of the country's imports consisted of soybean oil. Rapeseed oil and meal production and exports are expanding rapidly in competition with soybeans and soybean products. Rapeseed products are increasingly gaining world acceptance as edible oils and protein feedstuffs, as Canada and the EC have developed varieties in which the erucic acid content of the oil and sulfur compounds in the meal, factors which had previously limited their use, have been reduced.

After falling sharply during the first three quarters of 1986 because of burgeoning supplies, vegetable oil prices bottomed out during the fourth quarter, when the price of coconut oil increased by 67 percent and prices of other oils also increased.

In 1987 the annual index of prices of vegetable oils and protein meals, in terms of dollars, was 9 percent higher than in 1986, as higher average prices for coconut oil (49 percent), palm oil (33 percent), fish meal (20 percent), soybean meal (10 percent), and

soybeans (3 percent), more than offset the effects of lower prices for soybean oil (2 percent), groundnut oil (12 percent), and groundnut meal (2 percent).

During the first quarter of 1987, soybean oil prices declined steadily, while the prices of palm oil and coconut oil increased in January but declined in February and March. The decline in soybean oil prices partly reflected reportedly good prospects for substantial increases in soybean production in 1986/87 in major exporting countries in South America. As a result, the relative price between soybean oil and palm oil changed, with palm oil selling at a premium to soybean oil for the first time since June 1984. Higher average prices for palm oil were partly attributable to the expected decline in Malaysian production in 1986/87 as a result of decreased fertilizer application and below normal rainfall. Furthermore, the EC Commission proposed a plan to limit budgetary expenditures on oilseed production, including the imposition of a consumption tax on both imports and domestic production of vegetable oils.

The decline in soybean oil prices was reversed during the second quarter of 1987, when prices increased by 12 percent. The prices of soybeans and soybean meal rose by 10 percent and 11 percent, respectively. Prices of coconut oil, groundnut oil, and palm oil also increased modestly during the quarter. The price increases for the soybean complex were attributable to concerns over the effects of prolonged dry weather on the U.S. soybean growing area and survey results indicating reduced planting intentions in the United States. The increase in the prices of coconut oil and palm oil is attributable to the expectation of lower yields, partly as a result of below average rainfall from December 1986 to March 1987 in copra and palm oil producing areas in the Philippines and Malaysia, respectively.

During the third quarter of 1987, the overall index of vegetable oils and protein meals declined by 6 percent between June and August, before recovering somewhat in September. Palm oil and soybean oil prices declined by 8 percent and 6 percent, respectively, partly reflecting larger-than-expected palm oil production in Malaysia in June, alleviation of previous concerns over the effects of dry weather on much of the U.S. soybean crop, and a smaller-than-expected decline in U.S. soybean acreage below last year's level.

In the fourth quarter of 1987, the overall dollar index of vegetable oils and protein meals rose sharply by 10 percent, reflecting a 14 percent increase in the price of soybean meal as a result of large unexpected imports of soybeans and soybean meal by the U.S.S.R. and sharp price increases for palm oil (22 percent), soybean oil (11 percent), rapeseed oil (17 percent), and coconut oil (6 percent). The rise in vegetable oil prices, despite abundant world supplies, reflected substantial purchases by India because of drought damage to the country's groundnut crop and the earlier-than-expected seasonal decline in palm oil production in Malaysia.

Reflecting both higher unit values and volumes, export earnings from the major oilseeds and their products (soybeans, soybean oil, soybean meal, and palm oil) increased by 20 percent from $13 billion in 1986 to an estimated $15 billion in 1987 (Tables 20–23). This amount was still 12 percent lower than the $17 billion recorded in 1984. In terms of SDRs, export earnings increased by only 9 percent to SDR 12 billion in 1987, nearly 30 percent lower than the SDR 17 billion earned in 1984. About 56 percent of the increase

### Table 20. Soybeans: Export Earnings, 1984–87

| | 1984 | 1985 | 1986 | 1987[1] | 1984 | 1985 | 1986 | 1987[1] |
|---|---|---|---|---|---|---|---|---|
| | (Values in SDRs) | | | | (Values in U.S. dollars) | | | |
| **Earnings** (*in billions*) | **7.0** | **5.5** | **4.8** | **4.7** | **7.2** | **5.5** | **5.6** | **6.0** |
| Industrial countries | 5.4 | 3.8 | 3.8 | 3.6 | 5.5 | 3.8 | 4.4 | 4.6 |
| Developing countries | 1.6 | 1.7 | 1.0 | 1.1 | 1.7 | 1.7 | 1.2 | 1.4 |
| **Volumes** (*in millions of tons*) | **25.8** | **25.5** | **27.6** | **28.7** | **25.8** | **25.5** | **27.6** | **28.7** |
| Industrial countries | 19.7 | 17.1 | 21.7 | 22.0 | 19.7 | 17.1 | 21.7 | 22.0 |
| *United States* | *19.5* | *16.9* | *21.4* | *21.6* | *19.5* | *16.9* | *21.4* | *21.6* |
| *Other countries* | *0.2* | *0.2* | *0.3* | *0.4* | *0.2* | *0.2* | *0.3* | *0.4* |
| Developing countries | 6.1 | 8.4 | 5.9 | 6.7 | 6.1 | 8.4 | 5.9 | 6.7 |
| *Argentina* | *3.1* | *3.0* | *2.6* | *1.5* | *3.1* | *3.0* | *2.6* | *1.5* |
| *Brazil* | *1.6* | *3.5* | *1.2* | *3.3* | *1.6* | *3.5* | *1.2* | *3.3* |
| *Other countries* | *1.4* | *1.9* | *2.0* | *1.9* | *1.4* | *1.9* | *2.1* | *1.9* |
| **Unit values** (*a ton*) | **271** | **214** | **172** | **162** | **278** | **217** | **202** | **210** |
| Industrial countries | 271 | 219 | 173 | 163 | 278 | 222 | 203 | 211 |
| Developing countries | 269 | 204 | 170 | 160 | 276 | 207 | 199 | 207 |
| **Market prices** (*a ton*)[2] | **275** | **221** | **178** | **167** | **282** | **224** | **208** | **216** |

Sources: UN Food and Agriculture Organization, *1986 FAO Trade Yearbook* (Rome) for exports; data on volume of exports for 1987 from *Oil World: Statistical Update* (Hamburg); Commodities Division, IMF Research Department for market prices.
[1] Data on exports are estimates of Commodities Division, IMF Research Department.
[2] U.S. origin, c.i.f. Rotterdam.

### Table 21. Soybean Oil: Export Earnings, 1984–87

| | 1984 | 1985 | 1986 | 1987[1] | 1984 | 1985 | 1986 | 1987[1] |
|---|---|---|---|---|---|---|---|---|
| | (Values in SDRs) | | | | (Values in U.S. dollars) | | | |
| **Earnings** (*in billions*) | **2.8** | **2.2** | **1.0** | **1.2** | **2.9** | **2.3** | **1.2** | **1.6** |
| Industrial countries | 1.6 | 1.2 | 0.6 | 0.7 | 1.7 | 1.2 | 0.8 | 1.0 |
| Developing countries | 1.2 | 1.0 | 0.4 | 0.5 | 1.2 | 1.1 | 0.4 | 0.6 |
| **Volumes** (*in millions of tons*) | **4.0** | **3.5** | **2.9** | **3.9** | **4.0** | **3.5** | **2.9** | **3.9** |
| Industrial countries | 2.3 | 1.8 | 1.7 | 2.1 | 2.3 | 1.8 | 1.7 | 2.1 |
| *United States* | *1.0* | *0.6* | *0.5* | *0.7* | *1.0* | *0.6* | *0.5* | *0.7* |
| *Netherlands* | *0.3* | *0.3* | *0.3* | *0.4* | *0.3* | *0.3* | *0.3* | *0.4* |
| *Spain* | *0.4* | *0.3* | *0.3* | *0.4* | *0.4* | *0.3* | *0.3* | *0.4* |
| *Other countries* | *0.6* | *0.6* | *0.6* | *0.6* | *0.6* | *0.6* | *0.6* | *0.6* |
| Developing countries | 1.7 | 1.7 | 1.2 | 1.8 | 1.7 | 1.7 | 1.2 | 1.8 |
| *Argentina* | *0.5* | *0.5* | *0.7* | *0.7* | *0.5* | *0.5* | *0.7* | *0.7* |
| *Brazil* | *0.9* | *1.0* | *0.4* | *0.9* | *0.9* | *1.0* | *0.4* | *0.9* |
| *Other countries* | *0.3* | *0.2* | *0.1* | *0.2* | *0.3* | *0.2* | *0.1* | *0.2* |
| **Unit values** (*a ton*) | **700** | **630** | **360** | **310** | **720** | **640** | **420** | **400** |
| Industrial countries | 710 | 670 | 400 | 350 | 730 | 680 | 460 | 450 |
| Developing countries | 680 | 630 | 300 | 260 | 700 | 640 | 350 | 340 |
| **Market prices** (*a ton*)[2] | **707** | **567** | **292** | **258** | **725** | **576** | **342** | **334** |

Sources: UN Food and Agriculture Organization, *1986 FAO Trade Yearbook* (Rome) for exports; Commodities Division, IMF Research Department for market prices.
[1] Data on exports are estimates of Commodities Division, IMF Research Department.
[2] Dutch, f.o.b. ex-mill Rotterdam.

**Table 22. Soybean Meal: Export Earnings, 1984–87**

| | 1984 | 1985 | 1986 | 1987[1] | 1984 | 1985 | 1986 | 1987[1] |
|---|---|---|---|---|---|---|---|---|
| | (Values in SDRs) | | | | (Values in U.S. dollars) | | | |
| **Earnings** (*in billions*) | 4.2 | 3.5 | 3.5 | 4.2 | 4.3 | 3.6 | 4.1 | 5.4 |
| Industrial countries | 2.0 | 1.7 | 1.8 | 2.2 | 2.1 | 1.8 | 2.1 | 2.8 |
| Developing countries | 2.2 | 1.8 | 1.7 | 2.0 | 2.2 | 1.8 | 2.0 | 2.6 |
| **Volumes** (*in millions of tons*) | 20.3 | 22.1 | 21.3 | 25.5 | 20.3 | 22.1 | 21.3 | 25.5 |
| Industrial countries | 9.0 | 9.3 | 9.8 | 11.9 | 9.0 | 9.3 | 9.8 | 11.9 |
| *United States* | 4.5 | 4.7 | 6.0 | 6.6 | 4.5 | 4.7 | 6.0 | 6.6 |
| *Netherlands* | 1.7 | 1.7 | 1.4 | 1.7 | 1.7 | 1.7 | 1.4 | 1.7 |
| *Other countries* | 2.8 | 2.9 | 2.4 | 3.6 | 2.8 | 2.9 | 2.4 | 3.6 |
| Developing countries | 11.3 | 12.8 | 11.5 | 13.6 | 11.3 | 12.8 | 11.5 | 13.6 |
| *Brazil* | 7.6 | 8.6 | 6.5 | 7.8 | 7.6 | 8.6 | 6.5 | 7.8 |
| *Other countries* | 3.7 | 4.2 | 5.0 | 5.8 | 3.7 | 4.2 | 5.0 | 5.8 |
| **Unit values** (*a ton*) | 204 | 160 | 165 | 165 | 209 | 162 | 194 | 213 |
| Industrial countries | 223 | 183 | 183 | 183 | 229 | 186 | 215 | 236 |
| Developing countries | 188 | 142 | 150 | 149 | 193 | 144 | 176 | 193 |
| **Market prices** (*a ton*)[2] | 192 | 155 | 157 | 157 | 197 | 157 | 185 | 203 |

Sources: UN Food and Agriculture Organization, *1986 FAO Trade Yearbook* (Rome) for exports; Commodities Division, IMF Research Department for market prices.
[1] Data on exports are estimates of Commodities Division, IMF Research Department.
[2] U.S. origin, c.i.f. Rotterdam.

**Table 23. Palm Oil: Export Earnings, 1984–87**

| | 1984 | 1985 | 1986 | 1987[1] | 1984 | 1985 | 1986 | 1987[1] |
|---|---|---|---|---|---|---|---|---|
| | (Values in SDRs) | | | | (Values in U.S. dollars) | | | |
| **Earnings** (*in billions*) | 2.8 | 2.6 | 1.6 | 1.7 | 2.9 | 2.6 | 1.8 | 2.3 |
| Developing countries | 2.8 | 2.6 | 1.6 | 1.7 | 2.9 | 2.6 | 1.8 | 2.3 |
| **Volumes** (*in millions of tons*) | 4.3 | 5.2 | 6.3 | 6.5 | 4.3 | 5.2 | 6.3 | 6.5 |
| Developing countries | 4.3 | 5.2 | 6.3 | 6.5 | 4.3 | 5.2 | 6.3 | 6.5 |
| *Malaysia* | 3.0 | 3.2 | 4.3 | 4.5 | 3.0 | 3.2 | 4.3 | 4.5 |
| *Other countries* | 1.3 | 2.0 | 2.0 | 2.0 | 1.3 | 2.0 | 2.0 | 2.0 |
| **Unit values** (*a ton*) | 650 | 500 | 250 | 270 | 660 | 510 | 290 | 350 |
| **Market prices** (*a ton*)[2] | 711 | 493 | 219 | 265 | 729 | 501 | 257 | 343 |

Sources: UN Food and Agriculture Organization, *1986 FAO Trade Yearbook* (Rome) for exports; export data include only exports from palm oil producing countries; Commodities Division, IMF Research Department for market prices.
[1] Data on exports are estimates of Commodities Division, IMF Research Department.
[2] Sumatra/Malaysia, c.i.f. Northwest European ports.

in export proceeds was earned by the developing countries. Export volumes of the developing countries are estimated to have increased substantially in 1987, after declining in 1986. As a result of this and higher unit values, their share in total earnings increased from 43 percent in 1986 to 45 percent in 1987.

In 1987/88 world oilseed production, in terms of oil equivalent, is expected to increase by 5 percent to 56.6 million tons, a new record level (Table 18). Most of the increased output is attributable to rapeseed (35 percent) and soybeans (27 percent), although sunflowerseed and palm oil production are also expected to show important increases. Strong demand for soybean meal, especially in the United States and in the U.S.S.R., is expected to be reflected in increased

world soybean crushings and a further drawdown in stocks. Because soybean prices have been exceeding levels that trigger sales out of U.S. government stocks, these stocks have been reduced to very low levels. The growth in world consumption of vegetable oils is expected to increase from 3 percent in 1986/87 to about 5 percent in 1987/88. Of that growth, 43 percent is expected to be attributable to soybean oil, reflecting increased availability in Argentina, imports into India because of reduced vegetable oil production, and increased exports by the United States under the export enhancement program (EEP). Although world supplies are expected to remain abundant, projected consumption could exceed production and lead to a slight drawdown of vegetable oil stocks.

**Table 24. Soybeans: World Commodity Balance, 1981/82–87/88**

(In millions of tons)

| | October/September Crop Years | | | | | | |
|---|---|---|---|---|---|---|---|
| | 1981/82 | 1982/83 | 1983/84 | 1984/85 | 1985/86 | 1986/87[1] | 1987/88[2] |
| **Production** | **86.1** | **93.6** | **83.2** | **93.1** | **96.9** | **98.0** | **101.4** |
| Argentina | 4.2 | 4.2 | 7.0 | 6.8 | 7.3 | 7.3 | 9.0 |
| Brazil | 12.8 | 14.8 | 15.5 | 18.3 | 14.1 | 17.3 | 18.5 |
| China | 9.3 | 9.0 | 9.8 | 9.7 | 10.5 | 11.6 | 11.8 |
| United States | 54.1 | 59.6 | 44.5 | 50.6 | 57.1 | 52.8 | 51.8 |
| Other countries | 5.7 | 6.0 | 6.4 | 7.7 | 7.9 | 9.0 | 10.3 |
| **Crushings** | **72.3** | **76.2** | **70.9** | **73.8** | **76.9** | **84.3** | **86.8** |
| Brazil | 12.8 | 13.7 | 12.5 | 13.1 | 12.5 | 14.4 | 14.1 |
| European Community | 15.2 | 14.7 | 12.7 | 12.3 | 12.8 | 13.6 | 13.4 |
| United States | 28.0 | 30.2 | 26.8 | 28.0 | 28.7 | 32.1 | 32.1 |
| Other countries | 16.3 | 17.6 | 18.9 | 20.4 | 22.9 | 24.2 | 27.2 |
| **Noncrush use** | **15.1** | **15.1** | **16.2** | **15.0** | **14.4** | **16.7** | **17.2** |
| **Closing stocks** | **14.9** | **17.2** | **13.3** | **17.6** | **23.2** | **20.2** | **17.6** |
| United States | 6.9 | 9.4 | 4.8 | 8.6 | 14.6 | 11.9 | 8.3 |
| Other countries | 8.0 | 7.8 | 8.5 | 9.0 | 8.6 | 8.3 | 9.3 |

Source: U.S. Department of Agriculture, *Foreign Agriculture Circular: Oilseeds and Products* (Washington), various issues.

[1] Preliminary.

[2] U.S. Department of Agriculture forecast.

## Soybeans and Soybean Products

Soybeans are the single most important oilseed in terms of output, accounting for about one third of world production (Table 18). After declining in 1983/84, soybean production rose by 12 percent in the 1984/85 marketing year (October/September), 4 percent in 1985/86, and 1 percent in 1986/87 (Table 24). This strong recovery and continued expansion has exerted downward pressure on international market prices for all oils and meals. Sizable increases in production also were recorded for other oilseeds, such as rapeseed and palm oil. In terms of oil equivalent, however, the growth in soybean production alone accounted for 28 percent of the increase in world oilseed output in the period between 1983/84 and 1986/87.

Over one half of world soybean production is concentrated in the United States. Reflecting lower prices paid to farmers, soybean acreage in the United States declined by 8 percent in 1986/87. As a result, soybean production in the United States declined by 8 percent from the 1985/86 level (Table 24), despite the maintenance of the record yields of the previous year. The decline in U.S. production was more than offset, however, by increased soybean production in Brazil, China, and other countries. Production in Brazil, the world's second largest producer, recovered by 23 percent in 1986/87 because of favorable weather conditions throughout the growing season, which raised average yields by 23 percent; in 1985/86 a severe drought during the planting and growing season reduced planted area and yields.

World soybean crushings expanded by 10 percent in 1986/87 with 46 percent of that expansion occurring in the United States, where soybean crushings reached the highest level in over a decade. This was attributable to a combination of factors: larger-than-expected soybean meal imports by the U.S.S.R., increased meal imports relative to soybeans by the EC because large vegetable oil stocks in the EC had depressed crush margins, additional livestock feeding in Western Europe because of the severe winter, and increased domestic consumption in the United States, partly because of higher-than-expected poultry production. As a result of increased crushing, world stocks of soybean oil reached record levels, and over two fifths of those stocks are held in the United States. Consequently, while strong meal demand has been reflected in a strengthening of meal prices, soybean oil prices have weakened. Average soybean meal prices increased from $157 a ton in 1985 to $185 a ton in 1986 and to $203 a ton in 1987. In contrast, the soybean oil price fell from an average of $576 a ton in 1985 to $342 a ton in 1986 and $334 a ton in 1987.

In 1987/88, world soybean production is expected to increase by over 3 percent. Although soybean production in the United States is forecast at 51.8 million tons, 2 percent lower than in 1986/87, reflecting mainly a decline in soybean acreage,[33] it is expected to be offset by increased production in other countries.

---

[33] The decline in acreage was substantially smaller than had been expected, and this appears to have been prompted by a rise in soybean prices during the second quarter of 1987.

**Table 25.   Soybean Meal: World Commodity Balance, 1981/82–87/88**

(In millions of tons)

| | October/September Crop Years | | | | | | |
|---|---|---|---|---|---|---|---|
| | 1981/82 | 1982/83 | 1983/84 | 1984/85 | 1985/86 | 1986/87[1] | 1987/88[2] |
| **Production** | **57.3** | **60.5** | **55.3** | **58.2** | **60.6** | **66.3** | **68.5** |
| Brazil | 9.9 | 10.6 | 9.7 | 10.2 | 9.7 | 11.2 | 10.9 |
| European Community | 12.2 | 11.7 | 10.1 | 9.8 | 10.2 | 10.9 | 10.6 |
| United States | 22.4 | 24.2 | 20.7 | 22.3 | 22.6 | 25.2 | 25.4 |
| Other countries | 12.8 | 14.0 | 14.8 | 15.9 | 18.1 | 19.0 | 21.6 |
| **Consumption** | **57.8** | **59.8** | **54.8** | **58.5** | **60.5** | **66.0** | **68.5** |
| European Community | 19.7 | 18.1 | 17.3 | 18.0 | 18.7 | 19.3 | 19.0 |
| United States | 16.1 | 17.5 | 16.0 | 17.7 | 17.3 | 18.5 | 19.0 |
| Other countries | 22.2 | 24.2 | 21.5 | 22.8 | 24.5 | 28.2 | 30.5 |
| **Closing stocks** | **1.9** | **2.6** | **3.1** | **2.8** | **2.9** | **3.2** | **3.2** |

Source: U.S. Department of Agriculture, *Foreign Agriculture Circular: Oilseeds and Products* (Washington), various issues.

[1] Preliminary.

[2] U.S. Department of Agriculture forecast.

In Argentina, low grain prices and less attractive returns from other crops are expected to encourage expansion of soybean acreage. In Brazil, soybean acreage also is expected to increase in response to a high soybean-corn price ratio. In the EC, the main market for U.S. soybeans and soybean meal, surplus capacity to produce grains is expected to be shifted into oilseeds. EC production of soybeans is expected to increase by 68 percent to 1.5 million tons in 1987/88, when it will represent 13 percent of EC oilseed production, compared with 2 percent in 1983/84.

World consumption of soybean meal is expected to increase by 4 percent, compared with a 9 percent rise in 1986/87 (Table 25). In the United States, soybean meal consumption is expected to increase in 1987/88 mainly in response to increasing livestock numbers, especially hogs and poultry. In the EC, however, soybean meal consumption should decline as a result of an expected rise in the price of soybean meal compared with the price of feed wheat, reflecting the availability of rain-damaged grains at discounted prices, record supplies of rapeseed and sunflowerseed meals at relatively lower prices, and larger-than-expected output of field peas and beans. World soybean crushings are expected to increase by 3 percent, with increased crushings in Argentina, the U.S.S.R., and other countries offsetting the projected decline in crushings in Brazil and the EC. After declining by 13 percent in 1986/87, closing stocks of soybeans are expected to decline by an additional 13 percent in 1987/88, while soybean oil stocks are expected to decline by 5 percent (Table 26).

World export volumes of soybean meal and oil are estimated to have increased by 20 percent and 34 percent, respectively, in 1987. An important share of the expansion in meal and, to a lesser extent, in oil is attributable to the United States. After declining from 1.0 million tons in 1984 to 0.5 million tons in 1986, the volume of U.S. soybean oil exports is estimated to have increased by 30 percent in 1987, partly reflecting sales under the EEP.[34] The annual rate of growth in the volume of U.S. soybean meal exports has increased from 6 percent in 1985 to 26 percent in 1986 and an estimated 11 percent in 1987. One of the objectives of the U.S. Food Security Act of 1985, was to improve the competitiveness of U.S. exports of soybeans and their derivatives and increase market sales rather than government stockpiling. A gradual lowering of the price support level was expected to lead to increased demand and reduced supply.

Under the price support program for soybeans, a farmer can obtain a non-recourse loan[35] for a period of nine months from the Commodity Credit Corporation (CCC) at the announced loan rate using his soybeans as collateral. At the end of the nine-month period, the farmer may repay the loan with interest and sell the crop at market prices or forfeit the crop to the government. In contrast to price support programs for other crops, participants in the soybean program cannot receive cash deficiency payments and

---

[34] Almost all of the U.S. exports of soybean oil involve government assistance, including various export credit programs and the EEP. The EEP, which was mandated by Congress through fiscal 1988, provided for $1 to $1.5 billion to be used to subsidize U.S. exports, especially to countries in which the United States feels that it has lost market share to leading competitors. A provision in pending trade legislation before the U.S. Congress would extend the EEP for an additional two years and raise funding to a maximum of $2.5 billion. The EEP has substantially lowered U.S. export prices for wheat and other commodities, including soybean oil, through the payment of a bonus to the exporter, in the form of commodities from CCC inventories, which permits the exporter to reduce export prices.

[35] A loan issued with the commodity only as security.

**Table 26.  Soybean Oil: World Commodity Balance, 1981/82–87/88**

(In millions of tons)

| | October/September Crop Years | | | | | | |
| | 1981/82 | 1982/83 | 1983/84 | 1984/85 | 1985/86 | 1986/87[1] | 1987/88[2] |
|---|---|---|---|---|---|---|---|
| **Production** | **12.7** | **13.6** | **12.8** | **13.3** | **13.8** | **15.0** | **15.5** |
| Brazil | 2.4 | 2.6 | 2.4 | 2.5 | 2.4 | 2.7 | 2.6 |
| European Community | 2.6 | 2.6 | 2.3 | 2.2 | 2.3 | 2.4 | 2.3 |
| United States | 5.0 | 5.5 | 4.9 | 5.2 | 5.3 | 5.8 | 5.9 |
| Other countries | 2.7 | 2.9 | 3.2 | 3.4 | 3.8 | 4.1 | 4.7 |
| **Consumption** | **13.1** | **13.5** | **13.0** | **13.2** | **13.5** | **14.8** | **15.6** |
| Brazil | 1.5 | 1.6 | 1.5 | 1.6 | 1.9 | 2.0 | 1.9 |
| European Community | 1.7 | 1.5 | 1.4 | 1.4 | 1.4 | 1.5 | 1.4 |
| United States | 4.3 | 4.5 | 4.4 | 4.5 | 4.6 | 4.9 | 5.1 |
| Other countries | 5.6 | 5.9 | 5.7 | 5.7 | 5.6 | 6.4 | 7.2 |
| **Closing stocks** | **1.4** | **1.5** | **1.3** | **1.4** | **1.7** | **1.9** | **1.8** |

Source: U.S. Department of Agriculture, *Foreign Agriculture Circular: Oilseeds and Products* (Washington), various issues.

[1] Preliminary.

[2] U.S. Department of Agriculture forecast.

are not required to reduce acreage planted to soybeans. When market prices have fallen below the loan rate plus interest charges, farmers have forfeited large quantities to the CCC. These stocks are in turn sold by the CCC at given resale prices plus carrying charges. While the loan rate helps to provide a floor for soybean market prices, the resale price, plus carrying charges, helps to set a ceiling for soybean market prices. The loan rate for soybeans was initially set at $5.02 a bushel for 1986 and 1987 in the 1985 Farm Bill, but the Secretary of Agriculture was authorized to lower it by up to 5 percent to $4.77 a bushel. Effective September 12, 1986, the loan rate for the 1986 crop was lowered to $4.77 a bushel and, as a result of the implementation of the Gramm-Rudman law, which had been passed in December 1985, the effective loan rate for that crop was further reduced to $4.56 a bushel. The initial loan rate for the 1987 soybean crop has again been reduced from $5.02 a bushel to $4.77 a bushel but no further reduction was made on account of the Gramm-Rudman law. Effective September 1, 1987, the minimum price at which the CCC can sell its soybean stocks in the market was reduced sharply from the $5.58 a bushel ($205 a ton) level that was in effect through August 31 to $5.14 a bushel ($189 a ton).[36] Soybean prices have exceeded the CCC's minimum soybean release prices in recent months. Re-

flecting this, the CCC's soybean inventory has declined to an estimated 38 million bushels as of January 1, 1988, compared with 48 million bushels on December 1, 1987, and 311 million bushels on January 1, 1987.

Abundant supplies of soybean and other vegetable oils are expected to limit increases in the price of soybean oil during 1988. Reflecting an expected strong demand for imports of soybean oil from China, India, Pakistan, and countries in North Africa, partly because of sales under the EEP in the United States, a further buildup in soybean oil stocks is not expected. As the price of soybean meal is already high relative to prices for grains, any further increase is expected to be limited. Increased soybean and soybean meal imports by the U.S.S.R. are expected to be more than offset by smaller imports by the EC, reflecting increased availability of domestically produced protein meals and other feedstuffs.

## Palm Oil

After declining in 1986/87, palm oil production is expected to rise by 6 percent in 1987/88, resuming the long-term expansion in world palm oil production which began in 1970 (Table 27). Palm oil is second only to soybeans in production and trade. In 1986/87, soybeans accounted for 32 percent of world oilseed output, in terms of oil equivalent, and exports of soybeans and soybean oil accounted for 39 percent of world oilseed and oil exports. During the same year, palm oil represented 15 percent of world oilseed production and 22 percent of world exports of oilseeds and vegetable oils, in terms of oil equivalent.

[36] The CCC soybean release price for September was set at 105 percent of the county loan rate plus carrying charges of 13 cents a bushel. Based on the national average loan rate of $4.77 a bushel, the implied resale price for September 1977 would be $5.14. The CCC soybean release level increased to about $5.20 a bushel ($190.90 a ton) in October, with carrying charges set at nearly 19 cents a bushel, about the same level as in the previous year. In November and December, the soybean release price was increased to $5.25 a bushel ($193 a ton) and $5.31 a bushel ($195 a ton), respectively.

**Table 27.   Palm Oil: World Commodity Balance, 1981/82–87/88**

(In millions of tons)

| | October/September Crop Years | | | | | | |
|---|---|---|---|---|---|---|---|
| | 1981/82 | 1982/83 | 1983/84 | 1984 85 | 1985/86 | 1986/87[1] | 1987/88[2] |
| **Production** | **6.0** | **5.9** | **6.3** | **6.9** | **8.1** | **8.0** | **8.5** |
| Indonesia | 0.9 | 1.0 | 1.2 | 1.2 | 1.3 | 1.3 | 1.4 |
| Malaysia | 3.4 | 3.2 | 3.3 | 3.8 | 4.8 | 4.6 | 4.8 |
| Other countries | 1.7 | 1.7 | 1.8 | 1.9 | 2.0 | 2.1 | 2.3 |
| **Consumption** | **5.7** | **6.2** | **6.0** | **6.7** | **7.8** | **7.9** | **8.5** |
| European Community | 0.6 | 0.7 | 0.6 | 0.7 | 0.9 | 0.9 | 0.9 |
| India | 0.4 | 0.6 | 0.5 | 0.7 | 0.8 | 0.8 | 1.1 |
| Indonesia | 0.5 | 0.6 | 0.9 | 0.6 | 0.6 | 0.8 | 0.8 |
| Nigeria | 0.5 | 0.7 | 0.6 | 0.6 | 0.8 | 0.7 | 0.7 |
| Pakistan | 0.3 | 0.3 | 0.3 | 0.5 | 0.6 | 0.5 | 0.3 |
| Other countries | 3.4 | 3.3 | 3.1 | 3.6 | 4.1 | 4.2 | 4.7 |
| **Closing stocks** | **0.8** | **0.5** | **0.8** | **1.0** | **1.3** | **1.4** | **1.4** |

Sources: Based on statistics of U.S. Department of Agriculture, *Foreign Agriculture Survey: Oilseeds and Products* (Washington), various issues; and *Oil World: Statistics Update* (Hamburg), September 11, 1987 and October 18, 1986.

[1] Preliminary.

[2] Based on U.S. Department of Agriculture forecast.

Owing to the ease of substitution in consumption between palm oil and soybean oil, prices of these two oils tend to move together over price cycles. Between 1982 and 1984, palm oil traded at a small discount of $14 a ton, on average, to soybean oil in two out of three years. In 1985 and 1986, however, the strong recovery in Malaysian palm oil production and record stock accumulation resulted in a considerable widening of this discount to $75 a ton in 1985 and to $85 a ton in 1986. Nevertheless, prospects for abundant soybean oil supplies combined with declining palm oil output caused this price relationship to be temporarily reversed during the first quarter of 1987, when palm oil commanded a $22 premium over soybean oil. Palm oil again traded at a slight discount of $4 a ton during the second quarter of 1987, when weather-related concerns about U.S. soybean production caused soybean oil prices to rise sharply; a slight discount also prevailed during the third quarter. During the fourth quarter, however, palm oil prices surged, resulting in a premium for palm oil of $39 a ton over soybean oil. This reflected the earlier-than-expected seasonal decline in output in Malaysia and major palm oil purchases by India. With palm oil production expected to increase in 1987/88, and stocks expected to remain at about the previous year's level, palm oil was again traded at a discount to soybean oil in February 1988.

World production of palm oil declined by 1 percent in 1986/87 from the 1985/86 level, but remained 16 percent higher than in 1984/85. The slight production shortfall in 1986/87 was attributable to a sharp decline in palm oil yields in Malaysia following tree stress as a result of high yields during the preceding year, below-normal rainfall, and decreased fertilizer use, which can affect yields for over two years. After increasing by 26 percent in 1985/86, production in Malaysia, the world's leading producer, declined by 4 percent to 4.6 million tons in 1986/87. Despite a small decline in world output in 1986/87, production once again exceeded consumption, and led to a further rise in an already record level of accumulated stocks. Palm oil stocks as a percentage of palm oil consumption increased from 8 percent in 1982/83 to 18 percent in 1986/87. Prospects are for palm oil production to increase from 8.0 million tons in 1986/87 to 8.5 million tons in 1987/88. Despite a decline in average yield, production in Indonesia, the second largest producer, is expected to increase by 8 percent as a result of a large expansion of mature acreage.[37] Malaysian production is expected to increase by 4 percent, considerably less than the 26 percent increase recorded in 1985/86. In 1987/88, Indonesia and Malaysia together are expected to account for about 73 percent of world palm oil production.

World consumption of palm oil is expected to increase by 8 percent in 1987/88, compared with less than 2 percent during the previous year. While consumption in the EC and the United States is expected to decline as a result of an abundance of competitively priced rapeseed, sunflowerseed, and soybean oils, this decline is projected to be offset by increased consumption in China and India. The rise in palm oil consumption in these two countries is attributable to a number of factors, including market prices, the

---

[37] Indonesia has a total palm oil acreage of 620,000 hectares, of which an estimated 79 percent is mature. In Malaysia, palm oil acreage is 1.3 million hectares, with maturity estimated at 90 percent.

geographical proximity of consumers to exporters, providing a freight-cost advantage to Southeast Asian exporters over exporters in the EC and North America, and a domestic shortage of competing vegetable oils. Palm oil is expected to become the largest vegetable oil imported by China in 1987/88, when imports are expected to increase from 335,000 to 485,000 tons. In India, palm oil consumption is expected to expand from 831,000 tons in 1986/87 to 1.1 million tons in 1987/88. As a result of this increased consumption, closing world stocks of palm oil are expected to remain at about the previous year's level, but to decline from 18 percent to 16 percent of annual world consumption. Prospects for a decline in the stocks/consumption ratio are expected to augur well for palm oil prices, but the continued abundance of vegetable oil supplies are expected to limit any upward movement in prices in 1988.

## Coconut Oil

Between 1984 and 1986, the average annual price of coconut oil decreased from $1,155 a ton to $296 a ton, the lowest level since 1972, mainly reflecting a substantial recovery of copra production in the Philippines from a decline in 1983/84 caused by typhoon damage and drought. During the fourth quarter of 1986, however, coconut oil prices increased sharply and the recovery in prices continued during 1987, when they averaged $442 a ton. Coconut oil traded at a premium over soybean oil from 1978 to 1984, but was quoted at a discount from the second quarter of 1985 until the third quarter of 1986. Since then, coconut oil again has traded at a premium over soybean oil and the premium has widened from an average of $58 a ton in the fourth quarter of 1986 to an average of $140 a ton during the second half of 1987. The sharp rise in the price of coconut oil, despite the generally abundant supply of vegetable oils, can be attributed to the demand response of industrial soap and detergent producers to declining coconut oil supplies.[38] On average, coconut oil in 1986 continued to trade at a premium over palm kernel oil, a by-product of the palm oil industry and its closest substitute among the lauric oils, although the premium declined from an average of $118 a ton in 1985 to only $8 a ton in 1986. In 1987, coconut oil's premium increased, reaching an average of $28 a ton during the second half of the year. The volume of palm kernel oil exports represents over 50 percent of the volume of coconut oil exports,

and palm kernel oil accounts for over one third of the market for lauric oils, a share that has been increasing in recent years.

World copra production increased by 25 percent in 1984/85 and 14 percent in 1985/86 to reach a record high of 5.4 million tons. Production in the Philippines, the world's largest producer, increased from 1.2 million tons in 1983/84 to 1.8 million tons in 1984/85 and about 2.4 million tons in 1985/86. The Philippines accounted for 46 percent of output in 1985/86 and Indonesia, the second largest producer, for 24 percent. Reflecting excellent rainfall during the two previous seasons, copra yields in the Philippines in 1985/86 were 14 percent above the average level of the five preceding years, while the harvested area increased by 2 percent. The increase in copra production was reflected in an expansion of coconut oil production of 13 percent in 1984/85 and 27 percent in 1985/86. Coconut oil consumption also expanded rapidly in response to lower prices and record world availabilities but fell short of production. As a result, stocks increased from an average of 240,000 tons in 1983/84–84/85 to 390,000 tons in 1985/86.

In 1986/87 world copra production declined by about 12 percent to 4.7 million tons, mainly as a result of cyclical declines in copra yields in Indonesia and Sri Lanka.[39] Yields in Sri Lanka, a large exporter of coconut oil, were also adversely affected by severe drought in the period beginning August 1986. Coconut oil production declined by 12 percent in 1986/87. Reflecting both the fall in production and the sharp rise in coconut oil prices relative to other competing oils, world consumption declined in 1986/87. With production exceeding consumption, coconut oil stocks increased by 8 percent to a level 83 percent higher than in 1984/85.

Prospects are for a further decline of 5 percent in world copra production in 1987/88 to 4.5 million tons. Reflecting prolonged dry conditions in the Philippines during the period December 1986–June 1987 and typhoon-related damage to coconut trees, the Philippine crop is expected to decline by about 23 percent. About one fourth of the decline in production in the Philippines is expected to be offset by a 12 percent increase in output in Indonesia. Reduced world copra production is expected to be reflected in a 7 percent decline in coconut oil production. Although coconut oil consumption is currently forecast to remain at the 1986/87 level, it is expected to exceed coconut oil production. By the end of 1987/88, world stocks of coconut oil are expected to fall by 26 percent, but

---

[38] Coconut oil is high in lauric and myristic acids which, when used in soap, shampoo, and shaving cream, give good lathering properties.

[39] World copra production usually declines every third year following two years of higher yields. Prevailing drought conditions may prolong the decline in output beyond one year.

remain 35 percent above the 1984/85 level. While domestic consumption of coconut oil is expected to remain unchanged in the Philippines, it is expected to decline in Indonesia, where domestic pricing policies have encouraged a shift toward palm oil consumption and increased exports of coconut oil.

Since the autumn of 1986, with the steep rise in coconut oil prices relative to the prices of competing oils, the competitive position of coconut oil has deteriorated markedly. Between August 1986 and December 1987, the price of coconut oil increased by 151 percent, compared with increases of 119 percent for palm oil, 56 percent for rapeseed oil, 45 percent for soybean oil, and 30 percent for sunflowerseed oil. In August 1986 coconut oil traded at a discount of $93 to sunflowerseed oil, $60 to soybean oil, and $20 to rapeseed oil, and at a premium of $14 to palm oil. In December 1987, however, coconut oil commanded premiums over each of these oils ranging from $160 a ton for rapeseed oil to $97 a ton for palm oil. These developments, combined with the general oversupply of vegetable oils, could limit upward movement in coconut oil prices in 1988, as users of edible oils switch to lower-priced substitutes. Nevertheless, with the decline in the level of stocks as a percentage of consumption from 15 percent in 1986/87 to a forecast 11 percent in 1987/88, a further increase in prices is not unlikely.

## Groundnuts and Groundnut Oil

In terms of oil equivalent, groundnuts have accounted for about 11 percent of world oilseed production in recent years. Nearly half of that production is consumed directly as nuts, while the remainder is crushed to produce groundnut oil and meal. Groundnuts are 55 percent meal and 42 percent oil by weight. Groundnut oil accounts for about 6 percent of world production of vegetable oils, and groundnut meal accounts for 4 percent of world meal production.

Only about 11 percent of world production has entered international trade in recent years. Market structure and weather-related fluctuations in production have caused groundnut product prices to be particularly volatile. Changes in the volume of exports depend mainly upon production levels in a few important exporting countries. Variations in production in other large producing countries appear to have a relatively greater influence on domestic consumption levels and on the volume of substitutable imports.

The three largest producers of groundnuts in the world are China, India, and the United States. In 1986/87, China and India each accounted for 30 percent of world output, and the United States accounted for 9

percent. China and the United States are the main exporters of groundnuts for confectionary use. The major exporters of groundnut oil are Argentina, China, and Senegal, while India and Senegal are the major exporters of groundnut meal.[40]

Although India is the leading exporter of groundnut meal, the country is not a major exporter of groundnuts or groundnut oil. The projected poor 1987/88 groundnut crop in India, discussed below, is not, therefore, expected to have a substantial effect on world prices for groundnut oil. In addition, India is expected to meet domestic consumption requirements by importing lower-priced palm, soybean, and rapeseed oils, rather than by purchases of groundnut oil.

In line with the trend in prices of other vegetable oils, the average annual price of groundnut oil rose sharply in 1984, when it reached $1,017 per ton, but declined in 1985 and in 1986. In 1986, it was quoted at $569 a ton, 44 percent lower than in 1984. The market price for groundnut oil continued to decline in 1987, averaging $500 a ton or 12 percent lower than in the previous year.

Groundnut oil's competitive position in relation to other major vegetable oils improved during 1987 and this is expected to help maintain demand in important export markets. Exports to the EC are expected to remain at the 1986 level, despite abundant supplies of other vegetable oils in this market, including sunflowerseed oil, soybean oil, and rapeseed oil.[41] Although the average annual price of groundnut oil declined by 11 percent in 1985 and 37 percent in 1986, its premium over soybean oil increased from an average of 57 percent in 1985 to 66 percent in 1986. During 1987, however, groundnut oil's premium over soybean oil decreased to 50 percent. Groundnut oil's premium over sunflowerseed oil also decreased from 55 percent in 1986 to 39 percent in 1987.

World production of groundnuts and groundnut oil in 1986/87 remained at virtually the same level as in the previous year. An estimated 12 percent decline in groundnut production in China was largely offset by increased production in Argentina, India, Senegal, and Sudan. Increased availability of supplies in exporting countries, however, permitted exports of groundnuts and groundnut oil to increase by 4 percent in 1986/87, compared to an increase of 19 percent in 1985/86.

---

[40] India and Senegal account for about 40 percent and 20 percent, respectively, of world exports of groundnut meal. Since 1983, the EC, which accounts for about 48 percent of world imports, has ceased importing groundnut meal from India because of aflatoxin problems. Most of India's groundnut meal is traded on the basis of bilateral agreements with the U.S.S.R. and Eastern European countries.

[41] Groundnut oil enjoys a strong technical advantage to other vegetable oils in culinary use.

These increases in supply, combined with the increased availability of lower-priced competing oils, especially in the EC, the major importer of groundnuts and groundnut oil, exerted downward pressure on the price of groundnut oil in the period 1985–87. Production of sunflowerseed oil in the EC increased by 11 percent between 1984/85 and 1986/87, with most of the increase attributable to France, the single most important importer of groundnut oil in the world.

World output of groundnuts, in terms of oil equivalent, is projected to decline by 7 percent in 1987/88. While severe drought in June–August 1987 in major groundnut producing areas in India is expected to reduce groundnut output in that country by 15 percent, and drought conditions are expected to result in lower production in Senegal by 11 percent, groundnut production in China is expected to increase by 5 percent. Consequently, exports of groundnuts and groundnut oil, in terms of oil equivalent, are expected to decline by 4 percent in 1987/88 but to remain slightly above the 1985/86 level. Reflecting the decline in groundnut production, especially in India, groundnut meal output and the volume of groundnut meal exports are expected to decline by about 12 percent and 19 percent, respectively. The average annual price of groundnut meal has moved broadly in line with, and at a discount to, soybean meal. Since 1984, however, groundnut meal has traded at a widening discount to soybean meal, the discount increasing from 5 percent in 1984

to 10 percent in 1986 and 20 percent during 1987. Market prices for groundnut meal, after increasing by 14 percent in 1986, declined by 2 percent to $162 a ton in 1987.

## Rapeseed Oil

Rapeseed oil is currently the most competitive of the leading vegetable oils, underpricing both soybean and palm oil at Rotterdam. Rapeseed meal is gaining wider acceptance in producing countries and export markets as a feed ingredient.

World rapeseed production has been increasing rapidly (Table 28). As a share of world oilseed production, rapeseed is expected in 1987/88 to become the third most important oilseed. In terms of oil equivalent, production increased by 38 percent between 1983/84 and 1986/87, compared with increases of 16 percent for soybeans, 27 percent for palm oil, and 23 percent for sunflowerseed during that period. A further increase of 13 percent is expected in 1987/88.

China, the EC, and Canada together account for over two thirds of world rapeseed production. China, the world's leading producer, accounted for 31 percent of the increase in output in the three years ended 1986/87. While China exports large quantities of rapeseed meal, it exports little rapeseed and virtually no rape-

---

**Table 28. Rapeseed: World Commodity Balance, 1981/82–87/88**

(In millions of tons)

| | October/September Crop Years | | | | | | |
|---|---|---|---|---|---|---|---|
| | 1981/82 | 1982/83 | 1983/84 | 1984/85 | 1985/86 | 1986/87[1] | 1987/88[2] |
| **Production** | **12.3** | **14.8** | **14.3** | **17.0** | **18.6** | **19.5** | **22.3** |
| Canada | 1.8 | 2.2 | 2.6 | 3.4 | 3.5 | 3.8 | 3.5 |
| China | 4.1 | 5.7 | 4.3 | 4.2 | 5.6 | 5.9 | 6.1 |
| European Community | 2.0 | 2.7 | 2.4 | 3.4 | 3.6 | 3.7 | 6.0 |
| India | 2.4 | 2.2 | 2.6 | 3.1 | 2.6 | 3.0 | 3.1 |
| Other countries | 2.0 | 2.0 | 2.4 | 2.9 | 3.3 | 3.1 | 3.6 |
| **Crushings** | **12.0** | **13.8** | **13.3** | **15.4** | **16.8** | **18.2** | **19.2** |
| Canada | 0.9 | 0.9 | 1.2 | 1.3 | 1.2 | 1.6 | 1.4 |
| China | 3.7 | 5.1 | 3.8 | 3.8 | 5.0 | 5.3 | 5.4 |
| European Community | 2.3 | 2.7 | 2.9 | 3.5 | 3.9 | 4.0 | 4.8 |
| India | 2.2 | 2.0 | 2.1 | 2.9 | 2.6 | 2.7 | 2.8 |
| Japan | 1.2 | 1.2 | 1.3 | 1.4 | 1.4 | 1.6 | 1.6 |
| Other countries | 1.7 | 1.9 | 2.0 | 2.5 | 2.7 | 3.0 | 3.7 |
| **Noncrush use** | **0.9** | **1.1** | **1.2** | **1.2** | **1.6** | **1.4** | **2.2** |
| **Closing stocks** | **0.9** | **0.8** | **0.7** | **1.1** | **1.3** | **1.2** | **2.1** |
| European Community | 0.0 | 0.1 | 0.1 | 0.1 | 0.2 | 0.2 | 1.0 |
| Canada | 0.7 | 0.5 | 0.1 | 0.5 | 1.0 | 0.6 | 0.6 |
| Other countries | 0.2 | 0.2 | 0.5 | 0.5 | 0.1 | 0.4 | 0.5 |

Sources: U.S. Department of Agriculture, *Foreign Agriculture Circular: Oilseeds and Products* (Washington), various issues; and *Oil World: Statistics Update* (Hamburg), various issues.

[1] Preliminary.

[2] U.S. Department of Agriculture forecast.

**Table 29.   Rapeseed Oil: World Commodity Balance, 1981/82–87/88**

(In millions of tons)

| | October/September Crop Years | | | | | | |
|---|---|---|---|---|---|---|---|
| | 1981/82 | 1982/83 | 1983/84 | 1984/85 | 1985/86 | 1986/87[1] | 1987/88[2] |
| **Production** | **4.4** | **5.0** | **4.9** | **5.6** | **6.2** | **6.7** | **7.0** |
| Canada | 0.4 | 0.4 | 0.5 | 0.5 | 0.5 | 0.6 | 0.6 |
| China | 1.2 | 1.7 | 1.3 | 1.2 | 1.7 | 1.7 | 1.8 |
| European Community | 0.9 | 1.1 | 1.1 | 1.4 | 1.5 | 1.5 | 1.8 |
| India | 0.7 | 0.7 | 0.7 | 1.0 | 0.9 | 0.9 | 0.9 |
| Other countries | 1.2 | 1.1 | 1.3 | 1.5 | 1.6 | 2.0 | 1.9 |
| **Consumption** | **4.5** | **4.9** | **4.9** | **5.6** | **6.1** | **6.6** | **7.0** |
| China | 1.2 | 1.7 | 1.2 | 1.2 | 1.6 | 1.8 | 1.9 |
| European Community | 0.6 | 0.8 | 0.8 | 0.8 | 0.9 | 1.0 | 1.1 |
| India | 0.9 | 0.8 | 0.9 | 1.2 | 1.0 | 1.2 | 1.3 |
| Japan | 0.5 | 0.5 | 0.5 | 0.6 | 0.6 | 0.6 | 0.6 |
| Other countries | 1.3 | 1.1 | 1.5 | 1.8 | 2.0 | 2.0 | 2.1 |
| **Closing stocks** | **0.1** | **0.2** | **0.2** | **0.2** | **0.3** | **0.4** | **0.4** |

Sources: U.S. Department of Agriculture, *Foreign Agriculture Circular: Oilseeds and Products* (Washington), various issues; and *Oil World: Statistics Update* (Hamburg), various issues.

[1] Preliminary.

[2] U.S. Department of Agriculture forecast.

seed oil, as almost the entire production of rapeseed oil is consumed domestically (Tables 29 and 30). In 1987/88, rapeseed production in China is expected to increase by 3 percent, but the more rapid expansion of production in the EC is expected to reduce China's share in world output from 30 percent in 1986/87 to 27 percent. The EC and Canada contributed 25 percent and 23 percent, respectively, of the increase in rapeseed production during the period 1983/84–1986/87.

The EC's production of rapeseed increased by 54 percent in that three-year period and a further substantial increase of 62 percent is projected for 1987/88 alone. As a result, the EC's share of world rapeseed production, after increasing from 17 percent to 19 percent in the period 1983/84–1986/87, is expected to reach 27 percent in 1987/88. Rapeseed exports of countries in the EC have, however, been largely intra-community, but in 1987/88 the EC is expected to

**Table 30.   Rapeseed Meal: World Commodity Balance, 1981/82–87/88**

(In millions of tons)

| | October/September Crop Years | | | | | | |
|---|---|---|---|---|---|---|---|
| | 1981/82 | 1982/83 | 1983/84 | 1984/85 | 1985/86 | 1986/87[1] | 1987/88[2] |
| **Production** | **7.3** | **8.4** | **8.1** | **9.4** | **10.2** | **11.0** | **11.6** |
| Canada | 0.6 | 0.5 | 0.7 | 0.8 | 0.7 | 0.9 | 0.8 |
| China | 2.3 | 3.2 | 2.4 | 2.3 | 3.1 | 3.3 | 3.4 |
| European Community | 1.3 | 1.6 | 1.7 | 2.1 | 2.2 | 2.4 | 2.8 |
| India | 1.5 | 1.3 | 1.4 | 1.9 | 1.7 | 1.8 | 1.8 |
| Japan | 0.7 | 0.7 | 0.7 | 0.8 | 0.8 | 0.9 | 0.9 |
| Other countries | 0.9 | 1.1 | 1.2 | 1.5 | 1.7 | 1.7 | 1.9 |
| **Consumption** | **7.3** | **8.4** | **8.0** | **9.5** | **10.1** | **10.9** | **11.7** |
| Canada | 0.4 | 0.4 | 0.4 | 0.4 | 0.4 | 0.5 | 0.5 |
| China | 2.3 | 3.0 | 2.1 | 2.1 | 2.6 | 2.6 | 2.8 |
| European Community | 1.5 | 1.9 | 2.1 | 2.4 | 2.7 | 3.0 | 3.3 |
| India | 1.2 | 1.2 | 1.3 | 1.8 | 1.6 | 1.7 | 1.6 |
| Japan | 0.7 | 0.7 | 0.8 | 1.0 | 1.0 | 1.1 | 1.1 |
| Other countries | 1.2 | 1.2 | 1.3 | 1.8 | 1.8 | 2.0 | 2.4 |
| **Closing stocks** | **0.2** | **0.2** | **0.3** | **0.2** | **0.3** | **0.4** | **0.3** |

Sources: U.S. Department of Agriculture, *Foreign Agriculture Circular: Oilseeds and Products* (Washington), various issues; and *Oil World: Statistics Update* (Hamburg), various issues.

[1] Preliminary.

[2] U.S. Department of Agriculture forecast.

become a net exporter of rapeseed outside the EC. Thus far, Canada has been the main exporter of rapeseed, most of which has been exported to Japan, while the EC has been the leading exporter of rapeseed oil. Net exports of rapeseed oil by the EC are expected to represent 46 percent of world exports of rapeseed oil in 1987/88. However, the EC is still a net importer of rapeseed meal.

Production of oilseeds, mainly rapeseed and sunflowerseed, has increased sharply in the EC in response to the incentives offered under the EC's oilseeds policy, which has encouraged both a rapid expansion of oilseed production as well as an increase in the crushing and use of that production in the EC. This has been achieved through payments to EC processors, enabling them to purchase oilseeds from domestic producers at relatively high target prices and sell the oil and meal produced at world market prices. Despite recent reductions in support prices, the oilseeds sector is reportedly the third most costly to support, exceeded only by milk and cereals. The cost of the so-called deficiency payments or producer aids, which are made to the oilseed crusher, has increased from ECU 268 million in 1977 to ECU 1.7 billion in 1984, ECU 2.9 billion in 1986, and an estimated ECU 4 billion in 1987.[42]

To reduce the spiraling budgetary costs of community support for the oils and fats sector, the EC Commission, in February 1987, proposed a series of measures. Subsequently, effective July 1, 1987, the target price for rapeseed was reduced by 3 percent to ECU 450.2 a ton, which is more than twice the current world market price. To help control rapeseed production, a production threshold, or maximum guaranteed quantity (MGQ) level, was set at 3.5 million tons, and the producer support price declines by 1 percent for each 1 percent increase in production above the specified maximum guaranteed level. The maximum reduction in support prices, however, was set at 10 percent.[43] Since the EC's rapeseed crop (estimated at 5.9 million tons in 1987/88) is substantially in excess of the MGQ, support prices for the entire crop will be reduced by 10 percent below the target price.

In February 1988, at the EC summit meeting in Brussels, it was agreed to fix production thresholds, or the MGQs, for the years 1988/89, 1989/90, and 1990/

91 at 4.5 million tons annually for rapeseed, 2.0 million tons annually for sunflowerseed, and 1.3 million tons annually for soybeans, for all members combined, excluding Spain and Portugal. If actual output exceeds the MGQs, as is likely, the institutional support prices will be reduced by 0.45 percent for each 1 percent produced in excess of the MGQ in 1988/89 and by 0.5 percent for each 1 percent overproduced in subsequent marketing years. The new prices would come into effect on August 31, 1988, for rapeseed, September 30 for sunflowerseed, and October 31 for soybeans.

Reflecting the strong rise in production and exports and competition from abundant supplies of competing vegetable oils, the price of rapeseed oil declined sharply in 1985 and 1986 and continued to weaken in 1987. The average annual price of rapeseed oil decreased by 21 percent in 1985 and 43 percent in 1986. In that period, rapeseed oil traded at an average discount of about $35 a ton under soybean oil but at premia of $39 a ton and $50 a ton, respectively, over palm oil in 1985 and 1986. In 1987, the price of rapeseed oil averaged about 1 percent lower than in 1986, while palm oil prices strengthened. As a result, rapeseed oil traded at an average discount of $38 a ton under palm oil and $29 a ton under soybean oil during that period.

## Sunflowerseed Oil

After declining in 1986/87, world production of sunflowerseed is expected to increase to a record 20.5 million tons in 1987/88. The U.S.S.R., the EC, and Argentina are the three largest producers of sunflowerseed, accounting for 28 percent, 17 percent, and 12 percent of world output, respectively, in 1986/87. Argentina is the leading exporter of sunflowerseed oil and meal, while the EC, the United States, and Argentina together account for over 90 percent of gross exports of sunflowerseed. The EC, however, was a net importer of sunflowerseed until bumper crops have made the Community virtually self-sufficient in 1986/87. In 1987/88 the EC is expected to become a net exporter of sunflowerseed. The EC has been a net exporter of sunflowerseed oil since 1986/87. Net imports of sunflowerseed by the EC have decreased from 714,000 tons in 1984/85 to 49,000 tons in 1986/87, and net exports are projected at 26,000 tons in 1987/88. The EC nevertheless remains the world's largest net importer of sunflowerseed meal.

World production of sunflowerseed has increased rapidly from 15.5 million tons in 1983/84 to 19.5 million tons in 1985/86. In 1986/87 output decreased by 2 percent to 19.1 million tons. Most of the increase in world production between 1983/84 and 1985/86 was attributable to Argentina (54 percent) and the EC (25

---

[42] With the full integration of Spain and Portugal into the support systems of the Common Agricultural Policy (CAP) in 1991, the cost of the oils and fats sector could increase by an additional ECU 2 billion to ECU 6 billion.

[43] The threshold system for controlling production in the EC was introduced in 1982 for rapeseed and in 1984 for sunflowerseed. Total maximum production figures have been set each year. Formerly subsidies could be reduced, but by no more than 5 percent if producers exceeded the limit.

percent). In Argentina, area harvested increased from 2.0 million hectares in 1983/84 to 3.0 million hectares in 1985/86 and yields from an average of 1.1 tons a hectare to 1.4 tons a hectare over the same period. As a result, in 1985/86 Argentina's output rose by 97 percent to a record crop of 4.3 million tons. Production in the EC expanded by 57 percent between 1983/84 and 1985/86 to 2.8 million tons, of which two thirds was attributable to France, where the area harvested increased by 51 percent and yields by 19 percent. In 1986/87 sunflowerseed production expanded by over 18 percent to 3.3 million tons in the EC, but this was insufficient to offset a 49 percent decline in Argentina's output, as well as lower production in other countries, including the United States and China. The steep decline in Argentina's production reflected crop losses as a result of flood and wind damage and lower average yield. Area harvested is estimated to have fallen by 43 percent to 1.7 million hectares while yields declined by 11 percent.

In 1987/88, world production of sunflowerseed is expected to increase by over 7 percent to 20.5 million tons, thereby exceeding even the record level achieved in 1985/86. The increase is expected to result from a recovery of production in Argentina and the expansion of output in the U.S.S.R. and the EC, which are expected to more than offset lower production in the United States and several Eastern European countries.

EC production is expected to reach 3.7 million tons, or the equivalent of 18 percent of world output in 1987/88, compared with 11 percent of world production in 1983/84. In 1987/88, target and intervention prices in the EC for sunflowerseed remained unchanged at ECU 583.5 and ECU 534.7 a ton, and the MGQ was set at 3.95 million tons. As production is expected to remain below this threshold level, target prices are not expected to be reduced. For the years 1988/89–90/91, the MGQ for sunflowerseed, as mentioned earlier, has been fixed at 2 million tons annually, and, if output exceeds this level, support prices will be reduced by 0.5 percent for each 1 percent produced in excess of that amount in 1988/89 and by 0.5 percent for each 1 percent of overproduction in subsequent years.

Although sunflowerseed oil production and stocks declined in 1986/87, stocks remained 15 percent higher than in 1984/85. Reflecting this, the average annual price of sunflowerseed oil declined by 39 percent in 1986 and an additional 2 percent during 1987, and the competitive position of sunflowerseed oil relative to soybean oil, rapeseed oil, and groundnut oil declined. Between 1985 and 1987, sunflowerseed oil increased its premium over soybean oil from 5 percent to 10 percent and its premium over rapeseed oil from 12 percent to 21 percent, while its discount to groundnut oil declined from 35 percent to 28 percent. With the expected increase in export supplies from Argentina in 1988, improvement in the competitive position of sunflowerseed oil is not unlikely.

## Fish Meal

Fish meal is used in poultry, swine, and other animal feed as well as feed in aquaculture. After increasing by 15 percent in 1986, in line with the strengthening of other protein meal prices, the price of fish meal increased by an additional 19 percent during 1987 owing to a marked tightening of supply. In December 1987, the price of fish meal reached its most recent peak of $473 a ton, the highest level since January 1984, and 86 percent above the level recorded in July 1985. Fish meal generally is sold at a premium over soybean and other protein meals and, with its recent rise in price, fish meal's premium to soybean meal increased from an average of 74 percent ($136 a ton) in 1986 to an average of 89 percent ($180 a ton) during 1987. On a quarterly basis, fish meal's average premium over soybean oil rose from 80 percent in the first quarter of 1987 to over 100 percent in the third quarter and eased to 91 percent in the fourth quarter.

After increasing by 6 percent to a record level of 6.3 million tons in 1985/86, fish meal production declined by 7 percent to 5.9 million tons in 1986/87. The decline in production is mainly attributable to lower output in Chile and Peru, the world's two largest producers, reflecting poor fishing conditions as a result of the El Niño weather disturbances. Chilean production declined by an estimated 19 percent to 1 million tons, reflecting reduced catch because of poor fishing conditions combined with bans on fishing to protect its fish population during the spawning season. Nevertheless, a sharp drawdown in stocks enabled Chile to maintain export volume at only 1 percent below the 1985/86 level. Production in Peru declined by 25 percent to 0.7 million tons, but a substantial decline in stocks permitted export volume to increase by 3 percent in 1986/87. As a result of the decline in world output, combined with a continued high level of consumption, world stocks fell by 36 percent in 1986/87 to 0.45 million tons, the lowest level since 1982/83. World consumption of fish meal increased by 5 percent to 6.3 million tons in 1985/86 and declined to about 2 percent below that level in 1986/87. The Federal Republic of Germany and Taiwan Province of China are the largest importers of fish meal, accounting for about 12 percent each of world imports.

In 1987/88 world production of fish meal is expected to increase by 6 percent to 6.2 million tons. Higher consumption is currently expected to reduce stocks slightly below the low level at the end of 1986/87. EC production of poultry products is expected to continue to expand, although slower growth in pork output, accelerated growth in domestic production of oilseeds and pulses, and the recent sharp rise in fish meal prices relative to prices of other meals could cause a reduction in protein meal imports, including fish meal. Fish meal's reduced competitiveness in relation to soybean, rapeseed, and other oilseed meals could therefore encourage substitution in importing countries, thereby narrowing fish meal's premium over competing protein meals.

## Meat

The largest components of the global meat trade are beef and veal. In 1985 (the latest year for which complete data are available), exports of beef and veal amounted to 3.3 million tons (43 percent of the volume of global meat trade, including intra-EC trade), while pork exports were 2.1 million tons (28 percent). Although there has been a secular increase in global poultry production, the share of poultry in global meat trade has declined in recent years. In 1985 poultry exports of 1.5 million tons accounted for 19 percent of global meat trade, compared with 23 percent in 1981. The balance of meat trade is mostly lamb and mutton; exports in 1985 of 725,000 tons were 10 percent of global meat trade.

## Beef

After allowing for the secular decline in the demand for beef in industrial countries related to health concerns in favor of light meats, such as pork and especially poultry, the major influence on the price of internationally traded beef in recent years has been fluctuations in supply. Herd liquidation in the EC in response to measures to control the growth of dairy output led to heightened competition for export markets in 1984, and U.S. dollar prices fell to 103 cents a pound from an average of 111 cents a pound in 1983 (Table 31).[44] In 1985 herd rebuilding in Australia was interrupted by dry weather, while herd liquidation in the United States continued in response to the high indebtedness of producers and Government programs to curtail the output of dairy products. Prices fell further to an average of 98 cents a pound for the year. In 1986 the main influence on prices was the dairy

Table 31.    **Prices of Beef and Lamb, 1979-88**

| Year | | Beef[1] | Lamb[2] | Beef[1] | Lamb[2] |
|---|---|---|---|---|---|
| | | (*In SDRs a pound*) | | (*In U.S. dollars a pound*) | |
| 1979 | | 1.01 | 0.84 | 1.31 | 1.09 |
| 1980 | | 0.96 | 1.01 | 1.25 | 1.31 |
| 1981 | | 0.95 | 1.06 | 1.12 | 1.25 |
| 1982 | | 0.98 | 0.98 | 1.08 | 1.09 |
| 1983 | | 1.04 | 0.82 | 1.11 | 0.88 |
| 1984 | | 1.01 | 0.86 | 1.03 | 0.88 |
| 1985 | | 0.96 | 0.82 | 0.98 | 0.84 |
| 1986 | | 0.81 | 0.79 | 0.95 | 0.93 |
| 1987 | | 0.84 | 0.76 | 1.08 | 0.98 |
| 1986 | I | 0.88 | 0.76 | 0.99 | 0.85 |
| | II | 0.80 | 0.85 | 0.93 | 0.99 |
| | III | 0.76 | 0.81 | 0.91 | 0.97 |
| | IV | 0.81 | 0.74 | 0.97 | 0.89 |
| 1987 | I | 0.81 | 0.77 | 1.03 | 0.97 |
| | II | 0.83 | 0.77 | 1.08 | 1.00 |
| | III | 0.84 | 0.75 | 1.08 | 0.95 |
| | IV | 0.85 | 0.76 | 1.15 | 1.02 |
| 1988 | I | 0.85 | 0.82 | 1.16 | 1.12 |

Source: Commodities Division, IMF Research Department.
[1] Frozen boneless beef, Australian and New Zealand origin, f.o.b. U.S. ports.
[2] Frozen New Zealand lamb, grade PL, Smithfield market, London.

termination program under the 1985 U.S. farm bill which accelerated the rate of dairy cow slaughter in the United States and led to a sharp increase in U.S. beef exports.[45] The average price of beef in 1986 declined by a further 3 percent to 95 cents a pound, the lowest price recorded since 1978.

Prices strengthened to 105 cents a pound in the first half of 1987 in anticipation of a tightening of supplies with the imminent end of the dairy termination program and the possible limitation of imports from Australia and New Zealand under voluntary restraint agreements. Low grain prices also raised profitability of fattening cattle on feedlots, which, in turn, raised the demand for and prices of feeder cattle. Higher feeder cattle prices were then carried over to higher prices of finished cattle and meat, which were sustained by firm retail demand. Prices rose further to 108 cents a pound in the third quarter, reflecting a temporary ban by the United States on imports from Australia in August/September on account of an unacceptably high level of pesticide residues in some shipments and a reduction in the flow of imports from Australia in October and November under the voluntary restraint

---

[44] Price quotations refer to imported frozen boneless beef, separate, 85 percent lean, from Australia and New Zealand, f.o.b. U.S. ports. This is manufacturing grade beef generally used in hamburgers and sausages.

[45] The dairy termination program was a voluntary scheme in effect for 18 months from April 1986 whereby milk producers agree to sell for export or slaughter their herd in return for a cash payment. To alleviate the adverse impact of the program on domestic beef prices, the government agreed to purchase 180,000 tons of beef and to dispose of it about equally in export markets and in domestic food aid.

agreement. Prices peaked in November 1987 at 116 cents a pound but then weakened a little in December following U.S. government reports of higher-than-anticipated numbers of cattle on feedlots. For the year as a whole, beef prices were 14 percent higher than in 1986.

After rising by 2 percent in 1985, world production of beef and veal rose by an additional 1 percent in 1986, and remained unchanged in 1987 at 43.9 million tons. Higher beef production in Argentina, Australia, the EC, and the U.S.S.R. offset declines in Brazil and Eastern Europe in 1986. In 1987, higher output in Brazil, the EC, and the U.S.S.R. balanced lower slaughtering in countries entering the rebuilding phase of the cattle cycle—Argentina, Australia, Canada, and the United States. In the EC, output increased by 2 percent in 1986 in response to the dairy outgoers scheme which aims to compensate farmers for a 3 percent reduction in their milk production quotas in the two years to April 1988. Additional measures designed to reduce the flow of beef into intervention stores were introduced in December 1986, including an effective cut in intervention prices of between 10–15 percent. The impact of these measures on beef production in 1987 was offset by tighter controls on milk output (leading to increased slaughter) introduced at the same time,[46] and output is estimated to have increased by 1 percent. In the U.S.S.R., increased investment in the livestock sector resulted in higher cattle numbers and meat output in both years. Brazil's cattle slaughterings fell sharply (by 13 percent) in 1986 as producers withheld cattle from the market in protest against a freeze on prices. With domestic demand raised by high consumer purchasing power, Brazil changed from being the third largest net exporter of beef and veal in 1985 to the second largest net importer (after the United States) in 1986. The additional import demand did not, however, result in higher international prices because of competition between the EC and the United States to reduce Government stocks.[47] Brazilian meat output returned to normal in 1987 after the relaxation of price controls in March. Australian production of bovine meat rose by 10 percent in 1986 on account of additional slaughterings because of dry weather in the eastern states, but declined by an estimated 4 percent in 1987 as herds were rebuilt. United States production increased by 3 percent in 1986 and declined by an estimated 4 percent in 1987 under the influence of the dairy termination program.

The secular decline in global per capita consumption of beef and veal halted temporarily in 1985 at 35.9 pounds (carcass weight) as low prices stimulated consumption in the EC, Canada, and the United States. Although consumption increased further in 1986 throughout much of the world because of low prices, a sharp decline in Brazilian consumption related to reduced availability of domestic beef was mainly responsible for global per capita consumption resuming its downward trend, falling to 35.7 pounds. It is estimated that per capita consumption declined further in 1987 owing to higher prices and a further shift in demand from beef to pork and poultry, particularly in North America. In the United States, in terms of retail weight, estimates indicate that poultry consumption exceeded beef and veal consumption for the first time in 1987.

The outlook for 1988 is for global beef and veal production to remain almost unchanged from 1987, as higher output in the U.S.S.R. should balance reduced output in most other countries. Global per capita consumption is projected to decline further as competing meats will be in good supply, and this, together with large stocks of frozen beef available in the EC[48] should restrain any upward movement of prices.

## Lamb

After increasing by 2 percent in 1985, world production of sheep and goat meat fell by 6 percent in 1986 as higher output in Australia was offset by lower output in the EC, New Zealand, and the United States. In New Zealand, which accounts for about 14 percent of world sheepmeat production and about 70 percent of world exports, a seven-week strike by meatworkers in February–March, the on-going contraction of the sheep farming sector owing to the withdrawal of Government supports, and a greater emphasis on wool production led to a 16 percent reduction in output in 1986. Flock rebuilding with greater ewe retention in the EC and the United States resulted in a 3 percent and 6 percent fall in sheepmeat output, respectively. Sheepmeat production in Australia increased by 6 percent mainly because of drought-induced slaughter in the first half year, but also because the decline in New Zealand production opened up export opportunities in the United States market.[49]

---

[46] A 9.5 percent reduction in milk quotas is to take effect gradually in the period to mid-1989, and the levy on deliveries in excess of quotas was raised to 100 percent.

[47] Brazil purchased 90,000 tons of beef from the United States and 200,000 tons from the EC in 1986 at prices well below those prevailing in other markets. Shipments of U.S. beef were made about equally in 1986 and 1987.

[48] Intervention stocks of beef in the EC amounted to 741,000 tons at the end of 1985 and declined by about 200,000 tons during 1986, largely reflecting sales to Brazil. By the end of 1987, stocks again exceeded 700,000 tons.

[49] In the 12 months to May 1987, U.S. imports of lamb and mutton were 14 percent higher than in the preceding 12-month period. Between these two periods, imports from New Zealand were 62 percent lower, while imports from Australia were 55 percent higher.

The meatworkers strike in New Zealand occurred just before the seasonal peak in demand at Easter, and the shortage of supplies was mainly responsible for a sharp increase in prices, from 83 cents a pound in January 1986 to 108 cents a pound in June (Table 31).[50] Following the resumption of New Zealand exports, prices declined to 106 cents a pound in July, and then declined more rapidly, averaging just over 93 cents a pound in the second half year. For 1986 as a whole, prices averaged under 93 cents a pound, or 11 percent higher than in 1985. In the first half of 1987, prices averaged 98 cents a pound, boosted by seasonal demand. A peak of 101 cents a pound was recorded in May, after which prices weakened slightly, averaging 99 cents a pound in the second half year. For the year as a whole, prices were 5 percent higher than in 1986.

The overall rise in prices in 1986–87 was also attributable in part to increased consumption of lamb, especially in the United Kingdom, where demand was boosted by improved marketing and packaging in the form of boneless roast lamb. More strict attention by suppliers to religious requirements in slaughtering facilitated an increase in imports of lamb by Middle Eastern countries, and imported chilled lamb gained greater acceptance in Japan. On the other hand, lamb consumption per capita in the United States declined owing to an increase in price relative to pork and poultry.

World output of sheep and goat meat rose by an estimated 2 percent in 1987. Production in Australia increased by 7 percent owing both to rising sheep numbers as high wool prices and low cereal prices led to the expansion of forage for sheep and to an increased rate of slaughter of lambs to take advantage of high meat prices. In a reversal of trend, sheep numbers in New Zealand rose by 3 percent owing to high meat and wool prices, but production remained unchanged because of a higher rate of ewe retention. Low feed costs and improved returns resulted in continued flock buildup in the United States, and sheepmeat production declined by over 10 percent. Meat production is estimated to have increased marginally both in the EC and the U.S.S.R. as a result of previous flock expansion.

The outlook for sheepmeat production in 1988 is for only a modest increase. Although Australian pastures are close to their maximum carrying capacity, the rate of slaughter may be constrained by extremely favorable wool prices. New Zealand output may decline marginally because carrying capacity of pastures will be reduced by lower fertilizer application; many farmers are in a strained financial situation owing to high mortgage and other interest payments. Sheepmeat

---

[50] Price quotations refer to frozen New Zealand lamb, grade PL, Smithfield market, London (in U.S. cents).

prices in 1988 are expected to remain fairly stable at about the level prevailing at the end of 1987.

## Sugar

Sugar prices have been depressed in the 1980s because of high levels of production, slow growth of world sugar consumption, and a related buildup in stocks. At the same time, international trade in sugar beginning in 1983 has progressively declined in absolute terms. The free market price declined from an average of 29 U.S. cents a pound in 1980 to 4 cents a pound in 1985 and fluctuated between 5 and 7½ cents a pound in 1986 and 1987 (Table 32). World sugar production reached 101 million tons in 1981/82 and 1982/83 (September/August) (Table 33). Between then and 1986/87, despite the sharp decline in prices, world sugar production declined only twice—in 1983/84 and in 1985/86—and in both years the declines were largely attributable to adverse weather conditions. In 1986/87 world production was a record 103 million tons; a small decline is forecast for 1987/88. In the period from 1981/82 to 1986/87, world sugar consumption has increased by about 2 percent annually, averaging 96 million tons a year (Table 33). The level of stocks rose sharply from 18.6 million tons in 1980/81 to 31.6 million tons in 1982/83, but declined thereafter. End-of-period stocks averaged about 30 percent of world consumption during the period 1981/82–86/87, compared with a "normal" level of 24 percent. Meanwhile, the volume of world sugar exports declined from 31 million tons in 1982 to an estimated 28 million tons in 1987.

In 1986/87 world production increased by nearly 4 percent to 102.9 million tons. Most of the expansion was attributable to increased production in India, where output rose by 14 percent because of better weather and increased area under cultivation, and in the United States, where output grew by 13 percent to 6.2 million tons (the highest level since 1975/76) as a result of higher yields from a substantially larger harvested area. Production also increased in other countries, including Brazil and those in the EC, because of higher yields, and China, reflecting both an increase in yields and the use of improved cane varieties. The production increase was accompanied by a 3 percent growth in world consumption to 101.4 million tons. China alone accounted for 30 percent of the rise in world consumption in 1986/87, reflecting increased demand for refined sugar in China's expanding food-processing sector.

In 1987/88 world production is expected to decline by about 2 percent, mainly because of weather-related problems in some major producing countries, and is expected to fall short of consumption, which is pro-

**Table 32.  Prices of Sugar, 1979–88**

| Year | Free Market[1] | European Community[2] | United States[3] | Free Market[1] | European Community[2] | United States[3] |
|---|---|---|---|---|---|---|
| | *(In SDR 0.01 a pound)* | | | *(In U.S. cents a pound)* | | |
| 1979 | 7.5 | 14.9 | 12.0 | 9.7 | 19.3 | 15.5 |
| 1980 | 22.0 | 17.0 | 23.1 | 28.7 | 22.1 | 30.0 |
| 1981 | 14.3 | 16.1 | 16.7 | 16.9 | 18.9 | 19.7 |
| 1982 | 7.6 | 16.4 | 18.0 | 8.4 | 18.1 | 19.9 |
| 1983 | 7.9 | 16.4 | 20.6 | 8.5 | 17.6 | 22.0 |
| 1984 | 5.1 | 15.6 | 21.2 | 5.2 | 16.0 | 21.7 |
| 1985 | 4.0 | 15.9 | 20.0 | 4.1 | 16.1 | 20.4 |
| 1986 | 5.2 | 15.9 | 17.9 | 6.1 | 18.6 | 21.0 |
| 1987 | 5.2 | 16.2 | 16.9 | 6.8 | 20.9 | 21.8 |
| 1986 I | 5.2 | 16.1 | 18.6 | 5.8 | 18.1 | 20.9 |
| II | 6.4 | 16.4 | 18.0 | 7.5 | 19.0 | 20.9 |
| III | 4.4 | 15.8 | 17.4 | 5.3 | 19.0 | 20.9 |
| IV | 4.7 | 15.1 | 17.5 | 5.7 | 18.3 | 21.1 |
| 1987 I | 5.7 | 15.6 | 17.2 | 7.1 | 19.7 | 21.7 |
| II | 5.1 | 16.2 | 17.0 | 6.6 | 21.0 | 22.0 |
| III | 4.6 | 16.2 | 17.2 | 5.8 | 20.7 | 21.9 |
| IV | 5.5 | 16.7 | 16.2 | 7.4 | 22.4 | 21.7 |
| 1988 I | 6.5 | 16.8 | 16.1 | 8.9 | 20.9 | 22.0 |

Source: Commodities Division, IMF Research Department.

[1] International Sugar Agreement price which is an average of the New York contract No. 11 spot price and the London daily price, f.o.b. Caribbean ports.

[2] Unpacked sugar, c.i.f. European ports.

[3] U.S. future import price contract No. 14. Prior to June 1985, New York contract No. 12 spot price, c.i.f. Atlantic and Gulf of Mexico ports.

jected to expand by 1 percent. As a result of the projected production shortfall, world sugar stocks are expected to fall. The absolute level of reported stocks is expected to fall by 2 million tons and the stock/consumption ratio, which has been falling in recent years, is expected to decline further. The improvement in overall market balance is expected to result in higher prices.

After increasing by 26 percent in the first quarter of 1987 to 7.6 cents a pound in March, the average quarterly price of sugar on the free market declined by 7 percent during the second quarter and by a further 11 percent in the third quarter to a low of 5.6 cents a pound in August. The rise in prices in the early months of the year is mainly attributable to major purchases by the U.S.S.R. to supplement domestic production and normal purchases from Cuba, tight export availabilities in Brazil stemming from drought damage to production and sharply increasing domestic demand, and a poor supply situation in Cuba, because of low production in two successive years as a result of drought and hurricane damage. The fall in the free market price during the period March–August 1987 reflects increases in previously estimated production for 1986/87 and in projected output for 1987/88, indicating a continuation of the stock overhang. However, reports of possible weather-induced damage to sugar crops in major producing countries and an anticipated

stock drawdown in 1987/88 because world production is expected to decline below world consumption for the first time in over five years caused prices to move up in subsequent months, averaging 8.3 cents a pound in December 1987. For 1987 as a whole, the free market price of sugar averaged 11 percent higher than in 1986 but 39 percent lower than the average annual price in the period 1980–86 and 76 percent lower than in 1980.

Sharply lower prices in recent years have not had much of an impact on world sugar output mainly because of support prices in most industrial countries, and, to a lesser extent, in developing countries. These policies support production through government-administered prices and other production incentives and by preferential trade arrangements. A comparison of sugar prices in the United States and EC markets with free market prices is indicative of the degree of protection provided to domestic producers. In 1986 and 1987 the price in the U.S. market averaged about 21–22 cents a pound and the price of sugar in the EC averaged 19–20 cents a pound, compared to a free market price of 6–7 cents a pound.

Prices in the United States sugar market have been maintained at a relatively high level by means of guaranteed loans for domestic producers and of limiting the supply of sugar through import quotas. The Food Security Act of 1985 mandates that raw sugar prices be supported at no less than 18 cents a pound through

**Table 33. Sugar: World Commodity Balance, 1981/82–87/88**

(In millions of tons, raw value, unless otherwise indicated)

| | September/August Crop Years | | | | | | |
|---|---|---|---|---|---|---|---|
| | 1981/82 | 1982/83 | 1983/84 | 1984/85 | 1985/86 | 1986/87[1] | 1987/88[2] |
| **Production** | **100.6** | **101.3** | **96.5** | **100.3** | **99.3** | **102.9** | **101.3** |
| Australia | 3.4 | 3.5 | 3.4 | 3.5 | 3.4 | 3.8 | 3.4 |
| Brazil | 8.4 | 9.3 | 9.4 | 9.3 | 8.4 | 8.8 | 9.2 |
| China | 3.4 | 4.1 | 3.8 | 4.6 | 5.5 | 5.8 | 5.7 |
| Cuba | 8.2 | 7.2 | 8.3 | 8.1 | 7.1 | 7.2 | 7.3 |
| European Community | 17.1 | 16.0 | 13.3 | 14.4 | 14.4 | 14.9 | 13.4 |
| India | 9.7 | 9.5 | 7.0 | 7.1 | 8.0 | 9.1 | 8.9 |
| United States | 5.5 | 5.4 | 5.3 | 5.3 | 5.5 | 6.2 | 6.5 |
| U.S.S.R. | 6.4 | 7.4 | 8.7 | 8.6 | 8.7 | 8.7 | 8.3 |
| Other countries | 38.5 | 38.9 | 37.3 | 39.4 | 38.3 | 38.4 | 38.6 |
| **Consumption** | **90.5** | **93.8** | **95.9** | **96.5** | **98.4** | **101.4** | **102.7** |
| Brazil | 5.8 | 6.2 | 6.3 | 6.3 | 6.3 | 6.5 | 6.7 |
| China | 4.5 | 4.9 | 5.0 | 5.6 | 6.1 | 7.0 | 7.1 |
| European Community | 11.9 | 11.7 | 11.5 | 11.6 | 11.4 | 11.4 | 11.6 |
| India | 6.8 | 7.6 | 8.9 | 9.1 | 9.3 | 9.7 | 10.0 |
| United States | 8.4 | 8.0 | 7.9 | 7.2 | 7.3 | 7.4 | 7.4 |
| U.S.S.R. | 13.0 | 13.0 | 13.3 | 13.3 | 13.5 | 13.4 | 13.4 |
| Other countries | 40.1 | 42.4 | 43.0 | 43.4 | 44.5 | 46.0 | 46.5 |
| **Losses, discrepancy** | **0.0** | **−1.9** | **−3.4** | **−2.7** | **−2.5** | **−2.3** | **−0.8** |
| **Reported closing stocks** | **26.0** | **31.6** | **28.8** | **29.9** | **28.3** | **27.5** | **25.3** |
| Change from previous year | | | | | | | |
| (*in percent*) | 39.6 | 21.5 | −8.9 | 3.8 | −5.4 | −2.8 | −8.0 |
| Stocks/consumption ratio (*in percent*) | 29 | 34 | 30 | 31 | 29 | 27 | 25 |

Sources: Commodities Division, IMF Research Department for prices. Data for world commodity balance from U.S. Department of Agriculture, *Foreign Agriculture Circular: Sugar, Molasses, and Honey* (Washington), various issues.

[1] U.S. Department of Agriculture revised estimates.

[2] U.S. Department of Agriculture forecasts for production and Commodities Division, IMF Research Department forecasts for consumption and stocks.

1990. The Commodity Credit Corporation (CCC) guarantees nonrecourse commodity loans available to sugar processors, who can use sugar as collateral to receive the loans. Processors are permitted, without penalty, to forfeit the sugar used as collateral, and do so if market prices are not high enough to cover the loan proceeds and at least marketing expenses (insurance and transportation charges) and interest charges on the loan.[51] Since May 1982, the United States has maintained import quotas for sugar (Table 34) to maintain domestic prices high enough to prevent loan defaults.[52]

The relatively high sugar price in the United States and the relatively greater profitability of sugar production over production of alternative crops has been reflected in increased U.S. sugar production and increased substitution of more competitively priced high fructose corn syrup (HFCS) for sugar in processed foods. U.S. sugar consumption has fallen from nearly 9 million tons in 1980/81 to about 7 million tons annually on average in the years 1984/85–86/87, reflecting the displacement of sugar by caloric and also noncaloric sweeteners. Meanwhile, sugar production in 1987/88 is expected to be 18 percent higher than in 1985/86. Consequently, the U.S. import market has continued to contract, and it is possible that the United States

---

[51] For the 1987/88 crop, the loan rate has been set at 18 cents a pound for raw cane sugar and 21.16 cents a pound for refined beet sugar. The market stabilization price (MSP) has been set at 21.76 cents a pound, and import quotas were reduced to keep the spot market price at, or near, the MSP in order to prevent forfeitures. The prorated annual U.S. global sugar import quota has been reduced from 2,879,000 tons in 1983/84 to 685,000 tons in 1988. In December 1987, however, the United States government passed a spending bill which includes a provision permitting the Caribbean countries and the Philippines to export 290,000 short tons (263,000 metric tons) and 110,000 short tons (99,770 metric tons) of raw sugar, respectively, to the United States, over and above their 1988 quotas. This sugar would be refined and re-exported during fiscal year 1988. Sugar traders and refiners would receive generic certificates to bridge the gap between U.S. sugar prices and lower world sugar prices for refined sugar.

[52] In 1985 the U.S. global import quota for sugar was not sufficiently restrictive, and processors defaulted on $107.6 million in nonrecourse loans, with the CCC assuming title to the forfeited sugar and the responsibility for its storage and disposal. The CCC sold 150,000 tons of sugar, which had been acquired at 18 cents a pound, to China at 4.75 cents a pound and also sold some sugar domestically at 3 cents a pound for ethanol refining.

**Table 34.   U.S. Sugar Quota Allocations by Country, 1982/83–87/88[1]**

(In thousands of tons; raw value)

| Country | 10/01/82–09/30/83[2] | 09/26/83–09/30/84[3] | 10/01/84–11/30/85 (14 months) | 12/01/85–12/31/86 (13 months) | 01/01/87–12/31/87 | 01/01/88–12/31/88 |
|---|---|---|---|---|---|---|
| Argentina | 109.2 | 118.7 | 99.1 | 66.9 | 35.5 | 27.3 |
| Australia | 210.8 | 229.0 | 191.3 | 129.2 | 68.5 | 52.7 |
| Barbados | 17.8 | 19.3 | 16.1 | 11.3 | 6.8 | 5.2 |
| Belize | 27.9 | 30.4 | 25.3 | 17.1 | 9.1 | 7.0 |
| Bolivia | 20.3 | 22.1 | 18.4 | 12.5 | 6.8 | 5.2 |
| Brazil | 368.3 | 400.1 | 334.1 | 225.7 | 119.7 | 92.1 |
| Canada | 27.9 | 30.4 | 25.3 | 17.1 | 9.1 | 7.0 |
| Colombia | 60.9 | 66.2 | 55.3 | 37.4 | 19.8 | 15.2 |
| Congo | 0.0 | 15.2 | 11.3 | 11.3 | 6.8 | 5.2 |
| Costa Rica | 38.1 | 56.6 | 47.4 | 31.5 | 15.9 | 11.9 |
| Côte d'Ivoire | 15.0 | 15.2 | 11.3 | 11.3 | 6.8 | 115.2 |
| Dominican Republic | 447.1 | 485.7 | 405.5 | 274.0 | 145.3 | 111.7 |
| Ecuador | 27.9 | 30.4 | 25.3 | 17.1 | 9.1 | 7.0 |
| El Salvador | 66.0 | 80.9 | 67.6 | 45.4 | 23.6 | 17.9 |
| Fiji | 17.8 | 19.3 | 16.1 | 11.3 | 22.8 | 5.7 |
| Gabon | 0.0 | 0.0 | 11.3 | 11.3 | 6.8 | 5.2 |
| Guatemala | 121.9 | 132.5 | 110.6 | 74.7 | 39.6 | 30.5 |
| Guyana | 30.5 | 33.1 | 27.7 | 18.7 | 9.9 | 7.6 |
| Haiti | 15.0 | 15.2 | 11.3 | 11.3 | 6.8 | 5.2 |
| Honduras | 25.4 | 54.0 | 45.4 | 29.7 | 14.4 | 10.5 |
| India | 20.3 | 22.1 | 18.4 | 11.5 | 6.8 | 5.2 |
| Jamaica | 27.9 | 30.4 | 25.3 | 17.1 | 9.1 | 7.0 |
| Madagascar | 15.0 | 15.2 | 11.3 | 11.3 | 6.8 | 5.2 |
| Malawi | 17.8 | 26.6 | 32.1 | 15.6 | 8.3 | 6.3 |
| Mauritius | 27.9 | 30.4 | 25.3 | 27.7 | 9.9 | 7.6 |
| Mexico | 15.0 | 15.2 | 11.3 | 11.3 | 6.8 | 5.2 |
| Mozambique | 33.0 | 35.9 | 30.0 | 20.2 | 10.7 | 8.3 |
| Nicaragua | 53.3 | 5.4 | 5.4 | 0.0 | 0.0 | 0.0 |
| Panama | 73.7 | 80.0 | 66.8 | 45.1 | 23.9 | 18.4 |
| Papua New Guinea | 0.0 | 0.0 | 11.3 | 11.3 | 6.8 | 5.2 |
| Paraguay | 15.0 | 15.2 | 11.3 | 11.3 | 6.8 | 5.2 |
| Peru | 104.1 | 113.1 | 94.5 | 63.8 | 33.8 | 26.0 |
| Philippines | 342.9 | 372.6 | 311.1 | 210.1 | 130.4 | 100.3 |
| St. Kitts and Nevis | 15.0 | 15.2 | 11.3 | 11.3 | 6.8 | 5.2 |
| South Africa | 58.4 | 63.5 | 53.0 | 35.8 | 0.0 | 0.0 |
| Swaziland | 40.6 | 44.2 | 36.9 | 24.9 | 13.2 | 10.2 |
| Taiwan Province of China | 30.5 | 33.1 | 27.7 | 18.7 | 9.9 | 7.6 |
| Thailand | 35.6 | 38.6 | 32.2 | 21.8 | 11.6 | 8.9 |
| Trinidad and Tobago | 17.8 | 19.3 | 16.1 | 11.3 | 6.8 | 5.2 |
| Uruguay | 0.0 | 15.2 | 11.3 | 11.3 | 6.8 | 5.2 |
| Zimbabwe | 30.5 | 33.1 | 27.7 | 18.7 | 9.9 | 7.6 |
| Total | 2,622 | 2,879 | 2,426 | 1,675 | 908 | 685 |
| Total prorated to 12 months | 2,622 | 2,879 | 2,079 | 1,546 | 908 | 685 |
| Percentage change | 0.0 | 9.8 | −27.8 | −25.6 | −41.3 | −24.6 |

Source: U.S. Department of Agriculture. Converted at 1 short ton = .907 metric ton.

[1] Previous to these yearly quotas, quotas were in effect as follows: May 11, 1982–June 30, 1982, 199.6 thousand tons; July 1, 1982–September 30, 1982, 381.0 thousand tons.

[2] Does not reflect global reallocation of shortfalls (to Ecuador and Trinidad and Tobago) of a combined 45.7 thousand tons.

[3] Reflects global allocation of 90.7 thousand ton increase enacted on April 5, 1984.

may become a net exporter of domestically produced sugar within two to four years.

In the EC sugar market, domestic prices and production have been supported through a system of mechanisms, including quotas on domestic production and imports (Table 35). There are guaranteed prices, expressed in terms of ECUs, intervention purchases of domestic sugar, variable import levies that effectively eliminate all imports except those emanating from the African, Caribbean, and Pacific (ACP) countries, and a system of export refunds, or restitutions, which provide for the payment of refunds to exporters

## Table 35. European Community Sugar Quota Allocations by Country, 1981/82–87/88

(In thousands of tons; raw value)[1]

| Country | \multicolumn{7}{c}{July/June Quota Years} | | | | | | |
|---|---|---|---|---|---|---|---|
| | 1981/82 | 1982/83 | 1983/84 | 1984/85 | 1985/86 | 1986/87 | 1987/88[2] |
| Barbados | 53.6 | 53.6 | 53.6 | 54.4 | 54.4 | 54.7 | 54.7 |
| Belize | 42.8 | 42.8 | 42.8 | 43.6 | 43.6 | 43.9 | 43.9 |
| Congo | 5.4 | 5.4 | 8.7 | 10.9 | 10.9 | 11.1 | 11.1 |
| Côte d'Ivoire | 0.0 | 0.0 | 2.2 | 10.9 | 10.9 | 11.1 | 11.1 |
| Fiji | 177.8 | 177.8 | 177.8 | 179.2 | 179.2 | 179.7 | 179.7 |
| Guyana | 171.4 | 171.4 | 171.4 | 172.8 | 172.8 | 173.3 | 173.3 |
| India | 0.0 | 0.0 | 10.9 | 10.9 | 10.9 | 10.9 | 10.9 |
| Jamaica | 128.6 | 128.6 | 128.6 | 128.6 | 128.6 | 129.0 | 129.0 |
| Kenya | 0.1 | 4.3 | 4.3 | 5.4 | 5.4 | 0.0 | 0.0 |
| Madagascar | 10.9 | 10.9 | 10.9 | 11.5 | 11.5 | 11.7 | 11.7 |
| Malawi | 21.7 | 21.7 | 21.7 | 22.4 | 22.4 | 22.6 | 22.6 |
| Mauritius | 529.6 | 529.6 | 529.6 | 532.5 | 532.5 | 533.7 | 533.7 |
| St. Kitts and Nevis | 16.1 | 16.1 | 16.1 | 16.7 | 16.7 | 16.9 | 16.9 |
| Swaziland | 126.5 | 126.5 | 126.5 | 127.7 | 127.7 | 128.1 | 128.1 |
| Tanzania | 10.9 | 10.9 | 10.9 | 10.9 | 10.9 | 11.1 | 11.1 |
| Trinidad and Tobago | 75.0 | 75.0 | 75.0 | 47.3 | 47.3 | 47.6 | 47.6 |
| Zimbabwe | 6.6 | 27.2 | 27.2 | 32.6 | 32.6 | 32.9 | 32.9 |
| Total | 1,377 | 1,401 | 1,418 | 1,418 | 1,418 | 1,418 | 1,418 |

Sources: Regulation 3225/80 (Protocol No. 7) giving the text of the Second Lome Convention. Regulation 1255/82 on Zimbabwe's accession to the Lome Convention. Regulation 1243/84 partially restoring India's quota. Regulation 1764/84 giving the Côte d'Ivoire an ACP quota. Regulation 1763/84 giving full ACP membership to St. Christopher and Nevis, and Regulation 1256/82 doing the same for Belize. Council Decision 75/456/EEC of July 15, 1975 on India's sugar quota. Notices of the Commission in Official Journal C112 (May 13, 1978), C97 (April 18, 1979), C108 (April 29, 1982), C124 (May 15, 1982), and C328 (December 14, 1982). Reallocation of Trinidad's shortfall and Kenya's shortfall by Commission Decisions.
[1] Converted from white equivalent at 0.92 white ton = 1 raw ton.
[2] Estimated.

whenever export prices for quota sugar are below the guaranteed domestic prices.[53] The sugar regime has effectively insulated the EC sugar market from world sugar market conditions and has transformed the EC from a net importer of sugar in the 1970s to one of the world's four leading sugar exporters and the single largest exporter to the free market.

The EC sugar regime is largely self-financing. The main direct cost to the EC budget is the export refunds known as "restitutions," on the 1.4 million tons of ACP sugar (Table 35). Restitutions are paid to exporters in order to bridge the gap between the guaranteed domestic price and the world price. Restitutions are also paid on EC exports of sugar produced within the system of production quotas (about 2 million tons a year), and these are financed mainly by producer levies.[54] These levies, however, have been insufficient to cover the heavy cost of restitutions owing to depressed world prices.

Similarly in Japan, import stabilization fund, customs, and consumption taxes have increased the imported price of sugar substantially above the free market price; sugar production increased by 16 percent between 1982 and 1986, while consumption and net imports decreased by 6 percent and 19 percent, respectively, in that period.

As a consequence of the policy measures in many countries, in 1986 internationally traded sugar accounted for less than 27 percent of world production, and only 18 percent of production was traded at competitive prices on the free market. As countries have increasingly insulated producers and consumers

[53] The EC sugar regime is reviewed every five years. Production quotas have, however, remained effectively the same since 1981. There are two types of quotas, one which provides full price guarantees (known as A quota) and corresponds roughly to the Community's sugar consumption and the other (known as B quota), which provides a lower level of support for sugar that is largely exported. In addition, sugar is produced outside of quotas (known as C sugar), and this sugar does not attract support; it must either be exported or stored to become the first tranche of A quota sugar in the following year. In December 1985 the EC Farm Ministers agreed to extend the current sugar regime, which has been in operation since 1981/82, for an additional two years (1986/87 and 1987/88); production quotas were left unchanged at current levels.

[54] A levy of 2 percent of the intervention price is made on all sugar produced under quota. In addition, a levy of up to 37.5 percent can be made on sugar produced under the B quota. However, revenue generated by these levies has been insufficient to cover the heavy cost of export refunds as a result of depressed world market prices, and a cumulative deficit of about ECU 400 million was reached by the end of the 1986 budget period. In 1985, an additional levy, known as the elimination levy, was agreed upon to reduce the outstanding cumulative deficit over the five years to 1990/91. In February 1988, a supplementary levy was approved to ensure coverage of the deficit in each year, if the proceeds from the two production lines are insufficient. It was also agreed to maintain quotas at their present level through 1990/91.

from the sharp swings in free market prices, the absolute size of the residual free market has been reduced; net exports to the free market have fallen from about 22 million tons in 1982 to 18 million tons in 1986. About one fifth of international sugar trade is conducted under special long-term bilateral and multilateral supply and purchase arrangements. Importing countries typically pay higher than free market prices for imports under terms of such agreements. An example of special arrangement trading in sugar is the barter arrangement between Cuba, the world's leading sugar exporter, and the U.S.S.R., which acquires much of its imported sugar from Cuba at very high rates of compensation in the form of machinery and other goods. Another example is EC imports of sugar from ACP countries under the Sugar Protocol of the Lomé Convention. Net sugar imports by the U.S.S.R. have declined in recent years, from a record level of 7.1 million tons in 1982 to 5.2 million tons in 1986. This reflects increasing self-sufficiency, partly as a result of the recovery in output after three successive years of adverse weather conditions.

As a result of exports under such arrangements and to the preferential U.S. market, overall unit values of sugar exports have been considerably higher than prices on the free market. As purchase agreements are renewed, however, some reflect lower free market prices. Furthermore, as U.S. import quotas have been reduced, supplies in excess of quota limitations have had to be channeled to other free market outlets at substantially lower prices. The unit value of sugar exports of developing countries (excluding Cuba) has declined from an average of $545 a ton in 1980–81 to an estimated $218 in 1984–87 (Table 36). Reflecting this and lower export volumes since 1982, the value of sugar exports of developing countries has fallen from nearly $6 billion in 1980 to only $2.5 billion in 1986 and 1987.

Among developing countries, expanding domestic production has sharply reduced sugar imports by a number of countries. Mexico's imports declined from an average of 701,000 tons annually in the period 1980–83 to 273,000 tons in 1984, and since 1985 Mexico has been a net sugar exporter.

The shrinkage of world sugar trade reflecting structural changes in regard to both supply and demand, which appear to be extending the length of sugar price cycles, could limit the extent of future price increases.[55] Historically, high sugar prices have tended to induce over-expansion of production. Burdensome stocks and low prices help to discourage further increases in production, which tend to be inflexible in a downward direction. Increasing consumption helps to absorb excess supplies, and if this is accompanied by a large, typically weather-induced, shortfall in output in one or more major producers, prices may rise sharply. As a result, the sugar price cycle has typically involved a short period of high prices followed by a long period of low prices. The average length of time between peaks has been about 6 years, with the most recent peaks in 1974 and 1980, when prices averaged 30 cents a pound and 29 cents a pound, respectively.

Developments since the mid-1970s appear to have reduced the average potential response time of producers to higher prices. These include the expansion of output in the EC and its emergence as a major world exporter of sugar. The EC produces beet sugar, a crop whose production can be substantially increased in less than a year in response to appropriate price signals. Another potential supply response to high prices could be the cane used in Brazil's alcohol industry. About 40 percent of Brazil's cane production is used to produce sugar; some market analysts feel that a substantial rise in prices could induce Brazil to divert part of its sugarcane output from alcohol to sugar production, and this possibility should be factored into consideration of possible supply developments. Furthermore, the long period of low world market prices has caused many sugar exporters to maintain production by increasing efficiency and reducing production costs. Prices in the range of 7–10 cents a pound, basis New York, are now quoted as adequate to profitably export sugar. Higher prices could provide an incentive to such producers, and to those that cut back production as a result of adverse market developments, to expand output, or to increase it to former levels, both to increase rates of return and possibly also to recapture lost market shares.

The structure of the world sugar market has also changed substantially on the demand side. Whereas the industrial countries accounted for about two thirds of world imports in the mid-1970s, they accounted for only about 30 percent in 1986, with developing countries now accounting for the largest share. This is mainly attributable to the displacement of sugar by high fructose corn syrup, especially in the United States and to a lesser extent in Japan. In recent years, the U.S.S.R. has replaced the United States as the world's leading sugar importer, but the U.S.S.R.'s purchases on the free market have tended to fluctuate sharply, depending upon both domestic production prospects and production in Cuba, its major supplier. The shift in world import demand away from industrial countries, where price and income elasticities of demand are very low, to developing countries, where elasticities are relatively high, has made world demand

---

[55] A. C. Hannah, "The Sugar Cycle, Structural Change and International Sugar Agreements," F. O. Licht's *International Sugar Report*, Vol. 119, No. 14 (May 21, 1987), pp. 213–17.

**Table 36. Sugar: World Trade, 1984–87**

| | 1984 | 1985 | 1986 | 1987[1] | 1984 | 1985 | 1986 | 1987[1] |
|---|---|---|---|---|---|---|---|---|
| | (Values in SDRs) | | | | (Values in U.S. dollars) | | | |
| **Exports** | | | | | | | | |
| **Earnings** (*in billions*) | **9.8** | **8.8** | **8.0** | **7.6** | **10.1** | **8.9** | **9.4** | **9.8** |
| Industrial countries | 2.0 | 1.7 | 1.7 | 1.9 | 2.1 | 1.7 | 2.0 | 2.4 |
| Developing countries | 7.6 | 6.9 | 6.0 | 5.4 | 7.8 | 7.0 | 7.1 | 7.1 |
| U.S.S.R. and Eastern European countries | 0.2 | 0.2 | 0.3 | 0.3 | 0.2 | 0.2 | 0.3 | 0.3 |
| **Volumes** (*in millions of tons*) | **28.7** | **28.3** | **28.2** | **27.9** | **28.7** | **28.3** | **28.2** | **27.9** |
| Industrial countries | 8.3 | 8.1 | 8.8 | 9.3 | 8.3 | 8.1 | 8.8 | 9.3 |
| *France* | *2.9* | *2.4* | *2.2* | *2.0* | *2.9* | *2.4* | *2.2* | *2.0* |
| *Australia* | *2.4* | *2.5* | *2.8* | *2.8* | *2.4* | *2.5* | *2.8* | *2.8* |
| *Other* | *3.0* | *3.2* | *3.8* | *4.5* | *3.0* | *3.2* | *3.8* | *4.5* |
| Developing countries | 19.4 | 19.2 | 17.8 | 17.1 | 19.4 | 19.2 | 17.9 | 17.1 |
| *Brazil* | *3.2* | *2.7* | *2.4* | *2.3* | *3.2* | *2.7* | *2.4* | *2.3* |
| *Cuba* | *6.7* | *6.9* | *6.7* | *6.4* | *6.7* | *6.9* | *6.7* | *6.4* |
| *Other* | *9.5* | *9.6* | *8.7* | *8.4* | *9.5* | *9.6* | *8.8* | *8.4* |
| U.S.S.R. and Eastern European countries | 1.0 | 1.0 | 1.5 | 1.5 | 1.0 | 1.0 | 1.5 | 1.5 |
| **Unit values** (*a ton*) | **343** | **310** | **285** | **271** | **352** | **315** | **335** | **351** |
| Industrial countries | 248 | 213 | 198 | 200 | 254 | 216 | 232 | 258 |
| Developing countries | 391 | 359 | 339 | 318 | 401 | 365 | 397 | 412 |
| (Developing countries excluding Cuba) | 232 | 182 | 184 | 179 | 238 | 185 | 216 | 231 |
| U.S.S.R. and Eastern European countries | 205 | 167 | 188 | 170 | 210 | 170 | 220 | 220 |
| **Imports** | | | | | | | | |
| **Values** (*in billions*) | **10.5** | **9.0** | **8.6** | **7.6** | **10.8** | **9.2** | **10.1** | **9.8** |
| Industrial countries | 2.9 | 2.2 | 2.0 | 1.9 | 2.9 | 2.2 | 2.4 | 2.4 |
| Developing countries | 2.9 | 2.4 | 2.3 | 2.1 | 3.0 | 2.5 | 2.7 | 2.8 |
| U.S.S.R. and Eastern European countries | 4.7 | 4.4 | 4.3 | 3.6 | 4.9 | 4.5 | 5.0 | 4.6 |
| **Volumes** (*in millions of tons*) | **28.1** | **27.4** | **26.8** | **25.1** | **28.1** | **27.4** | **26.8** | **25.1** |
| Industrial countries | 9.3 | 8.5 | 8.0 | 7.4 | 9.3 | 8.5 | 8.0 | 7.4 |
| *United States* | *3.1* | *2.6* | *1.9* | *1.5* | *3.1* | *2.6* | *1.9* | *1.5* |
| *Japan* | *1.8* | *1.9* | *1.8* | *1.7* | *1.8* | *1.9* | *1.8* | *1.7* |
| *United Kingdom* | *1.4* | *1.1* | *1.3* | *1.4* | *1.4* | *1.1* | *1.3* | *1.4* |
| *Other* | *3.0* | *2.9* | *3.0* | *2.8* | *3.0* | *2.9* | *3.0* | *2.8* |
| Developing countries | 11.9 | 13.1 | 12.4 | 11.8 | 11.9 | 13.1 | 12.4 | 11.8 |
| U.S.S.R. and Eastern European countries | 6.9 | 5.8 | 6.4 | 5.9 | 6.9 | 5.8 | 6.4 | 5.9 |
| *U.S.S.R.* | *5.8* | *4.5* | *5.2* | *4.7* | *5.8* | *4.5* | *5.2* | *4.7* |
| *Other* | *1.1* | *1.3* | *1.2* | *1.2* | *1.1* | *1.3* | *1.2* | *1.2* |
| **Unit values** (*a ton*) | **373** | **330** | **322** | **302** | **383** | **335** | **378** | **390** |
| Industrial countries | 308 | 260 | 251 | 256 | 316 | 264 | 295 | 331 |
| Developing countries | 246 | 183 | 183 | 174 | 252 | 185 | 215 | 225 |
| U.S.S.R. and Eastern European countries | 680 | 768 | 679 | 615 | 697 | 779 | 797 | 795 |
| **Market prices** (*a ton*) | | | | | | | | |
| Free market[2] | 112 | 88 | 114 | 115 | 115 | 89 | 133 | 149 |
| European Community[3] | 345 | 350 | 350 | 357 | 353 | 355 | 410 | 462 |
| United States[4] | 468 | 442 | 394 | 372 | 479 | 449 | 462 | 481 |

Sources: UN Food and Agriculture Organization, *1986 FAO Trade Yearbook* (Rome), for exports and imports; Commodities Division, IMF Research Department for market prices.

[1] Data on exports and imports are estimates of Commodities Division, IMF Research Department.

[2] International Sugar Agreement price which is an average of the New York contract No. 11 spot price and the London daily price, f.o.b. Caribbean ports.

[3] Unpacked sugar, c.i.f. European ports.

[4] U.S. future import price contract No. 14. Prior to June 1985, New York contract No. 12 spot price, c.i.f. Atlantic and Gulf of Mexico ports.

for imported sugar more sensitive to movements in prices.

Free market prices are expected to improve in 1988 as a result of the expected reduction in world stocks, especially the expected decline in surplus stocks in exporting countries. Nevertheless, the extent and duration of the price rise is expected to be limited. Structural changes in the market, such as the increased share of beet sugar in world trade as a result of the expansion of beet sugar production in the EC and the development of the sugar cane-based alcohol industry in Brazil, have reduced the potential response time required by producers to adjust to changing price signals. World beet and cane processing capacity, which already substantially exceeds consumption, is still continuing to expand. Furthermore, because of the marked rise in the share of developing countries in world sugar imports in recent years, the elasticity of market demand with respect to price has increased, and any major price increase could result in reduced purchases. In addition, a strong rise in world prices in 1988–89 could encourage further major shifts in consumption away from sugar toward high fructose corn syrup and high intensity sweeteners. HFCS could potentially displace sugar in markets other than those in the United States and Japan, and, over the longer term, trade in crystar (crystaline corn fructose) and low-calorie sweeteners could increase.

## Bananas

The volume of world exports of bananas increased by 5 percent in 1986 to 7.4 million tons; it is estimated to have increased further in 1987. Ninety-five percent of world exports come from developing countries, of which the members of the UPEB (Union de Paises Exportadores de Banano) account for more than 50 percent. With the exception of Colombia and Guatemala for which export volumes were unchanged, member countries of UPEB registered substantial increases in 1987 exports: Costa Rica, 5 percent; Honduras, 15 percent; and Panama, 19 percent. Ecuador, normally accounting for about 20 percent of total trade, is estimated to have exported 1.4 million tons. In 1986, exports of the Philippines rose by 12 percent to 900,000 tons and by the Caribbean countries by 18 percent to 535,000 tons.

By far the biggest importers are the industrial countries, representing 93 percent of the total world import demand in 1986. Imports of the United States at 2.7 million tons were unchanged compared with 1985, while the imports of the EC increased by 6 percent to 2.4 million tons, and Japan increased imports by 12 percent to 760,000 tons. Except for Portugal and Spain, all member countries of the EC increased their imports individually; per capita imports also rose, with the Federal Republic of Germany reaching 10.5 kilograms, the highest level in the EC and close to that of the United States.

U.S. dollar prices on average in 1987 were 5 percent lower than in 1986. Prices in deutsche mark fell in 1987 by 4 percent; in Japan prices in Japanese yen fell at least 15 percent, whereas in French ports, prices in French francs rose by 3 percent. Prices in terms of dollars rose substantially in Europe: in the Federal Republic of Germany by 14 percent and in France by 18 percent, whereas in Japan they remained virtually unchanged (Table 37).

Different price movements for bananas in different countries not only reflect exchange rate changes but also are an indication of the segmentation of this market. In many cases, importing countries have long-standing bilateral trade relations with individual exporting countries. For example, shipments to continental France come mainly from the Overseas Departments and from Cameroon and Côte d'Ivoire under preferential import regimes. Caribbean countries are the major suppliers for the British market, providing about 225,000 tons out of a total import demand of 350,000 tons in 1987 under special arrangements. Japan, a country without quantitative import restrictions on bananas but with significant duties, is supplied with bananas to a large extent by the Philippines. In the case of the Federal Republic of Germany, there are no particular bilateral links to banana-producing countries and no quantitative import restrictions. The German market is mainly supplied from the same sources as the U.S. market, that is, the countries in Latin America. Even differences in seasonal policy patterns can be related partly to this segmentation. The pattern of German prices is similar to the U.S. price pattern, while French prices seem to move within a more narrow range. Price movements throughout the year in Japan differ considerably from those in the United States and Europe, with the tendency toward one peak around mid-year. In Japan the traditional peak demand during the second quarter of the year is only partly in line with the production cycle in the Philippines, where peaks occur in both the second and fourth quarters.

Mainly because of the increasing variety of competing fruit, import demand for bananas in the traditional major markets may only have a limited growth potential. Substantial increases of imports into the EC and Japan in 1986 and 1987, contrasting with the stagnation in previous years, could be misleading if interpreted as long-term trends. Lower-than-expected availabilities of competitive fruit owing to a severe winter in 1985/86, as well as the generally favorable import prices for bananas and the alleviation of some

## Table 37. Bananas: Prices in Selected Markets, 1985–87

(A ton)

| | Year | Average | Jan. | Feb. | Mar. | April | May | June | July | Aug. | Sept. | Oct. | Nov. | Dec. |
|---|---|---|---|---|---|---|---|---|---|---|---|---|---|---|
| **New York** | | | | | | | | | | | | | | |
| In U.S. dollars | 1985 | 378 | 376 | 443 | 454 | 484 | 457 | 380 | 321 | 422 | 362 | 278 | 275 | 285 |
| | 1986 | 382 | 329 | 386 | 500 | 578 | 387 | 345 | 331 | 321 | 424 | 375 | 294 | 311 |
| | 1987 | 362 | 357 | 402 | 420 | 373 | 402 | 355 | 410 | 304 | 328 | 247 | 381 | 356 |
| **Hamburg** | | | | | | | | | | | | | | |
| In deutsche mark | 1985 | 1,340 | 1,287 | 1,494 | 1,877 | 2,011 | 1,803 | 1,509 | 1,168 | 1,100 | 1,223 | 822 | 937 | 848 |
| | 1986 | 1,210 | 1,185 | 1,323 | 1,447 | 1,685 | 1,523 | 1,540 | 879 | 1,066 | 1,054 | 1,002 | 855 | 947 |
| | 1987 | 1,160 | 775 | 1,197 | 1,410 | 1,282 | 1,288 | 1,521 | 1,323 | 1,264 | 1,129 | 1,020 | 909 | 811 |
| In U.S. dollars | 1985 | 455 | 406 | 454 | 567 | 652 | 579 | 493 | 400 | 394 | 431 | 311 | 361 | 377 |
| | 1986 | 557 | 485 | 567 | 639 | 741 | 684 | 689 | 408 | 517 | 517 | 500 | 422 | 475 |
| | 1987 | 632 | 396 | 655 | 769 | 708 | 721 | 836 | 716 | 632 | 583 | 568 | 505 | 497 |
| **French ports** | | | | | | | | | | | | | | |
| In French francs | 1985 | 4,970 | 4,500 | 4,890 | 5,750 | 5,790 | 5,490 | 4,940 | 4,610 | 4,610 | 4,760 | 4,920 | 4,710 | 4,660 |
| | 1986 | 5,060 | 4,760 | 5,080 | 5,600 | 5,490 | 5,210 | 5,300 | 4,710 | 4,820 | 5,020 | 5,020 | 4,870 | 4,820 |
| | 1987 | 5,210 | 4,700 | 4,840 | 5,620 | 5,420 | 5,330 | 5,550 | 5,540 | 5,520 | 5,450 | 5,360 | 4,970 | 4,220 |
| In U.S. dollars | 1985 | 553 | 464 | 486 | 569 | 615 | 580 | 529 | 519 | 541 | 550 | 610 | 597 | 605 |
| | 1986 | 731 | 635 | 709 | 804 | 763 | 732 | 743 | 680 | 717 | 752 | 767 | 735 | 737 |
| | 1987 | 864 | 759 | 795 | 921 | 899 | 893 | 914 | 901 | 883 | 882 | 895 | 871 | 763 |
| **Japanese ports** | | | | | | | | | | | | | | |
| In thousands of Japanese yen | 1985 | 105 | 88 | 89 | 95 | 122 | 131 | 133 | 116 | 107 | 118 | 107 | 79 | 73 |
| | 1986 | 84 | 73 | 80 | 87 | 96 | 99 | 114 | 108 | 84 | 77 | 64 | 61 | 65 |
| | 1987 | 71 | 58 | 62 | 74 | 85 | 79 | 76 | 68 | 65 | 72 | 72 | 73 | 73 |
| In U.S. dollars | 1985 | 439 | 346 | 342 | 367 | 486 | 519 | 536 | 480 | 450 | 500 | 497 | 388 | 358 |
| | 1986 | 498 | 366 | 433 | 484 | 548 | 592 | 676 | 683 | 544 | 500 | 412 | 375 | 401 |
| | 1987 | 496 | 375 | 404 | 488 | 594 | 562 | 526 | 453 | 441 | 503 | 503 | 540 | 570 |

Sources: UN Food and Agriculture Organization, *FAO Monthly Bulletin of Statistics* (Rome), and Commodities Division, IMF Research Department.

of the supply problems that were evident in the early 1980s, contributed to the far-above-average increase. A return to the high growth rates of the 1970s in markets in eastern Europe and the U.S.S.R. can only be expected in the event of major changes in foreign trade regimes of these countries. In any event, these countries account for only about 3 percent of world trade. Even imports into the United States, growing throughout the whole postwar period, seem to have lost some strength after the per capita import reached a level above 11 kilograms in the mid-1980s. Plans for substantial expansion of production in the Caribbean and some UPEB countries could, therefore, contribute to an underlying tendency for growth in supply to exceed growth in consumption and to a deterioration of already weak price prospects for bananas.

# III

# Beverages

This section discusses market developments for coffee, tea, and cocoa.[56] In the short run, demand for these three commodities tends to be stable and strongly price inelastic. Supply, however, is subject to cyclical fluctuations owing to the perennial nature of the three crops and the resulting lagged response of production to prices. In addition, the three commodities are vulnerable to weather-related short-run supply fluctuations. Consequently, supply changes tend to be the main determinants of price fluctuations. On the demand side there is little substitution in consumption among the three commodities, except during periods of very large price movements, when there has been evidence of limited substitution between coffee and tea in some consuming countries.

Partly because of the dominant role of supply factors, beverage prices have tended to move independently of prices of other primary commodities. As the weight of coffee in the overall index for beverages is much larger than the combined weights of cocoa and tea, movements in coffee prices have a relatively large effect on the movement of the overall beverage price index. This pattern was evident in 1986 and 1987 when the index of dollar prices of beverages moved in a direction opposite to the index of dollar prices of all commodities (Tables 3 and 38 and Chart 5). In 1986 the index of dollar prices of beverages rose by 15 percent when the index of dollar prices of all commodities excluding beverages declined by 7 percent, while in 1987 the index of dollar prices of beverages fell by 28 percent when the index of dollar prices of all commodities excluding beverages rose by 16 percent. The index of SDR prices of beverages remained unchanged in 1986 and fell by 35 percent in 1987. These price changes were primarily the result of changes in the supply of beverages. The index of world beverage production fell by 11 percent in 1986 before

---

[56] Cocoa is included in this group because of its traditional association with coffee and tea as a beverage and because it shares with them certain characteristics with respect to supply. It should be noted, however, that the beverage use of cocoa is secondary to its use in chocolate confectionery.

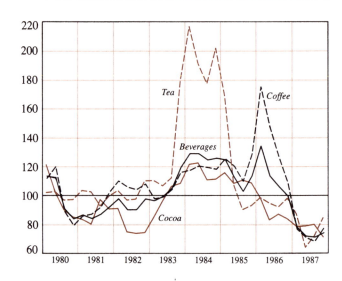

**Chart 5. Prices of Beverages, 1980–87**

(In SDRs; indices: 1980 = 100)

recovering by 17 percent in 1987 (Table 39). Similarly, the index of world beverage supply declined by 5 percent in 1986 before recovering by 8 percent in 1987. The 15 percent increase in the index of dollar prices of beverages in 1986 was largely the result of a sharp drop in world coffee production in the 1986/87 (October/September) coffee year. Similarly, the sharp drop in the index of dollar prices of beverages in 1987 was mainly attributable to a large recovery in world coffee production.

## Coffee

A rapid rise in coffee prices that started in late October 1985 brought to an end a five-year period of relatively stable prices. The dollar price for arabica coffee increased by more than 75 percent over the next four months, while the price for robusta coffee increased by more than 50 percent. Prices of coffee remained relatively high through most of 1986, but by

**Table 38. Prices of Beverages, 1979–88**

| Years | Index of Prices of Beverages[1] | "Other mild" arabica[2] (Pound) | Robusta[3] (Pound) | Tea[4] (Kilogram) | Cocoa Beans[5] (Ton) |
|---|---|---|---|---|---|
| | *(1980 = 100)* | | *(In SDRs)* | | |
| 1979 | 115.3 | 1.35 | 1.28 | 1.67 | 2,549 |
| 1980 | 100.0 | 1.18 | 1.13 | 1.71 | 2,000 |
| 1981 | 87.5 | 1.09 | 0.87 | 1.71 | 1,761 |
| 1982 | 93.8 | 1.27 | 1.01 | 1.75 | 1,578 |
| 1983 | 105.0 | 1.23 | 1.16 | 2.17 | 1,982 |
| 1984 | 127.0 | 1.41 | 1.35 | 3.37 | 2,337 |
| 1985 | 113.3 | 1.43 | 1.19 | 1.95 | 2,220 |
| 1986 | 113.3 | 1.64 | 1.26 | 1.64 | 1,763 |
| 1987 | 73.8 | 0.87 | 0.79 | 1.32 | 1,545 |
| 1986 I | 134.2 | 2.07 | 1.50 | 1.69 | 1,970 |
| II | 113.4 | 1.74 | 1.22 | 1.62 | 1,665 |
| III | 106.1 | 1.50 | 1.18 | 1.58 | 1,745 |
| IV | 99.5 | 1.28 | 1.17 | 1.68 | 1,679 |
| 1987 I | 78.0 | 0.91 | 0.85 | 1.49 | 1,574 |
| II | 71.9 | 0.84 | 0.79 | 1.10 | 1,581 |
| III | 71.2 | 0.81 | 0.75 | 1.23 | 1,602 |
| IV | 74.1 | 0.91 | 0.78 | 1.45 | 1,427 |
| 1988 I | 73.7 | 0.97 | 0.75 | 1.46 | 1,330 |
| | *(1980 = 100)* | | *(In U.S. dollars)* | | |
| 1979 | 114.4 | 1.74 | 1.66 | 2.16 | 3,293 |
| 1980 | 100.0 | 1.54 | 1.47 | 2.23 | 2,603 |
| 1981 | 79.3 | 1.28 | 1.03 | 2.02 | 2,077 |
| 1982 | 79.6 | 1.40 | 1.11 | 1.93 | 1,742 |
| 1983 | 86.1 | 1.32 | 1.24 | 2.32 | 2,119 |
| 1984 | 100.0 | 1.44 | 1.38 | 3.46 | 2,396 |
| 1985 | 88.3 | 1.46 | 1.21 | 1.98 | 2,255 |
| 1986 | 101.8 | 1.93 | 1.48 | 1.93 | 2,068 |
| 1987 | 73.3 | 1.12 | 1.02 | 1.71 | 1,998 |
| 1986 I | 116.0 | 2.33 | 1.68 | 1.90 | 2,217 |
| II | 101.1 | 2.02 | 1.42 | 1.89 | 1,934 |
| III | 98.0 | 1.80 | 1.42 | 1.90 | 2,099 |
| IV | 92.1 | 1.55 | 1.41 | 2.03 | 2,024 |
| 1987 I | 75.6 | 1.14 | 1.08 | 1.88 | 1,984 |
| II | 71.5 | 1.09 | 1.02 | 1.43 | 2,046 |
| III | 69.8 | 1.03 | 0.96 | 1.57 | 2,046 |
| IV | 76.4 | 1.23 | 1.05 | 1.95 | 1,916 |
| 1988 I | 77.4 | 1.33 | 1.02 | 1.99 | 1,819 |

Source: Commodities Division, IMF Research Department.
[1] The weights in the index are as follows: coffee, 63 percent; tea, 11 percent; and cocoa beans, 26 percent.
[2] Central American and Mexican origin, average of prices ex-dock New York and ex-dock Bremen/Hamburg.
[3] African origin, average of prices of ex-dock New York and ex-dock Le Havre/Marseilles.
[4] Any origin, average London auction prices.
[5] International Cocoa Organization daily prices, averages of three nearest trading months on New York Cocoa Exchange and London Cocoa Terminal Market, c.i.f. U.S. and European ports.

mid-1987 had fallen to low levels similar to those recorded in the early 1980s.

The largest coffee producing countries are Brazil, Colombia, Indonesia, Côte d'Ivoire, and Mexico. In recent years, total annual world coffee production has tended to fluctuate around a level of 90 million 60-kilogram bags (5.4 million tons). Owing to the long gestation period for this tree crop, the time lags between price changes and production adjustments can be quite long. Consequently, the short-term price elasticity of supply tends to be quite low—about 0.06, while the long-term price elasticity of supply is about 0.3. Consumption in producing countries is important only in Brazil, India, Indonesia, and Mexico, and most of the world's coffee is exported in the form of beans to the industrialized countries of North America, Western Europe, and Eastern Europe. The demand for coffee is not very responsive to price changes; the world short-term price elasticity of demand is about −0.19 while the long-term elasticity has been estimated

**Table 39. Movements in the Prices of Beverages and Related Economic Indicators, 1980–87**

(Annual percentage changes)

| | 1980 | 1981 | 1982 | 1983 | 1984 | 1985 | 1986 | 1987 |
|---|---|---|---|---|---|---|---|---|
| Prices of beverages[1] | | | | | | | | |
| In SDRs | − 13.2 | − 12.5 | 7.3 | 11.9 | 20.9 | − 10.8 | 0.0 | − 34.8 |
| In U.S. dollars | − 12.6 | − 20.7 | 0.4 | 8.2 | 16.1 | − 11.7 | 15.3 | − 28.0 |
| Real[2] | − 20.5 | − 17.8 | 2.6 | 11.4 | 19.6 | − 12.4 | − 2.2 | − 35.9 |
| Consumer price index in seven industrial countries | | | | | | | | |
| In SDRs | 11.4 | 13.2 | 6.7 | 5.0 | 4.6 | 3.5 | 1.0 | 0.4 |
| In U.S. dollars | 12.2 | 2.6 | − 0.1 | 1.7 | 0.3 | 2.5 | 16.7 | 10.7 |
| Real GNP in seven industrial countries | 1.2 | 1.7 | − 0.4 | 2.8 | 5.2 | 3.2 | 2.8 | 3.1 |
| World consumption of beverages[3] | | | | | | | | |
| Index of consumption | 1.7 | 2.4 | 2.3 | 0.0 | 3.4 | − 1.2 | 1.9 | 1.1 |
| World supply of beverages[3] | | | | | | | | |
| Index of production | 3.7 | 9.5 | − 13.3 | 5.4 | 9.2 | 4.2 | − 10.7 | 17.3 |
| Index of supply[4] | 5.4 | 12.4 | − 2.4 | 1.1 | 4.1 | 2.3 | − 4.6 | 8.3 |
| Index of closing stocks | 23.9 | 33.6 | − 8.8 | − 7.9 | − 4.3 | 14.6 | − 14.2 | 23.7 |

Sources: Commodities Division and Current Studies Division, IMF Research Department.

[1] Refers to IMF world index of prices of beverages. These percentages differ from those reported in the *World Economic Outlook* which refer to the price index of beverages *exported by developing countries*.

[2] Index of dollar prices of beverages deflated by the index of dollar unit values of manufactured exports.

[3] Overall indices constructed using the same weights for the indices of individual commodities as in overall (world) price index. Crop year data for agricultural commodities are given under the earlier calendar year, e.g., crop year 1980/81 under 1980. The commodity coverage of the indices of consumption and stocks is less comprehensive than the coverage of the indices of production and supply.

[4] Supply is defined as production plus *beginning*-of-year stocks.

at − 0.23. The income elasticity of demand, on the other hand, is about 0.45 for the world as a whole and is much higher in Japan (2.0), Eastern Europe (1.0), and the EC (0.60).

Export quotas under the 1976 and 1983 International Coffee Agreements had a major bearing on coffee market developments in the 1980s. When export quotas were first imposed in October 1980, the composite indicator price[57] of the International Coffee Organization (ICO) remained outside the agreement's price range of $1.20–1.40 a pound because of relatively large stocks in consuming countries. A frost in Brazil in July 1981 and export quotas were instrumental in keeping prices relatively stable between mid-1981 and October 1985. The disparity between world coffee production and consumption was absorbed by a large buildup in coffee stocks in exporting countries (Table 40).

A sharp rise in prices that began in late October

---

[57] The International Coffee Organization's (ICO) composite indicator is an average of the ICO indicator prices for robusta and "other milds." Both are physical prices for specific grades of coffee. The robusta indicator is an average of prices ex-dock New York (Angola Ambriz 2BB, Côte d'Ivoire Grade II, and Uganda Standard) and ex-dock Le Havre/Marseille (Côte d'Ivoire Superior Grade II, Cameroon Superior Grade I, Central African Superior, and Madagascar Superior Grade II). The "other milds" indicator is an average of prices of arabica coffee ex-dock New York (El Salvador Central Standard, Guatemala Prime Washed, Mexico Prime Washed), and ex-dock Bremen/Hamburg (El Salvador High Grown, Guatemala Hard Bean, and Nicaragua Strict High Grown).

1985 was caused by a prolonged period of dry weather in the major Brazilian coffee producing states of Minas Gerais, Paraná, and São Paulo, which delayed and severely reduced flowering and fruit set on coffee plantations. Despite the arrival of rains in November and early December, prices continued to rise. Estimates by the coffee trade and government agencies indicated that the 1986 Brazilian coffee crop (during the April 1986 to March 1987 Brazilian crop year) was likely to amount to less than one half of the 1985 crop of 30 million bags. Prices, which averaged $1.27 cents a pound in October 1985, rose to $1.41 in November and $1.75 cents a pound in December. Three successive quota increases totaling 5 million bags or about 8.6 percent of the initial 1985/86 quota of 58 million bags did little to check the upward spiral in prices. Large-scale precautionary and speculative purchases resulting from continued concern about the size of the 1986 Brazilian crop helped to drive prices to an average level of $2.04 a pound in January 1986, which was the highest average monthly price since mid-July 1977. Quotas under the International Coffee Agreement were suspended on February 18, 1986, because the ICO had exhausted all its means of defending the ceiling price ($1.40 a pound) of the price stabilization range.

The prospect of a shortage of arabica coffee as a result of the Brazilian drought caused the price differential between arabica and robusta coffees to widen.

**Table 40.   Coffee: World Commodity Balance, 1981/82–87/88**

(In millions of 60-kilogram bags)

| | October/September Crop Years | | | | | | |
|---|---|---|---|---|---|---|---|
| | 1981/82 | 1982/83 | 1983/84 | 1984/85 | 1985/86 | 1986/87 | 1987/88[1] |
| **Production** | **91.2** | **90.8** | **85.9** | **88.0** | **89.8** | **77.7** | **97.9** |
| Brazil | 26.7 | 23.4 | 24.7 | 25.9 | 30.3 | 15.3 | 35.0 |
| Colombia | 14.5 | 12.3 | 13.0 | 11.0 | 11.8 | 11.0 | 10.7 |
| Other countries[2] | 50.0 | 55.1 | 48.2 | 51.1 | 47.7 | 51.4 | 52.2 |
| **Consumption** | **84.6** | **86.5** | **84.9** | **85.8** | **85.0** | **85.5** | **86.6** |
| Exporting countries | 19.6 | 20.2 | 18.7 | 19.4 | 19.5 | 19.7 | 20.1 |
| *Brazil* | *7.7* | *7.7* | *7.3* | *7.0* | *7.0* | *7.0* | *7.2* |
| *Colombia* | *1.9* | *1.9* | *1.6* | *1.8* | *2.0* | *1.7* | *2.0* |
| *Other countries[2]* | *10.0* | *10.6* | *9.8* | *10.6* | *10.5* | *11.0* | *10.9* |
| Importing countries | 65.0 | 66.3 | 66.2 | 66.4 | 65.5 | 65.8 | 66.5 |
| *ICO members[3]* | *56.0* | *56.8* | *56.2* | *55.9* | *57.0* | *57.5* | *56.0* |
| *Nonmembers[4]* | *9.0* | *9.5* | *10.0* | *10.5* | *8.5* | *8.3* | *10.5* |
| **Losses[5]** | **1.3** | **1.4** | **1.4** | **1.4** | **1.4** | **1.5** | **1.6** |
| **Closing stocks** | **62.0** | **64.9** | **64.5** | **65.3** | **68.7** | **59.4** | **69.1** |
| In exporting countries | 49.6 | 54.3 | 51.4 | 50.9 | 50.0 | 43.1 | 50.8 |
| *Brazil* | *17.3* | *15.5* | *12.8* | *13.4* | *14.3* | *9.0* | *15.0* |
| *Colombia* | *10.1* | *11.3* | *12.7* | *12.3* | *10.6* | *10.0* | *10.7* |
| *Other countries* | *22.2* | *27.5* | *25.9* | *25.2* | *25.1* | *24.1* | *25.1* |
| Other stocks | 12.4 | 10.6 | 13.1 | 14.4 | 18.7 | 16.3 | 18.3 |
| *Inventories in importing countries* | *5.0* | *4.4* | *5.0* | *5.4* | *7.3* | *5.2* | *7.0* |
| *Stocks in free ports* | *2.0* | *1.9* | *2.6* | *2.8* | *3.7* | *3.8* | *3.8* |
| *Afloat, etc.[6]* | *5.4* | *4.3* | *5.5* | *6.2* | *7.7* | *7.3* | *7.5* |

Source: Based on statistics of the International Coffee Organization (ICO).

[1] Projections of Commodities Division, IMF Research Department.

[2] Includes estimates for producing countries which are not members of ICO, as follows: production, 0.2 million bags a year; consumption, 0.1 million bags a year; and exports, 0.1 million bags a year.

[3] Net imports adjusted for changes in visible inventories.

[4] Estimates based on data on exports to nonmembers and data on consumption by nonmembers.

[5] Calculated as 1 percent of supply, that is, beginning stocks plus production.

[6] Based on September exports and partly residual.

Precautionary purchases by roasters transferred stocks from producing countries to consuming countries. Substantial exports to nonquota markets at discounts of up to 50 percent had been common during the period when export quotas were in effect, but with the suspension of export quotas, the volume exports to nonquota markets declined sharply, and the differential in export unit values from sales to quota and nonquota markets narrowed considerably.

An increase in export volumes following the suspension of quotas and a lack of demand from roasters in consuming countries who had already built up substantial stocks caused prices to weaken during the latter part of March 1986. Despite the approach of the frost season in Brazil and the increased vulnerability to frost of the drought-weakened trees, prices continued to decline through July 1986 because of unusually warm weather in Brazil and expectations that the long-term effects of the 1985 drought would be quite small. Prices recovered slightly in August when estimates of the 1986 Brazilian harvest were reduced substantially. In the event, the 1986 Brazilian harvest amounted to 11 million bags, as opposed to estimates of 16 million

bags in late 1985. Concern about the effects of dry weather on the 1987 Brazilian crop and purchases of coffee by Brazil on the terminal markets caused prices to strengthen further in September 1986 when the ICO indicator price rose to $1.87 a pound.

During the 1986/87 coffee year, the main factors influencing coffee price movements were the outcome of ICO discussions pertaining to the reintroduction of coffee export quotas, the relatively high level of coffee stocks in consuming countries, and the prospects for the 1987 Brazilian coffee crop. At its September 1986 meeting in London, the International Coffee Council failed to agree on a new quota allocation for the remaining three years of the 1983 International Coffee Agreement. Consumers did not agree to a producer proposal to maintain the 1985/86 quota distribution for the 1986/87 coffee year. The relatively high level of market prices at that time may have reduced the urgency to agree on a new quota system. Instead, the Council decided that the Executive Board of the ICO should meet in special session if the 15-day average of the composite indicator price was to fall to $1.45 a pound.

Fears of a second year of drought in the Brazilian coffee belt subsided when an unusually dry spell was broken by normal rains in late October 1986. With ample rainfall from then on, there was a rapid recovery in the coffee trees and in the prospects for the 1987 Brazilian coffee crop, which was then forecast to exceed 30 million bags. Despite a decline in coffee prices from the very high levels in early 1986, import demand remained weak because of a relatively high level of stocks in consuming countries. Weak import demand combined with a favorable supply outlook, caused the composite indicator price to decline from $1.63 a pound in October to $1.30 a pound in December.

A fall in the composite indicator price to $1.45 a pound triggered a meeting of the Executive Board of the ICO in mid-December 1986. The meeting decided only to keep the market situation under review. By early January 1987, when the composite indicator price had fallen to almost $1.20 a pound, officials from eight major exporting countries met in London and decided to convene a meeting of the 50 exporting members of the ICO to discuss matters relating to the reintroduction of quotas. A special session of the Council in February 1987 ended without a consensus on the distribution of quotas. The principal difficulty was the criteria to be used in allocating export quotas. Brazil and a number of larger producing countries were in favor of retaining the old formula under which export quotas were based on historic trade shares of the 1960s and 1970s. Seeking greater access to the types and qualities of coffee that they desired, consuming countries for the first time became more directly involved in the quota negotiation process. These countries were in favor of allocating quotas on the basis of more recent trends in export performance and in the stock levels carried over from the previous marketing year. A group of six producing countries, where production had expanded rapidly in recent years, supported the consumer position.

Following the failure of the special ICO Council to arrive at an agreement, the composite indicator price fell by 15 cents to about $1.00 a pound. Increased supplies from origin and limited demand owing to continued destocking by roasters and dealers caused prices to hover around $1.00 a pound in March and April. In May, though there was no major change in market fundamentals, prices recovered to an average level of $1.11 a pound owing largely to the depreciation of the U.S. dollar. With an increase in coffee supplies resulting from a complete recovery in the 1987 Brazilian coffee crop to 35 million 60-kilogram bags and the question of export quotas being put off until at least the beginning of the 1987/88 coffee year, prices fluctuated between $0.95 and $1.01 cents a pound in June, July, and August.

The prospect of a reintroduction of export quotas from October 1987, the beginning of the 1987/88 coffee year, caused prices to recover from the fourth week of August onward. During the first half of September, Latin American coffee exporters agreed on a quota stance for the ICO meetings, which were scheduled for the third week of September. During the fourth week of September, all the producer members of the ICO, with the exception of Indonesia, agreed on a formula for the reintroduction of export quotas. After protracted negotiations between producers and consumers, on October 5, the International Coffee Council agreed to reintroduce export quotas from October 6 onward. The initial global quota for the 1987/88 coffee year was set at 58 million bags or at the same level as the initial global quota for the 1985/86 coffee year. The Council agreed on an objective to stabilize prices in a range between $1.20 and $1.40 a pound. As the composite indicator price was substantially below $1.20 a pound when quotas were reintroduced, the Council also agreed on transitional arrangements to cut quotas during the first quarter of the 1987/88 coffee year. In a departure from past practice, the Council also agreed on a new formula for the allocation of export quotas during the 1988/89 coffee year. The formula, which takes account of recent trends in exportable production, exports, and of the level of stocks, addresses the concerns of some consuming and producing countries about the current system of quota allocation.

Despite the reintroduction of quotas, followed by a quota cut of 1.5 million bags in early October 1987 and two additional quota cuts of 1.0 million bags each in early January, the 15-day moving of the average of the composite indicator price remained below the agreed floor price of $1.20 a pound until late February 1988.

Responding to the high coffee prices that prevailed during the mid-1970s, world coffee production increased from an average level of 69.3 million bags during the three coffee years 1975/76–77/78 to an average level of 91.5 million bags during the three coffee years 1983/84–85/86. Production of arabica coffee increased by 36 percent during this period while robusta coffee production increased by 27 percent. Regionally, the largest production increases were recorded in South America and Asia. Production in Central America and the Caribbean showed a small increase, while production in Africa remained virtually unchanged. Among the major producing countries, substantial production increases were recorded in Brazil, Colombia, and Indonesia; if allowance is made for the effects of a severe drought in 1983/84, production in Côte d'Ivoire remained virtually unchanged during this period.

The effects of a severe drought in Brazil, which

caused total world coffee production to decline sharply from 89.8 million bags in 1985/86 to 77.7 million bags in 1986/87, underscores the key role that Brazil continues to play in world coffee market developments. Owing to a large increase in coffee production and exports from other countries, Brazil's share in total exports has declined from about 50 percent in the early 1950s to its current level of about 25 percent. At the same time, the cushion to variations in world coffee production provided in the earlier period by the level of stocks in Brazil has been sharply reduced because Brazilian stocks have declined from the equivalent of over one year's total world coffee consumption in the early 1960s to their current level of about 35 percent of total world coffee consumption. The shift in the focus of Brazilian coffee production from the frost-prone southern states of Paraná and São Paulo to the states of Minas Gerais and Espírito Santo does not seem to have substantially reduced the variability in total Brazilian coffee production. Recent experience indicates that coffee production in Minas Gerais, which currently accounts for about one third of total Brazilian coffee production, is susceptible to both frosts and droughts.

Growth in world coffee consumption has lagged behind the relatively rapid rate of growth in world coffee production, because of the impact of changes in beverage consumption tastes and high retail prices for coffee. Despite promotional efforts, the ICO's winter 1986 study on coffee consumption indicates that per capita consumption in the United States had declined to 1.74 cups a day as compared with 1.99 cups a day in 1984 and 3.12 cups a day in 1962. The declining trend in U.S. coffee consumption has been slightly more than offset by consumption growth in Western Europe and Japan. Consequently, world coffee consumption has increased, but at an annual rate of less than 1 percent during the period 1980/81 to 1986/87.

The level of world coffee stocks increased sharply from 27.0 million bags in 1979/80 to 41.7 million bags in 1980/81 when export quotas were first imposed under the 1976 International Coffee Agreement. Stock levels remained high during the five subsequent coffee years when export quotas remained in effect. These stocks, which were equivalent to about a year's world coffee consumption, were largely held in coffee exporting countries. With the suspension of export quotas in February 1986 and the sharp fall in the 1986 Brazilian crop, the level of world stocks fell from 68.7 million bags in 1985/86 to 59.4 million bags in 1986/87.

World coffee production is expected to reach a record 98 million bags in 1987/88 largely because the 1987 Brazilian crop, estimated at 35 million bags, is expected to be about two and a half times as large as the drought-reduced 1986 crop. Since world coffee consumption in 1987/88 is expected to increase by about only 1 percent to 86.6 million bags, world coffee stocks are expected to increase by 16 percent to 69.1 million bags. Despite this large expected increase in stock levels, export quotas under the ICO are expected to stabilize prices near the lower end of the $1.20–1.40 a pound price range specified in the agreement.

After rising to 71.1 million bags in 1985, owing in part to precautionary purchases by importers in the final quarter of 1985, the volume of world coffee exports declined by 9 percent to 64.6 million bags (3.9 million tons) in 1986. Among the primary commodities exported by non-oil exporting developing countries, coffee is the largest single source of foreign exchange earnings. The coffee earnings of these countries increased from $10.8 billion in 1985 to $14.2 billion in 1986 as a result of the sharp rise in coffee prices during 1986. In 1987, despite an expected recovery in export volume to 72.2 million bags (4.4 million tons), export earnings are expected to fall by about 30 percent to $10 billion because of sharply lower prices. In terms of SDRs earnings are expected to decline by 36 percent from SDR 12.1 billion in 1986 to SDR 7.7 billion in 1987 (Table 41).

## Tea

Tea prices, which peaked at $4.29 a kilogram in January 1984, started declining sharply during the second quarter of 1985 as a result of an increase in world tea production. Prices were relatively stable in 1986 when they averaged $1.93 per kilogram, but fell further during 1987 to average $1.71 per kilogram for the year.[58]

The boom in tea prices that started in the fourth quarter of 1983 was caused by a low level of world inventories and concern about prospective supplies owing to low rainfall in Sri Lanka and a drought in southern India. A partial ban on the export of CTC (crush, tear, and curl) teas by India, beginning in January 1984, also contributed to the rise in prices. In the event, world tea production in 1983 was about 5 percent higher than in 1982; production in Sri Lanka declined by about 5 percent, but production in northern India, which increased by 7 percent, more than compensated for a 7 percent reduction in the south Indian crop (Table 42). Prices remained firm during 1986 because of strong import demand to rebuild depleted stocks in consuming countries and because of continued uncertainty about the availability of export supplies from India.

---

[58] Price quotations refer to the London auction price, average all teas.

## Table 41.   Coffee: Export Earnings, 1984–87

| | 1984 | 1985 | 1986 | 1987 | 1984 | 1985 | 1986 | 1987 |
|---|---|---|---|---|---|---|---|---|
| | *(Values in SDRs)* | | | | *(Values in U.S. dollars)* | | | |
| **Earnings** (*in billions*) | **10.4** | **10.7** | **12.1** | **7.8** | **10.6** | **10.8** | **14.2** | **10.0** |
| Developing countries | 10.4 | 10.7 | 12.1 | 7.8 | 10.6 | 10.8 | 14.2 | 10.0 |
| *To ICO members*[1] | *9.4* | *9.5* | *11.0* | *7.0* | *9.6* | *9.6* | *12.9* | *9.0* |
| *To nonmembers of ICO* | *1.0* | *1.2* | *1.1* | *0.8* | *1.0* | *1.2* | *1.3* | *1.0* |
| **Volumes** (*in thousands of tons*) | **4.1** | **4.3** | **3.9** | **4.4** | **4.1** | **4.3** | **3.9** | **4.4** |
| Developing countries | 4.1 | 4.3 | 3.9 | 4.4 | 4.1 | 4.3 | 3.9 | 4.4 |
| *To ICO members*[1] | *3.5* | *3.7* | *3.5* | *3.9* | *3.5* | *3.7* | *3.5* | *3.9* |
| *To nonmembers of ICO* | *0.6* | *0.6* | *0.4* | *0.5* | *0.6* | *0.6* | *0.4* | *0.5* |
| **Unit values** (*a ton*) | **2,530** | **2,500** | **3,120** | **1,780** | **2,590** | **2,520** | **3,660** | **2,280** |
| To ICO countries | 2,670 | 2,560 | 3,160 | 1,810 | 2,730 | 2,600 | 3,710 | 2,310 |
| To nonmembers of ICO[2] | 1,640 | 1,900 | 2,800 | 1,540 | 1,680 | 1,930 | 3,280 | 1,990 |
| **Market prices** | | | | | | | | |
| ICO daily composite indicator (*a ton*) | | | | | | | | |
| Other milds[3] | 3,100 | 3,160 | 3,620 | 1,920 | 3,180 | 3,210 | 4,250 | 2,480 |
| Robusta[4] | 2,970 | 2,630 | 2,790 | 1,750 | 3,050 | 2,670 | 3,270 | 2,260 |

Sources: Export data are based on statistics of the International Coffee Organization (ICO); Commodities Division, IMF Research Department for market prices.

[1] Includes exports of an estimated 0.1 million bags a year from nonmembers of ICO.

[2] Export quotas were in effect from October 1980 to February 1986 and again beginning October 1987. Unit values of exports to members and nonmembers are assumed equal in the absence of quotas.

[3] Ex-dock New York and Bremen/Hamburg.

[4] Ex-dock New York and Le Havre/Marseilles.

## Table 42.   Tea: World Commodity Balance, 1981–87

(In thousands of tons)

| | 1981 | 1982 | 1983 | 1984 | 1985 | 1986 | 1987[1] |
|---|---|---|---|---|---|---|---|
| **Production** | **1,870** | **1,930** | **2,040** | **2,170** | **2,330** | **2,290** | **2,360** |
| Green tea | 420 | 480 | 520 | 520 | 550 | 560 | 570 |
| *China* | *270* | *330* | *330* | *340* | *360* | *370* | *380* |
| *Other countries* | *150* | *150* | *190* | *180* | *190* | *190* | *190* |
| Black tea | 1,450 | 1,450 | 1,520 | 1,650 | 1,780 | 1,730 | 1,790 |
| *India* | *550* | *550* | *580* | *640* | *650* | *620* | *660* |
| *Kenya* | *90* | *100* | *120* | *120* | *150* | *140* | *160* |
| *Sri Lanka* | *210* | *190* | *180* | *210* | *220* | *210* | *210* |
| *Other countries* | *600* | *610* | *640* | *680* | *770* | *760* | *760* |
| **Consumption** (*black and green*) | **1,920** | **1,930** | **2,030** | **2,160** | **2,260** | **2,280** | **2,340** |
| Tea producing countries[2] | 1,160 | 1,200 | 1,190 | 1,230 | 1,310 | 1,320 | 1,360 |
| *China* | *250* | *290* | *280* | *280* | *300* | *310* | *320* |
| *India* | *360* | *370* | *370* | *430* | *440* | *430* | *440* |
| *Japan* | *110* | *110* | *100* | *90* | *90* | *90* | *100* |
| *U.S.S.R.* | *210* | *200* | *150* | *150* | *160* | *170* | *180* |
| *Other countries* | *230* | *230* | *290* | *280* | *300* | *320* | *320* |
| Tea importing countries[3] | 760 | 730 | 840 | 930 | 950 | 960 | 980 |
| *Asian countries* | *200* | *190* | *230* | *260* | *260* | *260* | *270* |
| *United Kingdom* | *180* | *170* | *170* | *200* | *180* | *180* | *180* |
| *Other countries* | *380* | *370* | *440* | *470* | *510* | *520* | *530* |
| **Implied change in total stocks** | **0** | **0** | **10** | **10** | **70** | **10** | **20** |
| **Closing stocks in the United Kingdom** | **58** | **67** | **56** | **62** | **56** | **54** | **60** |

Sources: Estimates of Commodities Division, IMF Research Department, derived from statistics of the International Tea Committee and the UN Food and Agriculture Organization.

[1] Estimated by Commodities Division, IMF Research Department.

[2] For India, adjustments have been made for stock changes; for other countries domestic consumption is derived as production less exports plus imports.

[3] Net imports adjusted for stock changes where possible. Covers only countries which do not produce tea on a large scale.

Responding to the stimulus of high prices, tea production increased by 6 percent in 1984; most of the increase in production came from "coarse picking" of more leaves than normal. While the upward trend in production in Kenya was temporarily halted in 1984 because of a drought, production in India and Sri Lanka increased by 10 percent and 17 percent, respectively. Increased production resulting from the high tea prices of 1983 and 1984 and favorable weather in major producing countries brought the tea price boom to an end in 1985, when world tea production rose by 7 percent to a record 2.33 million tons. Tea production in Kenya, which had declined the year before, increased by 25 percent and there were large production increases in a number of the smaller tea producing countries, such as Argentina, Indonesia, and Rwanda. Prices, which averaged $3.46 a kilogram in 1984, declined to $1.98 a kilogram in 1985.

In 1986 world tea production declined by 35,000 tons to 2.3 million tons because of lower black tea production in many major and minor producing countries. Production in India declined by 5 percent to 620,000 tons because of adverse weather conditions in northern India. Output in Sri Lanka declined by 4 percent while production in Kenya declined by 7 percent, also on account of adverse weather conditions. On the other hand, production in China, which consists mainly of green tea, increased by 5 percent to a record 480,000 tons. Prices in 1986 averaged $1.93 a kilogram or about 3 percent lower than in 1985.

The pattern of tea consumption in industrial countries differs from that in developing countries. In major tea drinking industrial countries, such as Australia, Canada, and the United Kingdom, consumption has been declining, while in the developing tea producing countries and developing tea importing countries tea consumption has been increasing rapidly. Between 1961 and 1984 per capita tea consumption declined at an annual rate of 2 percent in the United Kingdom, the world's largest tea importing country. During the same period per capita consumption increased at an annual rate of 2 percent in Egypt, 3 percent in India, and 5 percent in Pakistan. Import demand for tea increased in 1985 and 1986 because of lower tea prices; purchases by industrial countries are estimated to have risen by about 9 percent in 1986 owing to sharply higher imports by the United Kingdom and the United States. World tea consumption is estimated to have exceeded world tea production by 70,000 tons in 1985, but in 1986 the surplus of production over consumption is estimated to have been only 10,000 tons.

Tea production is estimated to have recovered to 2.36 million tons in 1987, largely because of favorable weather conditions in Kenya. In India the tea crop escaped the effects of drought; ideal growing conditions especially in northern India are estimated to have boosted production to a record 660,000 tons. Tea prices declined sharply from an average of $1.88 a kilogram during the first quarter of 1987 to $1.43 during the second quarter, mainly because of the availability of large supplies of low quality plain teas in London and because of a decision by Pakistan in late March 1987 to suspend purchases of Kenyan tea. During the third quarter, prices recovered slightly owing to greater availability of good quality north Indian and Kenyan teas and a reduction in the supplies of poorer quality grades that had been holding prices down. Prices recovered further during the fourth quarter because of a seasonal rise in demand for tea.

Despite an estimated 3 percent increase in world tea production in 1987, world tea production and consumption were in better balance because the lower tea prices caused an increase in tea consumption in both tea producing and tea importing countries. An implied stock increase of 20,000 tons is estimated for 1987.

The tea price boom caused earnings from tea exports to rise sharply, from $1.7 billion in 1983 to a record $2.5 billion in 1984 (Table 43). In 1985, however, despite an increase in export volume, earnings declined to $2.0 billion. Weak prices caused earnings to decline further to $1.7 billion in 1986 and to an estimated level of $1.6 billion in 1987. Owing to the depreciation of the dollar since the end of 1984, earnings in terms of SDRs have declined much more sharply—from SDR 2.0 billion in 1985 to an estimated level of SDR 1.2 billion in 1987.

## Cocoa

Cocoa is a tree crop, which takes about 10 years to reach maximum yields; the newer high yielding hybrid varieties reach peak yields at about seven years of age. Owing to the perennial nature of the crop and its relatively long gestation period, cocoa producers tend to adjust to prices only after relatively long time lags. Since production in the short run can only be changed by varying the intensity of input use or by varying thoroughness of harvesting, the short-run price elasticity of cocoa supply tends to be quite low.[59] In the longer run, production can be more readily varied by increasing or decreasing the area under cocoa cultivation. Consequently, the long-run price elasticity of cocoa supply tends to be higher.[60] The relatively high long-run supply elasticity has imparted a cyclical

[59] Estimates of the short-run price elasticity of cocoa supply vary between 0.10 and 0.26.

[60] Estimates of the long-run price elasticity of cocoa supply range between 0.13 and 0.59.

**Table 43: Tea: Export Earnings, 1984–87**

| | 1984 | 1985 | 1986 | 1987 | 1984 | 1985 | 1986 | 1987 |
|---|---|---|---|---|---|---|---|---|
| | *(Values in SDRs)* | | | | *(Values in U.S. dollars)* | | | |
| **Earnings** (*in billions*) | **2.5** | **2.0** | **1.5** | **1.2** | **2.5** | **2.1** | **1.7** | **1.5** |
| Developing countries | 2.5 | 2.0 | 1.5 | 1.2 | 2.5 | 2.1 | 1.7 | 1.5 |
| **Volumes** (*in thousands of tons*) | **990** | **990** | **1,020** | **1,000** | **990** | **990** | **1,020** | **1,000** |
| Developing countries | 990 | 990 | 1,020 | 1,000 | 990 | 990 | 1,020 | 1,000 |
| *India* | *220* | *220* | *200* | *210* | *220* | *220* | *200* | *210* |
| *Kenya* | *100* | *120* | *130* | *130* | *100* | *120* | *130* | *130* |
| *Sri Lanka* | *200* | *200* | *210* | *210* | *200* | *200* | *210* | *210* |
| *Other countries* | *470* | *450* | *480* | *450* | *470* | *450* | *480* | *450* |
| **Unit values** (*a ton*) | **2,510** | **2,040** | **1,450** | **1,200** | **2,570** | **2,070** | **1,700** | **1,550** |
| **Market prices** (*a ton*)[1] | **3,370** | **1,950** | **1,640** | **1,320** | **3,460** | **1,980** | **1,930** | **1,710** |

Sources: Export data are estimates of Commodities Division, IMF Research Department, derived from statistics of the International Tea Committee and the UN Food and Agriculture Organization; Commodities Division, IMF Research Department for market prices.

[1] London auction price, average all teas.

pattern to cocoa production and prices; low production and high prices encourage increased plantings which, after a lag, result in much higher production and lower prices.

World cocoa market developments during the 1980s reflected the lagged response of world cocoa production to the high real cocoa prices in the late 1970s. Production increases, especially in the Côte d'Ivoire, Brazil, and Malaysia, caused world cocoa output to increase from 1.50 million tons in the 1978/79 cocoa year (October/September) to an estimated 2.06 million tons in the 1987/88 cocoa year. Growth in world cocoa consumption, on the other hand, lagged well behind the growth in world cocoa production. As a result, closing stocks are expected to increase from 0.38 million tons at the end of the 1978/79 cocoa year to 0.88 million tons at the end of the 1987/88 cocoa year.

In the period prior to August 1981 when the 1980 International Cocoa Agreement (ICCA) became operational, cocoa market prices were well below both the agreement's lower intervention price of $1.10 a pound ($2,425 a ton) and the minimum price of $1.00 a pound ($2,205 a ton).[61] Buffer stock purchases of 100,000 tons of cocoa between September 1981 and March 1982 failed to raise the price above the lower intervention price. Buffer stock purchases which were suspended in March 1982 due to a lack of funds were not resumed during the rest of the life of the 1980 Agreement.

Improved crop prospects in West Africa and concern about consumer ratification of the 1986 ICCA caused prices to weaken to $2,024 a ton during the first quarter

of the 1986/87 cocoa year.[62] The 100,000 tons of cocoa purchased by the buffer stock of the 1980 International Cocoa Agreement were transferred to the 1986 ICCA, which entered into force provisionally on January 20, 1987. At its meeting in January 1987 the International Cocoa Council was unable to agree on buffer stock intervention rules. As a result prices continued to fall during the first quarter of 1987. In March, the Council approved a new set of buffer stock intervention rules which permitted buffer stock purchases to commence on May 18 to support the agreement's lower intervention trigger price of SDR 1,600 a ton. By June 22, when the buffer stock had purchased 75,000 tons of cocoa, buffer stock purchases were suspended pending an International Cocoa Council decision on a revision of the trigger prices for buffer stock operations. Prices averaged $2,046 (SDR 1,577) a ton during the second half of the 1986/87 cocoa year. The International Cocoa Council met in July, September, and December 1987, but failed to reach an agreement on lowering the price range for buffer stock operations. The collapse of the December talks caused cocoa prices to fall sharply to a five-year low of $1,860 (SDR 1,340) a ton. Buffer stock purchases were suspended from late June 1987 until mid-January 1988 because the International Cocoa Council was unable to arrive at a decision on lowering the price range.[63]

At a special session in mid-January 1988, however, the Council agreed to revise the lower intervention price to SDR 1,485 and lifted the suspension on buffer stock purchases. At the same meeting the Council also

[61] Price quotations refer to the ICCO daily price, which is the average of the nearest three active future trading months on the New York Cocoa Exchange *at noon* and on the London Cocoa Terminal market *at closing time*.

[62] For a description of the main economic provisions of the 1986 Agreement see International Monetary Fund, *Primary Commodities: Market Developments and Outlook*, World Economic and Financial Surveys (Washington), May 1987, p. 71.

[63] At its meeting in September 1987 the Council decided to reduce the cocoa export levy from $45 a ton to $30 a ton effective January 1988.

agreed to adopt the rules for a scheme to withhold up to 120,000 tons of cocoa from the market. As a result of further purchases by the buffer stock manager, by the end of February 1988 the buffer stock had reached its maximum capacity of 250,000 tons. These actions provided little support to the market because of the prospect of a large surplus of production over consumption in 1987/88. By the end of February, prices had fallen to $1,712 (SDR 1,260) a ton, the lowest level in more than five years.

The largest increases in cocoa production in the 1980s were recorded in the Côte d'Ivoire, Brazil, and Malaysia. Officially sponsored large-scale new plantings with hybrid varieties and rehabilitation programs in the Côte d'Ivoire and Brazil during the late 1970s and early 1980s contributed significantly to increased production in these countries. An increase in the total land area planted to cocoa, from 0.95 million hectares in 1976/77 to 1.35 million hectares in 1985/86, caused production in the Côte d'Ivoire to increase from 230,000 tons to 580,000 tons over the same period. Owing to the efforts of the agricultural extension service and the cocoa research institute, about half of the new area was planted with high yielding hybrid varieties. An increase in planted area in Brazil from 0.49 million hectares in 1976/77 to 0.70 million hectares in 1985/86 was also largely responsible for a 25 percent increase in production in that country. The area planted with hybrid varieties increased from 60,000 hectares to 340,000 hectares during the same period. In addition to a large proportion of hybrid varieties, Brazil also has the youngest stock of trees of all the traditional major cocoa producing countries; about 40 percent of the trees are less than 10 years old. The availability of large areas of undeveloped land suitable for cocoa cultivation and a long tradition of tree crop production enabled Malaysia to exploit rapidly the technological advantages of the earlier maturing and much higher yielding hybrid varieties. The area under cocoa, all of it planted with hybrid varieties, increased from 40,000 hectares in 1976 to 310,000 hectares in 1986. As these new plantings came into bearing and the productivity of the trees increased with maturity, production increased from 12,000 tons in 1974/75 to 160,000 tons in 1986/87. In 1986/87 Malaysia replaced Nigeria as the world's fourth largest cocoa producer.[64]

Cocoa beans and the semi-finished cocoa products produced by grinding cocoa[65] are largely consumed in the industrial countries and the U.S.S.R. In these countries, chocolate and cocoa-based confectionery products tend to compete with a wide range of other confectionery and snack foods. Despite the availability of these substitutes and a tendency for manufacturers to vary the cocoa content of their products in line with movements in the cocoa price, price elasticity of demand for cocoa is quite low.[66] Similarly, the income elasticity of demand for cocoa also tends to be quite low in the major cocoa consuming countries.[67] In the period since the 1981–82 recession, though real GDP in the main cocoa consuming countries has grown and cocoa prices in real terms have declined quite sharply in the period since 1983/84, world cocoa consumption has only increased at a relatively modest rate in the period 1984/85–86/87. With world cocoa production exceeding world cocoa consumption in each year beginning 1984/85, closing stocks increased from 460,000 tons at the end of the 1983/84 crop year to 760,000 tons by the end of the 1986/87 crop year (Table 44). Most of the world's cocoa stocks are held in the form of cocoa beans in the major importing countries. The ratio of total world stocks to world consumption increased from 0.27 in 1983/84 to 0.41 in 1986/87. Owing to a continuing excess of production over consumption, stocks are expected to increase to 880,000 tons by the end of the 1987/88 crop year. Of this amount, the 630,000 tons expected to be held as "free stocks" by the cocoa trade and cocoa end users will have a direct impact on market prices because they are readily available to the market. By the end of February the buffer stock of the International Cocoa Agreement had reached its maximum capacity of 250,000 tons. These stocks would be unavailable to the market unless prices rise high enough to trigger buffer stock sales.

In dollar terms, earnings of developing countries from exports of cocoa beans and cocoa products increased from $3.6 billion in 1985 to $3.7 billion in 1986 because of a 2 percent increase in export unit value; export volume was virtually the same in both years (Table 45). In 1987 earnings of developing countries from exports of cocoa beans and cocoa products

---

[64] Ghana and Nigeria were the world's largest and second largest cocoa producers, respectively, during the 1960s and the early 1970s. However, high domestic rates of inflation during the late 1970s and early 1980s rapidly eroded the purchasing power of relatively low nominal producer prices for cocoa in these countries. The resulting fall in real producer prices for cocoa caused production in these countries to decline sharply during this period. Ghana's share in total world production declined from 24 percent in 1973/74 to 11 percent in 1983/84. Ghanaian production, however, recovered sharply in 1985/86 and 1986/87, largely because of substantial increases in real producer prices.

[65] Cocoa products are obtained by "grinding" cocoa beans. They consist of cocoa butter, cocoa powder and cake, and cocoa paste, all of which are derived entirely from cocoa beans (apart from small amounts of other vegetable fats which some countries permit to be included in cocoa butter). Roughly 80 percent of a cocoa bean is used to make these products, the remaining 20 percent is waste or a low-valued by-product.

[66] The short-run world price elasticity has been estimated at about −0.20 while the long-run price elasticity of demand has been estimated to be about −0.30.

[67] The world income elasticity of demand for cocoa has been estimated to be about 0.3.

**Table 44.   Cocoa Beans: World Commodity Balance, 1981/82–87/88**

(In thousands of tons)

| | 1981/82 | 1982/83 | 1983/84 | 1984/85 | 1985/86 | 1986/87 | 1987/88[1] |
|---|---|---|---|---|---|---|---|
| | | | | October/September Crop Years | | | |
| **Gross production** | **1,730** | **1,530** | **1,510** | **1,960** | **1,960** | **1,980** | **2,060** |
| Brazil | 300 | 330 | 300 | 410 | 370 | 360 | 390 |
| Cameroon | 120 | 110 | 110 | 120 | 120 | 120 | 120 |
| Côte d'Ivoire | 470 | 360 | 410 | 570 | 580 | 580 | 600 |
| Ecuador | 90 | 40 | 40 | 130 | 110 | 90 | 80 |
| Ghana | 230 | 180 | 160 | 180 | 220 | 230 | 220 |
| Malaysia | 60 | 70 | 80 | 100 | 120 | 160 | 180 |
| Nigeria | 180 | 160 | 120 | 150 | 120 | 110 | 130 |
| Other countries | 270 | 280 | 290 | 300 | 320 | 330 | 340 |
| **Production adjusted for loss in weight** | **1,710** | **1,510** | **1,490** | **1,940** | **1,940** | **1,960** | **2,040** |
| **Grinding** (*consumption*) | **1,580** | **1,630** | **1,700** | **1,850** | **1,820** | **1,870** | **1,920** |
| Cocoa bean producing countries | 470 | 480 | 510 | 600 | 620 | 580 | 600 |
| European Community | 570 | 580 | 610 | 640 | 630 | 660 | 680 |
| United States | 200 | 190 | 210 | 190 | 190 | 220 | 230 |
| U.S.S.R. | 130 | 150 | 140 | 170 | 140 | 160 | 150 |
| Other countries | 210 | 220 | 230 | 250 | 240 | 250 | 260 |
| **Closing stocks** | **790** | **670** | **460** | **550** | **670** | **760** | **880** |
| Commercial stocks | 690 | 570 | 360 | 450 | 570 | 585 | 630 |
| ICCO buffer stock | 100 | 100 | 100 | 100 | 100 | 175 | 250 |

Source: International Cocoa Organization (ICCO), *Quarterly Bulletin of Cocoa Statistics* (London), various issues.
[1] Projected by Commodities Division, IMF Research Department.

**Table 45.   Cocoa: Export Earnings, 1984–87**

| | 1984 | 1985 | 1986 | 1987[1] | 1984 | 1985 | 1986 | 1987[1] |
|---|---|---|---|---|---|---|---|---|
| | (*Values in SDRs*) | | | | (*Values in U.S. dollars*) | | | |
| **Earnings** (*in billions*) | | | | | | | | |
| **Beans** | **2.5** | **2.6** | **2.3** | **2.1** | **2.6** | **2.6** | **2.7** | **2.7** |
| Developing countries | 2.5 | 2.6 | 2.3 | 2.1 | 2.6 | 2.6 | 2.7 | 2.7 |
| **Products[2]** | **1.7** | **2.0** | **1.7** | **1.5** | **1.8** | **2.0** | **2.0** | **2.0** |
| Developing countries | 0.9 | 1.0 | 0.8 | 0.7 | 0.9 | 1.0 | 1.0 | 0.9 |
| Industrial countries | 0.8 | 1.0 | 0.9 | 0.8 | 0.9 | 1.0 | 1.0 | 1.0 |
| **Volumes** (*in thousands of tons*) | | | | | | | | |
| **Beans** | **1,230** | **1,280** | **1,300** | **1,350** | **1,230** | **1,280** | **1,280** | **1,300** |
| **Products[2]** | **610** | **650** | **650** | **660** | **610** | **650** | **650** | **660** |
| Developing countries | 340 | 370 | 380 | 370 | 340 | 370 | 380 | 370 |
| Industrial countries | 270 | 280 | 270 | 290 | 270 | 280 | 270 | 290 |
| **Unit values** (*a ton*) | | | | | | | | |
| **Beans** | **2,040** | **2,030** | **1,800** | **1,550** | **2,090** | **2,060** | **2,110** | **2,000** |
| **Products[2]** | **2,860** | **3,010** | **2,670** | **2,320** | **2,930** | **3,060** | **3,130** | **3,000** |
| Developing countries | 2,680 | 2,680 | 2,250 | 1,900 | 2,750 | 2,720 | 2,640 | 2,460 |
| Industrial countries | 3,070 | 3,450 | 3,252 | 2,850 | 3,150 | 3,500 | 3,810 | 3,690 |
| **Market prices of cocoa beans** (*a ton*)[3] | **2,340** | **2,220** | **1,760** | **1,550** | **2,400** | **2,260** | **2,070** | **2,000** |

Sources: UN Food and Agriculture Organization, *1986 FAO Trade Yearbook* (Rome) for exports; for cocoa beans, export data include only exports from cocoa bean producing countries; Commodities Division, IMF Research Department for market prices.
[1] Data on exports are estimates of Commodities Division, IMF Research Department.
[2] Cocoa products are obtained by grinding cocoa beans. They consist of cocoa butter, cocoa powder and cake and cocoa paste, all of which are derived entirely from cocoa beans.
[3] Averages of ICCO daily prices.

are estimated to have declined to $3.6 billion because an estimated 5 percent fall in export unit values more than offset increased volumes. Owing to the depreciation of the U.S. dollar, the decline in earnings of developing countries from the export of cocoa beans and cocoa products was much larger in terms of SDRs. Earnings declined from SDR 3.6 billion in 1985 to an estimated SDR 2.8 billion in 1987.

Provided weather conditions remain normal, the near-term outlook is for world cocoa production to continue to exceed world cocoa consumption. As total stocks rise to the equivalent of more than four months of consumption, prices can be expected to remain under downside pressure during 1987/88.

# IV

# Agricultural Raw Materials

The strength of prices of most agricultural raw materials in 1987 contrasts sharply with their weakness during 1985 and 1986 (Table 46 and Chart 6). As discussed in this section, prices of logs, natural rubber, cotton, wool, and hides all increased by large percentages in 1987. The tobacco market also appeared more active than for a number of years, but this change was not reflected in prices because of the persistence of large stocks. The markets for jute and sisal, however, remained weak, although some longer-term adjustments appear to be taking place.

The prices of agricultural raw materials in 1986–87 appear to have provided leading indicators of movements in other commodity prices. The price index for agricultural raw materials, whether measured in terms of SDRs or dollars, fell to its most recent trough in the third quarter of 1986 and rose to a record high in the final quarter of 1987 (Table 46). The sharp upturn in this index became evident in the final quarter of 1986, whereas a comparable upturn in the price index for minerals and metals only became evident in the second quarter of 1987. Weaker and possibly unsustained upturns in the price indices for food commodities and beverages occurred only in the final quarter of 1987 (see Tables 3, 8, and 38). An examination of monthly movements in the index of prices of agricultural raw materials suggests that the fourth quarter of 1987 might represent a peak in the series. In the first quarter of 1988 the index fell by about 8 percent from the level of the fourth quarter of 1987.

The lead that prices of agricultural raw materials appears to have had in this period over the prices of other commodities, however, can to a considerable degree be traced to fortuitous rather than systemic factors. The group index is dominated by movements in the prices of logs and cotton, with weights of 45 percent and 17 percent, respectively. The price increase for logs was associated both with supply restrictions as a consequence in part of conservation measures in exporting countries and with strong demand in a major import market—Japan. The supply factors appear to be specific to the market for logs,

while strong growth in demand in the Japanese market could affect on a wide range of primary commodites. The sharp rise in the price of cotton was largely the result of adverse weather leading to a very low U.S. production, extraordinary measures to reduce stocks in China, and larger-than-expected increases in consumption worldwide, triggered by lower prices. These reasons appear largely specific to cotton although the underestimation of demand response to a period of substantially lower prices may have wider application relevance.

It might be reasoned that the prices for agricultural raw materials react faster to changed conditions than those for other commodities because of competition with synthetic materials. Nevertheless, the sharp decline in 1986 in the price of petroleum (Table 47)—the base for most synthetic materials competing with agricultural raw materials—would suggest at least a potential weakening of the competitive edge of agricultural raw materials in 1987 and hence a tendency toward decreasing rather than increasing prices. The nature of these competitive relationships would need to be examined in greater depth before any conclusions are drawn.

## Hardwood

U.S. dollar prices of hardwood logs, which had been declining intermittently since the second half of 1985, rose by 46 percent in 1987.[68] The price increase was sharp particularly in the second half of the year, with the prices reaching a historic peak of $306 a cubic meter in November. Prices, however, began to weaken toward the end of the year as log stocks climbed rapidly. The major factors contributing to the price increase in 1987 were an upsurge in housing starts in

---

[68] No comprehensive price data for hardwood logs are available owing to the many species traded. The price of a major species of hardwood logs, Malaysian meranti, in the largest importing country, Japan, is assumed to be representative of log export prices industrywide.

**Table 46.  Prices of Agricultural Raw Materials, 1979–87**

| Years | Index of Prices of Agricultural Raw Materials[1] | Logs[2] (Cubic meter) | Tobacco[3] (Pound) | Natural Rubber[4] (Pound) | Medium-Staple Cotton[5] (Pound) | Fine Wool[6] (Kilogram) | Jute[7] (Ton) | Sisal[8] (Ton) | Hides[9] (Pound) |
|---|---|---|---|---|---|---|---|---|---|
| | *(1980 = 100)* | | | | *(In SDRs)* | | | | |
| 1979 | 92.6 | 132 | 1.04 | 0.44 | 0.60 | 4.06 | 298 | 551 | 0.57 |
| 1980 | 100.0 | 150 | 1.10 | 0.50 | 0.72 | 4.59 | 241 | 588 | 0.35 |
| 1981 | 96.5 | 132 | 1.36 | 0.43 | 0.71 | 5.20 | 236 | 547 | 0.35 |
| 1982 | 98.6 | 141 | 1.66 | 0.35 | 0.66 | 5.19 | 256 | 539 | 0.35 |
| 1983 | 103.9 | 136 | 1.74 | 0.45 | 0.79 | 5.05 | 279 | 534 | 0.42 |
| 1984 | 115.9 | 163 | 1.81 | 0.42 | 0.79 | 5.45 | 518 | 570 | 0.57 |
| 1985 | 99.7 | 134 | 1.82 | 0.34 | 0.59 | 4.88 | 574 | 517 | 0.50 |
| 1986 | 87.7 | 129 | 1.40 | 0.31 | 0.41 | 3.97 | 232 | 439 | 0.55 |
| 1987 | 105.9 | 171 | 1.22 | 0.35 | 0.58 | 5.52 | 248 | 396 | 0.62 |
| 1986 I | 92.3 | 137 | 1.51 | 0.31 | 0.47 | 4.20 | 287 | 447 | 0.52 |
| II | 89.0 | 131 | 1.45 | 0.30 | 0.39 | 4.15 | 252 | 448 | 0.58 |
| III | 82.4 | 121 | 1.34 | 0.32 | 0.33 | 3.65 | 201 | 433 | 0.55 |
| IV | 86.9 | 128 | 1.29 | 0.32 | 0.45 | 3.88 | 191 | 426 | 0.53 |
| 1987 I | 91.9 | 141 | 1.23 | 0.32 | 0.51 | 4.25 | 225 | 404 | 0.52 |
| II | 96.7 | 141 | 1.20 | 0.33 | 0.57 | 5.45 | 237 | 394 | 0.64 |
| III | 112.6 | 179 | 1.22 | 0.37 | 0.66 | 6.18 | 266 | 399 | 0.67 |
| IV | 122.4 | 220 | 1.21 | 0.36 | 0.56 | 6.13 | 263 | 385 | 0.64 |
| 1988 I | 110.9 | 179 | 1.18[10] | 0.37 | 0.50 | 7.66 | 271 | 380 | 0.65 |
| | *(1980 = 100)* | | | | *(In U.S. dollars)* | | | | |
| 1979 | 92.0 | 170 | 1.35 | 0.57 | 0.77 | 5.25 | 385 | 713 | 0.73 |
| 1980 | 100.0 | 196 | 1.43 | 0.65 | 0.94 | 5.97 | 314 | 765 | 0.46 |
| 1981 | 87.5 | 156 | 1.61 | 0.51 | 0.84 | 6.13 | 278 | 645 | 0.42 |
| 1982 | 83.7 | 156 | 1.83 | 0.39 | 0.73 | 5.73 | 283 | 595 | 0.39 |
| 1983 | 85.2 | 145 | 1.86 | 0.48 | 0.84 | 5.40 | 298 | 571 | 0.45 |
| 1984 | 91.4 | 167 | 1.86 | 0.43 | 0.81 | 5.59 | 531 | 584 | 0.59 |
| 1985 | 77.7 | 136 | 1.84 | 0.34 | 0.60 | 4.95 | 583 | 525 | 0.51 |
| 1986 | 78.9 | 151 | 1.64 | 0.37 | 0.48 | 4.65 | 272 | 515 | 0.64 |
| 1987 | 105.5 | 221 | 1.57 | 0.45 | 0.75 | 7.13 | 321 | 512 | 0.80 |
| 1986 I | 79.8 | 153 | 1.70 | 0.35 | 0.53 | 4.72 | 323 | 503 | 0.58 |
| II | 79.4 | 152 | 1.69 | 0.35 | 0.45 | 4.82 | 293 | 520 | 0.67 |
| III | 76.2 | 145 | 1.61 | 0.38 | 0.39 | 4.39 | 241 | 521 | 0.67 |
| IV | 80.4 | 154 | 1.56 | 0.39 | 0.55 | 4.68 | 230 | 513 | 0.64 |
| 1987 I | 89.0 | 178 | 1.56 | 0.41 | 0.65 | 5.36 | 283 | 510 | 0.65 |
| II | 96.1 | 183 | 1.55 | 0.43 | 0.74 | 7.06 | 307 | 510 | 0.83 |
| III | 110.6 | 229 | 1.56 | 0.47 | 0.85 | 7.89 | 339 | 510 | 0.85 |
| IV | 126.1 | 296 | 1.62 | 0.48 | 0.76 | 8.22 | 353 | 517 | 0.86 |
| 1988 I | 116.6 | 245 | 1.61[10] | 0.50 | 0.69 | 10.50 | 370 | 520 | 0.89 |

Source: Commodities Division, IMF Research Department.

[1] The weights in the index are as follows: logs, 45 percent; cotton, 17 percent; wool, 10 percent; natural rubber, 11 percent; tobacco, 11 percent; hides, 5 percent; jute and sisal, less than 1 percent.
[2] Malaysian meranti logs, average wholesale price, Japan.
[3] United States, average, estimated prices received by producers.
[4] Malaysian RSS1, f.o.b. Malaysia/Singapore ports.
[5] Liverpool Index A, c.i.f. Liverpool.
[6] U.K. Dominion, 64's clean, dry combed basis.
[7] Bangladesh BWD, f.o.b. Chittagong/Chalna.
[8] East African origin, ungraded, c.i.f. European ports.
[9] U.S. wholesale price, f.o.b. shipping point, Chicago.
[10] January–February average.

Japan and the restrictive log export policies of major hardwood producing countries in Southeast Asia. Prices of sawnwood[69] recovered by about 4 percent in 1987 to $279 a cubic meter owing in part also to restrictions on sawnwood exports imposed by producing countries in Southeast Asia.

Hardwood log production is estimated to have declined marginally, from 255 million cubic meters in 1986 to 254 million cubic meters in 1987. The share of tropical hardwood logs (which are produced entirely

[69] Malaysian meranti, select and better quality, c.i.f. French ports.

**Chart 6. Prices of Agricultural Raw Materials, 1980–87**

(In SDRs; indices: 1980 = 100)

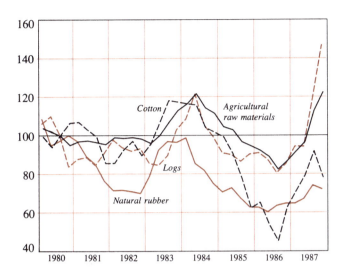

in developing countries) in total hardwood log production remained broadly unchanged in 1987 at 68 percent (Table 48). Logging activities in the Malaysian State of Sabah were hindered by unusually heavy rainfall during the first half of the year and shipping delays owing to typhoons caused a slower turnaround time for many vessels in Southeast Asia. In the Philippines, the policy banning log exports remained in force, while Indonesia continued its policy of progressively halting log exports in order to promote domestic production of plywood and other finished products. While production of tropical hardwood declined by a small percentage in 1987, hardwood log production in industrial countries in 1987 remained unchanged from 1986. The major factor accounting for this development was a sluggish demand for timber owing to a fall in housing starts caused by the continued high level of real interest rates in the United States and the generally fragile state of business expectations prevailing in most industrial countries. Forest fires and dry weather in Canada and the United States kept loggers out of the woods, and as a result, log supplies from these two major industrial country producers of hardwood remained tight throughout much of 1987. Sawnwood production rose in 1987 reflecting a shift away by timber producers in Southeast Asia from logs toward the higher-priced sawnwood.

Consumption of hardwood is estimated to have increased considerably in Japan in 1987 owing to an upturn in housing construction. In the first nine months of the year, housing starts in Japan reached 1.2 million units, which was about 20 percent higher than in the same period a year earlier. Housing construction

activity in Japan was boosted in part by the emergency economic measures introduced by the Japanese Government in May to expand, inter alia, government loans for new housing at concessional interest rates. For 1987 as a whole, housing starts are estimated to have risen by about 20 percent to 1.6 million units. In contrast, housing starts in the United States fell by 10 percent in 1987 to 1.6 million units owing mainly to steady increases in mortgage rates. Consumption of hardwood in the United States in 1987, however, did not appear to have fallen by as much as indicated by the decline in housing starts. The decline in the number of single and two-family houses, which of all types of dwellings use the most volume of forest products per unit, was less than the decline in the number of multi-family housing complexes. The average size of the single family house continued to increase. Also, there was a strong rise in repair and modernization work on existing buildings, particularly in the dwelling sector.

In 1987, export volumes of hardwood logs increased marginally (Table 49), partly in response to the sharp increase in prices. As in recent years, tropical hardwood producers continued to be the world's major exporter of hardwoods, while industrial countries, in particular Japan, remained the major importers. Throughout the year, exports of tropical hardwoods, most of which were priced in U.S. dollars, were favorably affected by the depreciation of the U.S. dollar against the currencies of main importing countries. Japan's imports of hardwood logs are estimated to have increased by about 10 percent in 1987 to 15 million cubic meters. Malaysia and Indonesia continued to be the major suppliers of logs to Japan. In contrast to logs, exports of sawnwood fell slightly in 1987, reflecting a continuation of the depressed level of activity in important end-use sectors, notably joinery and furniture. In addition, in late 1986, Indonesia imposed restrictions on exports of sawn timber from certain species and similar steps were taken by the Malaysian State of Sarawak in July 1987. While the high price in the final quarter of 1987 occasioned by shortages in the Japanese market was not sustained in January 1988, average hardwood log prices in 1988 are expected to be higher than the average for 1987 because of the combined influences of a further increase in housing starts in Japan and the tightness in the supply of logs from the traditional producers in Southeast Asia. The projected increase in housing starts in Japan would be predicated largely on the continued availability of concessional funds from the Government. Housing starts in the United States are expected to stagnate at the current level in 1988 as mortgage rates are expected to remain at relatively high levels. On the supply side, the policies restricting the export of logs from the major producers are expected to remain

**Table 47.  Movements in Prices of Agricultural Raw Materials and Related Economic Indicators, 1980–87**

(Annual percentage changes)

|  | 1980 | 1981 | 1982 | 1983 | 1984 | 1985 | 1986 | 1987 |
|---|---|---|---|---|---|---|---|---|
| Prices of agricultural raw materials[1] |  |  |  |  |  |  |  |  |
| In SDRs | 7.9 | −3.5 | 2.2 | 5.3 | 11.6 | −14.0 | −12.0 | 20.8 |
| In U.S. dollars | 8.7 | −12.5 | −4.3 | 1.9 | 7.2 | −15.0 | −1.6 | 33.6 |
| Real[2] | −1.3 | −9.1 | −2.2 | 4.9 | 10.3 | −15.6 | −14.0 | 18.8 |
| Unit value of petroleum exports |  |  |  |  |  |  |  |  |
| In SDRs | 62.3 | 21.3 | 2.2 | −9.0 | 2.1 | −4.1 | −56.5 | 16.7 |
| In U.S. dollars | 63.5 | 9.9 | −4.3 | −11.9 | −2.1 | −5.0 | −49.8 | 28.6 |
| Unit value of manufactured exports |  |  |  |  |  |  |  |  |
| In SDRs | 9.6 | 6.0 | 4.5 | 0.4 | 1.2 | 2.1 | 2.1 | 1.7 |
| In U.S. dollars | 10.4 | −3.9 | −2.1 | −2.8 | −3.0 | 1.1 | 18.0 | 12.0 |
| Domestic prices in seven industrial countries |  |  |  |  |  |  |  |  |
| Consumer price index |  |  |  |  |  |  |  |  |
| In SDRs | 11.4 | 13.2 | 6.7 | 5.0 | 4.6 | 3.5 | 1.0 | 0.4 |
| In U.S. dollars | 12.2 | 2.6 | −0.1 | 1.7 | 0.3 | 2.5 | 16.7 | 10.7 |
| GNP deflator |  |  |  |  |  |  |  |  |
| In SDRs | 8.8 | 11.9 | 6.5 | 5.1 | 4.0 | 3.1 | 2.1 | 0.3 |
| In U.S. dollars | 9.6 | 1.4 | −0.3 | 1.8 | −0.2 | 2.2 | 18.0 | 10.6 |
| Economic activity in seven industrial countries |  |  |  |  |  |  |  |  |
| Real GNP | 1.2 | 1.7 | −0.4 | 2.8 | 5.2 | 3.2 | 2.8 | 3.1 |
| Industrial production | −0.2 | 0.6 | −3.8 | 3.8 | 8.5 | 2.8 | 1.0 | 3.3 |
| Domestic fixed investment | −2.2 | −0.2 | −5.2 | 3.9 | 9.6 | 4.5 | 2.8 | 3.3 |
| World consumption of agricultural raw materials[3] |  |  |  |  |  |  |  |  |
| Index of consumption | 0.7 | 0.2 | 2.6 | 2.7 | 5.0 | 5.3 | 3.3 | 0.6 |
| World supply of agricultural raw materials[3] |  |  |  |  |  |  |  |  |
| Index of production | −0.8 | 1.6 | 0.2 | 1.5 | 9.0 | −0.3 | −3.6 | 3.0 |
| Index of supply[4] | −1.1 | 0.4 | 0.0 | 3.0 | 6.5 | 3.0 | 1.4 | −0.6 |
| Index of closing stocks | 1.5 | 8.6 | 4.2 | −3.7 | 35.5 | 3.7 | −17.3 | −8.6 |

Sources: Commodities Division and Current Studies Division, IMF Research Department.

[1] Refers to IMF world index of prices of agricultural raw materials. These percentages differ from those reported in the *World Economic Outlook* which refer to the index of commodities *exported by developing countries.*

[2] Index of dollar prices of agricultural raw materials deflated by the index of dollar unit values of manufactured exports.

[3] Overall indices constructed using the same weights for the indices of individual commodities as in overall (world) price index. Crop year data for agricultural commodities are given under the earlier calendar year, e.g., crop year 1980/81 under 1980. The commodity coverage of the indices of consumption and stocks is less comprehensive than the coverage of the indices of production and supply.

[4] Supply is defined as production plus *beginning*-of-year stocks.

in force and are expected to support a modest increase in log prices. The price of sawnwood is also projected to increase in 1988 broadly in line with the increase in the log prices.

Because much of the increase in the price of hardwood logs occurred only late in 1987, earnings from the exports of hardwood logs are estimated to have increased by only 9 percent in terms of dollars in 1987 and to have remained unchanged in terms of SDRs (Table 49). Earnings measured in dollars from exports of sawnwood made from hardwood are estimated to have increased in 1987 by 4 percent but earnings in SDR terms remained unchanged. The higher market prices prevailing late in 1987, however, are likely to

be reflected in substantially higher export earnings in 1988.

## Tobacco

In 1987 world production of tobacco is estimated to have risen by about 6 percent to 6.5 million tons. While world consumption is estimated to have remained close to the previous year's level of 6 million tons (Table 50). Estimates of the volume of world exports of unmanufactured tobacco vary but are close to the level of 1986 of 1.3 million tons (Table 51). World stocks are calculated to have been reduced from 5.9 million tons at the beginning of 1987 to 5.7

## Table 48. Hardwood Logs and Sawnwood: World Production, 1981–87

(In millions of cubic meters)

| | 1981 | 1982 | 1983 | 1984 | 1985 | 1986[1] | 1987[1] |
|---|---|---|---|---|---|---|---|
| **Logs** | **249** | **238** | **249** | **256** | **255** | **255** | **254** |
| Industrial countries | 68 | 56 | 61 | 63 | 63 | 63 | 63 |
| Developing countries | 147 | 149 | 155 | 159 | 158 | 158 | 157 |
| *Brazil* | *14* | *14* | *14* | *14* | *14* | *14* | *14* |
| *China* | *17* | *17* | *18* | *20* | *21* | *21* | *20* |
| *Indonesia* | *23* | *22* | *26* | *27* | *24* | *24* | *24* |
| *Malaysia* | *27* | *30* | *33* | *32* | *31* | *31* | *31* |
| *Other* | *66* | *66* | *64* | *66* | *68* | *68* | *68* |
| U.S.S.R. and Eastern European countries | 34 | 33 | 33 | 34 | 34 | 34 | 34 |
| **Sawnwood** | **111** | **107** | **110** | **115** | **117** | **118** | **120** |
| Industrial countries | 35 | 29 | 30 | 31 | 31 | 31 | 32 |
| Developing countries | 58 | 60 | 63 | 66 | 68 | 69 | 70 |
| *Brazil* | *8* | *8* | *8* | *8* | *8* | *9* | *9* |
| *China* | *8* | *9* | *9* | *10* | *10* | *10* | *10* |
| *Indonesia* | *5* | *7* | *6* | *7* | *7* | *7* | *7* |
| *Malaysia* | *6* | *6* | *7* | *7* | *7* | *7* | *7* |
| *Other* | *31* | *30* | *33* | *34* | *36* | *36* | *37* |
| U.S.S.R. and Eastern European countries | 18 | 18 | 18 | 18 | 18 | 18 | 18 |

Source: UN Food and Agriculture Organization, *1985 Yearbook of Forest Products* (Rome).

[1] Estimated by Commodities Division, IMF Research Department.

## Table 49. Hardwood Logs and Sawnwood: Export Earnings, 1984–87

| | 1984 | 1985 | 1986[1] | 1987[1] | 1984 | 1985 | 1986[1] | 1987[1] |
|---|---|---|---|---|---|---|---|---|
| | *(Values in SDRs)* | | | | *(Values in U.S. dollars)* | | | |
| **Logs** | | | | | | | | |
| **Earnings** (*in billions*) | **2.1** | **2.1** | **1.9** | **1.9** | **2.1** | **2.1** | **2.2** | **2.4** |
| Industrial countries | 0.3 | 0.3 | 0.2 | 0.2 | 0.3 | 0.3 | 0.3 | 0.3 |
| Developing countries | 1.8 | 1.8 | 1.7 | 1.7 | 1.8 | 1.8 | 1.9 | 2.1 |
| **Volumes** (*in million cubic meters*) | **29.5** | **30.1** | **30.5** | **31.0** | **29.5** | **30.1** | **30.5** | **31.0** |
| Industrial countries | 2.7 | 2.8 | 2.5 | 2.5 | 2.7 | 2.8 | 2.5 | 2.5 |
| Developing countries | 26.8 | 27.3 | 28.0 | 28.5 | 26.8 | 27.3 | 28.0 | 28.5 |
| *Malaysia* | *16.9* | *19.6* | *19.1* | *19.5* | *16.9* | *19.6* | *19.1* | *19.5* |
| *Other* | *9.9* | *7.7* | *8.9* | *9.0* | *9.9* | *7.7* | *8.9* | *9.0* |
| **Unit values** (*a cubic meter*) | **69** | **69** | **61** | **60** | **71** | **70** | **72** | **77** |
| Industrial countries | 105 | 102 | 95 | 87 | 107 | 104 | 112 | 112 |
| Developing countries | 66 | 65 | 58 | 58 | 68 | 66 | 68 | 74 |
| **Market prices** (*a cubic meter*)[2] | **163** | **134** | **129** | **171** | **167** | **136** | **151** | **221** |
| **Sawnwood** | | | | | | | | |
| **Earnings** (*in billions*) | **2.5** | **2.3** | **1.9** | **1.9** | **2.5** | **2.3** | **2.3** | **2.4** |
| Industrial countries | 0.7 | 0.7 | 0.6 | 0.5 | 0.7 | 0.7 | 0.7 | 0.6 |
| Developing countries | 1.8 | 1.6 | 1.4 | 1.4 | 1.8 | 1.6 | 1.6 | 1.8 |
| **Volumes** (*in million cubic meters*) | **12.6** | **11.7** | **11.5** | **11.0** | **12.6** | **11.7** | **11.5** | **11.0** |
| Industrial countries | 3.1 | 2.8 | 2.2 | 2.0 | 3.1 | 2.8 | 2.2 | 2.0 |
| Developing countries | 9.5 | 8.9 | 9.3 | 9.0 | 9.5 | 8.9 | 9.3 | 9.0 |
| *Malaysia* | *2.8* | *2.7* | *2.6* | *2.8* | *2.8* | *2.7* | *2.6* | *2.8* |
| *Other* | *6.7* | *6.2* | *6.7* | *6.2* | *6.7* | *6.2* | *6.7* | *6.2* |
| **Unit values** (*a cubic meter*) | **200** | **190** | **170** | **170** | **200** | **200** | **100** | **220** |
| Industrial countries | 240 | 250 | 250 | 250 | 250 | 250 | 300 | 330 |
| Developing countries | 180 | 180 | 150 | 150 | 190 | 180 | 170 | 190 |
| **Market prices** (*a cubic meter*)[3] | **300** | **272** | **227** | **213** | **307** | **276** | **266** | **275** |

Sources: UN Food and Agriculture Organization, *1985 Yearbook of Forest Products* (Rome), for exports; Commodities Division, IMF Research Department for market prices.

[1] Data on exports are estimates of Commodities Division, IMF Research Department.

[2] Malaysian meranti logs, average wholesale price in Japan.

[3] Malaysian meranti, select and better quality, c.i.f. French ports.

**Table 50. Tobacco: World Leaf Production, 1981–87**

(In thousands of tons)

|  | 1981 | 1982 | 1983 | 1984 | 1985 | 1986 | 1987[1] |
|---|---|---|---|---|---|---|---|
| **World** | **5,990** | **6,890** | **6,000** | **6,460** | **7,020** | **6,110** | **6,460** |
| Industrial countries | 1,430 | 1,350 | 1,160 | 1,280 | 1,160 | 990 | 970 |
| *United States* | *930* | *900* | *650* | *780* | *690* | *540* | *560* |
| *Others* | *500* | *450* | *510* | *500* | *470* | *450* | *410* |
| Developing countries | 4,080 | 5,000 | 4,260 | 4,610 | 5,260 | 4,520 | 4,820 |
| *China* | *1,520* | *2,200* | *1,400* | *1,820* | *2,450* | *1,730* | *2,090* |
| *Brazil* | *370* | *420* | *390* | *410* | *410* | *390* | *410* |
| *Greece* | *120* | *120* | *120* | *140* | *150* | *150* | *130* |
| *India* | *480* | *520* | *580* | *490* | *490* | *440* | *450* |
| *Malawi* | *50* | *60* | *70* | *70* | *70* | *70* | *70* |
| *Turkey* | *180* | *210* | *230* | *180* | *170* | *170* | *170* |
| *Zimbabwe* | *80* | *90* | *100* | *120* | *110* | *120* | *140* |
| *Others* | *1,280* | *1,380* | *1,370* | *1,380* | *1,410* | *1,450* | *1,360* |
| U.S.S.R. and Eastern European countries | 480 | 540 | 580 | 570 | 600 | 600 | 670 |
| *U.S.S.R.* | *270* | *310* | *390* | *340* | *380* | *380* | *380* |
| *Others* | *210* | *230* | *190* | *230* | *220* | *220* | *290* |

Source: UN Food and Agriculture Organization, *FAO Production Yearbook*, years 1984–86.
[1] Estimated by Commodities Division, IMF Research Department.

**Table 51. Tobacco: Export Earnings, 1984–87**

|  | 1984 | 1985 | 1986 | 1987[1] | 1984 | 1985 | 1986 | 1987[1] |
|---|---|---|---|---|---|---|---|---|
|  | *(Values in SDRs)* | | | | *(Values in U.S. dollars)* | | | |
| **Earnings** (*in billions*) | **4.0** | **4.0** | **3.3** | **3.0** | **4.1** | **4.1** | **3.9** | **3.9** |
| Industrial countries | 1.8 | 1.8 | 1.4 | 1.2 | 1.9 | 1.9 | 1.7 | 1.6 |
| Developing countries | 2.0 | 2.0 | 1.7 | 1.6 | 2.0 | 2.0 | 1.9 | 2.1 |
| U.S.S.R. and Eastern European countries | 0.2 | 0.2 | 0.2 | 0.2 | 0.2 | 0.2 | 0.3 | 0.2 |
| **Volumes** (*in thousands of tons*) | **1,400** | **1,390** | **1,300** | **1,310** | **1,400** | **1,390** | **1,300** | **1,310** |
| Industrial countries | 440 | 420 | 400 | 390 | 440 | 420 | 400 | 390 |
| *United States* | *250* | *250* | *220* | *220* | *250* | *250* | *220* | *220* |
| *Other countries* | *190* | *170* | *190* | *170* | *190* | *170* | *190* | *170* |
| Developing countries | 880 | 890 | 810 | 840 | 880 | 890 | 810 | 840 |
| *Brazil* | *190* | *200* | *180* | *180* | *190* | *200* | *180* | *180* |
| *Malawi* | *70* | *60* | *60* | *60* | *70* | *60* | *60* | *60* |
| *Zimbabwe* | *90* | *100* | *100* | *110* | *90* | *100* | *100* | *110* |
| *Other countries* | *530* | *530* | *480* | *490* | *530* | *530* | *480* | *490* |
| U.S.S.R. and Eastern European countries | 80 | 80 | 90 | 80 | 80 | 80 | 90 | 80 |
| **Unit values** (*a ton*) | **2,890** | **2,870** | **2,550** | **2,320** | **2,970** | **2,920** | **3,000** | **3,000** |
| Industrial countries | 4,240 | 4,370 | 3,500 | 3,150 | 4,350 | 4,440 | 4,110 | 4,080 |
| Developing countries | 2,240 | 2,190 | 2,050 | 1,930 | 2,300 | 2,230 | 2,410 | 2,500 |
| U.S.S.R. and Eastern European countries | 2,650 | 2,580 | 2,780 | 2,330 | 2,720 | 2,630 | 3,260 | 3,010 |
| **Market prices** (*a ton*)[2] | **3,990** | **4,000** | **3,080** | **2,680** | **4,090** | **4,060** | **3,610** | **3,470** |

Sources: UN Food and Agriculture Organization, *1986 FAO Trade Yearbook* (Rome) for exports; Commodities Division, IMF Research Department for market prices.
[1] Data on exports are estimates of Commodities Division, IMF Research Department.
[2] United States, average estimated prices received by producers.

million tons by the end of the year. In the United States, the stock was estimated to decline from 2 million on July 1, 1987 to approximately 1.5 million toward the beginning of 1988. Notwithstanding these developments, stocks of unmanufactured tobacco at the beginning of 1988 were sufficient to cover 12 months' usage by the world's tobacco manufacturing industry.

Auction prices for unmanufactured tobacco in 1987 were rather mixed reflecting mainly the type and quality of tobacco offered and marketing arrangements. In Malawi, auction prices increased by 37 percent in terms of kwacha (20 percent in U.S. dollars), whereas in Zimbabwe, auction prices declined by about 30 percent both in terms of Zimbabwe dollars and U.S. dollars. The average price in the flue-cured auction markets in the United States increased from $1.52 a pound in 1986 to $1.60 a pound in 1987.

Export earnings in dollar terms in 1987 are estimated to have remained nearly unchanged compared to 1986; in SDR terms, a further decrease is estimated—the decline, however, is relatively small in relation to the substantial drop between 1985 and 1986 (see Table 51). It is estimated that developing countries improved their export earnings in terms of dollars, whereas industrial countries may have lost some ground owing mainly to a lower volume of exports.

With respect to consumption of cigarettes, the prevailing trend continued; demand in developing countries increased owing to rising incomes, increasing urbanization, and other socio-economic factors, whereas consumption in industrial countries was reduced because of heavier taxes, higher retail prices, and enhanced anti-smoking restrictions. Taxes and excise duties on cigarettes are, however, being increasingly used as revenue sources in developing countries such as Argentina, India, and the Philippines. Cigarette consumption in China, the world's largest producer and consumer, increased at an average yearly rate of 9 percent throughout the 1980s. In Brazil, cigarette sales grew by 15 percent in 1986, but may have fallen in 1987. Cigarette sales in Indonesia were expected to register a 6 percent increase in 1987. In the United States, major increases of cigarette production are expected to be channeled to export markets similar to the jump in shipments to Japan and other Asian countries in 1987, reflecting primarily the recent trade liberalizations of these markets, but also exchange rate changes. The volume of U.S. exports of cigarettes rose from 64 billion pieces in 1986 to 100 billion pieces in 1987, valued at $2 billion compared with $1.3 billion in 1986.

Reflecting this consumption demand, world production of cigarettes is estimated to have risen to more than 5,000 billion pieces in 1987. This fourth consecutive annual increase was principally the result of a yearly 10 percent output growth in China since 1984. Cigarette production also increased in most other Asian countries, while production in South America and Africa increased by 8 percent and 4 percent, respectively. Most European manufacturers, however, reduced their production. In 1988, world cigarette production is expected to increase by around 2 percent to 5,200 billion pieces.

World tobacco production is expected to follow a moderately expansionary path. After a sharp upturn in 1987, production in China may grow at a somewhat slower rate in 1988. Production in the United States may increase again in 1988 when the national crop quota of 352,000 tons will be 21,800 tons higher than last year. In addition the average yield goal has been increased and price supports are also above their 1987 level. In 1987 planted area in Zimbabwe increased by 16 percent, but hot, dry conditions toward the end of the growing period limited the size of the crop and reduced leaf quality. With a return to more normal weather conditions, Zimbabwe should realize a larger crop in 1988. Malawi's leaf harvest may also increase in 1988. Brazil is also expected to have a larger tobacco crop in 1988, up 2 percent to 415,000 tons.

Prices of unmanufactured tobacco are estimated to move upwards in a narrow range in 1988, reflecting mainly the expected improved quality. Prices of the U.S. burley tobacco auction market in the 1988 (January-February) season averaged $3.45 a kilogram, the same level as in the previous year. Zimbabwe's flue-cured tobacco auction opened in April 1988 with prices substantially higher than in the previous year, although the difference primarily reflected higher quality leaf.

## Natural Rubber

The market for natural rubber has remained weak in recent years, with natural rubber production generally outpacing consumption. An excess of production over consumption and an increase in stocks was responsible for a 29 percent decline in dollar prices from 1983 to 1985. In 1985 the International Natural Rubber Organization (INRO) made substantial buffer stock purchases in order to defend the floor price under the 1979 International Natural Rubber Agreement (INRA). Natural rubber prices recovered during the next two years, aided in part by a sharp growth in demand in China and by weather-induced supply shortages in major rubber producing countries.

After recovering somewhat in the previous year, the price of first quality ribbed smoked sheets (RSS1), f.o.b. Malaysia, rose sharply in 1987. In terms of monthly movements, the price, which remained stable at around 41 U.S. cents a pound during the first three months, began to increase at the onset of the wintering period,[70] and advanced rapidly thereafter to reach a level of 48 cents a pound in September. This increase of 23 percent over the same period in 1986 was caused by drought-induced supply disruptions in Indonesia and Thailand, which coincided with a surge in demand from China. A shortage of RSS1 arising from a continued shift from sheet rubber to the production of latex concentrates in Malaysia was also an important factor contributing to the price rise of RSS1. The price increase was more pronounced for lower grade tire rubbers, such as Thai RSS3 and Technically Specified Rubber (TSR) 20, as well as for latex concentrates which are used for the manufacture of surgical gloves and condoms. In October the price of RSS1 retreated

---

[70] A seasonal reduction in the latex output of rubber trees which normally occurs in the second quarter of the year.

steadily partly as a result of sales from the INRO buffer stock. The price remained in the range of 47–50 cents a pound in the period October 1987 through January 1988. For 1987 as a whole, the dollar price of RSS1 increased by 22 percent to average 44.7 cents a pound.

Movements of natural rubber prices in 1987 in terms of the market indicator price (MIP) of INRA[71] were broadly similar to those of RSS1. A shortage of supplies resulting from droughts in Indonesia and Thailand during the first half of the year caused the MIP to rise steadily during the first eight months of the year. By the end of August, the MIP, upon which INRO's buffer stock operations are based, reached 232.7 M/S cents a kilogram, marginally surpassing the "may sell" level of 232 M/S cents a kilogram, and remained above the "may sell" level throughout September. After a further rise to over 239 M/S cents a kilogram in the first half of October, the MIP retreated slowly; the average for the month as a whole was 237 M/S cents a kilogram. In early November the MIP fell below the "may sell" level for the first time in nearly three months partly because of uncertainties associated with the sharp drop in stock market prices. Prices recovered during the latter part of the month, however, and for the month as a whole the MIP averaged 232 M/S cents a pound. Sales from the buffer stock which commenced in early September were reported to have amounted to about 70,000 tons (20 percent of the buffer stock) through October. Buffer stock sales ended in early November when the MIP fell below the "may sell" level.

World production and consumption for natural rubber were closely balanced in 1987, and commercial stocks rose only moderately (Table 52). As a result of drought-induced slowdowns in the growth of production in Indonesia and Thailand in the first half of the year, world production is estimated to have risen by only 1 percent to 4.5 million tons. World consumption of natural rubber rose by 2 percent in 1987 with the main impetus for growth coming from China, where both tire production and vehicle output are estimated to have risen by 22 percent; imports of natural rubber by China increased 50 percent to about 315,000 tons. In the United States (which accounts for 17 percent of world consumption), natural rubber consumption rose by 4 percent aided by strong demand in the replacement tire market; during the period January–September 1987 total tire production rose by 15 percent, while total vehicle output fell by 4 percent. In

Japan (which accounts for 12 percent of world consumption), the growth of tire exports slowed down because of an appreciation in the yen but the expansion of domestic demand supported a 2 percent rise in rubber consumption. Consumption in Europe as a whole remained broadly unchanged.

Commercial stocks as a proportion of world consumption declined steadily from 44 percent in the early 1980s to 32 percent in 1985. The stock-consumption ratio, which rose slightly in 1986 partly as a result of a stock buildup in China, remained unchanged in 1987 at around 33 percent. Sustained conditions of high real interest rates, falling prices, ready availability of supplies for immediate needs because of improvement in the frequency, speed, and turnaround time of ocean transportation, and better inventory management are responsible for the steady fall in stocks in relation to consumption in recent years.

Although the volume of exports remained unchanged in 1987, earnings from natural rubber exports increased by 24 percent in terms of U.S. dollars because of higher export unit values (Table 53). The increase in export earnings in terms of SDRs in 1987 was 12 percent. The share of TSRs in total natural rubber trade is estimated to have increased to 50 percent, while that of RSS is estimated to have fallen to about 35 percent. TSR 20, RSS1, and RSS3 now account for about two thirds of natural rubber exports. The United States, which accounts for over 20 percent of total world natural rubber imports, obtained 60 percent of its imports from Indonesia. Japan, which accounts for 15 percent of total world natural rubber imports, obtained 70 percent of its imports from Thailand. Imports by China, mostly from Indonesia and Thailand, grew sharply to reach an estimated level of 315 thousand tons or 9 percent of total world exports of natural rubber.

Natural rubber prices are expected to increase modestly in 1988. Barring unfavorable weather conditions, high prices that prevailed in 1987 are expected to stimulate production, particularly in Indonesia and Thailand, where the effects of the planting programs undertaken in the 1970s are expected to raise output considerably throughout the remainder of the 1980s. Demand for natural rubber is also expected to grow as tire production, which accounts for about 70 percent of natural rubber use, is expected to rise in the United States and Japan.

The 1979 International Natural Rubber Agreement expired on October 22, 1987, and the 1987 Agreement is expected to come into force provisionally in the latter part of 1988. During the interim period of about 14 months, all the relevant provisions of the 1979 INRA relating to the administration and operation of the buffer stock will continue to be applicable. How-

---

[71] The MIP is defined in the 1979 International Natural Rubber Agreement (INRA) as the average official price for RSS1, RSS3, and TSR 20 rubber on the Kuala Lumpur, London, New York, and Singapore markets, expressed in equally weighted Malaysian and Singapore cents per kilogram.

## Table 52. Natural Rubber: World Commodity Balance, 1981–87

(In thousands of tons)

| | 1981 | 1982 | 1983 | 1984 | 1985 | 1986 | 1987[1] |
|---|---|---|---|---|---|---|---|
| **Production** | **3,700** | **3,750** | **4,030** | **4,260** | **4,330** | **4,440** | **4,470** |
| Indonesia | 870 | 880 | 1,000 | 1,120 | 1,130 | 1,040 | 1,100 |
| Malaysia | 1,510 | 1,490 | 1,560 | 1,530 | 1,470 | 1,540 | 1,550 |
| Thailand | 500 | 550 | 590 | 630 | 730 | 780 | 810 |
| Other countries | 820 | 830 | 880 | 980 | 1,000 | 1,080 | 1,010 |
| **Consumption** | **3,700** | **3,660** | **3,990** | **4,240** | **4,350** | **4,400** | **4,500** |
| European Community | 760 | 730 | 740 | 760 | 790 | 810 | 830 |
| Japan | 440 | 440 | 500 | 520 | 540 | 540 | 550 |
| United States | 630 | 580 | 660 | 750 | 760 | 740 | 770 |
| Other countries | 1,870 | 1,910 | 2,090 | 2,210 | 2,260 | 2,310 | 2,350 |
| **Closing stocks** | **1,630** | **1,720** | **1,760** | **1,780** | **1,760** | **1,800** | **1,790** |
| Commercial stocks[2] | 1,630 | 1,490 | 1,490 | 1,510 | 1,400 | 1,440 | 1,480 |
| INRA buffer stock | 0 | 230 | 270 | 270 | 360 | 360 | 310 |

Source: International Rubber Study Group, *Rubber Statistical Bulletin* (London), various issues.
[1] Estimates by Commodities Division, IMF Research Department.
[2] Stocks in store are lower than cumulative net buffer stock purchases due to defaults, cancellations, rejections, losses, and damage.

## Table 53. Natural Rubber: Export Earnings, 1984–87

| | 1984 | 1985 | 1986 | 1987[1] | 1984 | 1985 | 1986 | 1987[1] |
|---|---|---|---|---|---|---|---|---|
| | *(Values in SDRs)* | | | | *(Values in U.S. dollars)* | | | |
| **Earnings (*in billions*)** | **3.4** | **2.7** | **2.5** | **2.8** | **3.5** | **2.7** | **2.9** | **3.6** |
| Developing countries | 3.4 | 2.7 | 2.5 | 2.8 | 3.5 | 2.7 | 2.9 | 3.6 |
| **Volumes (*in millions of tons*)** | **3.6** | **3.6** | **3.7** | **3.7** | **3.6** | **3.6** | **3.7** | **3.7** |
| Developing countries | 3.6 | 3.6 | 3.7 | 3.7 | 3.6 | 3.6 | 3.7 | 3.7 |
| *Indonesia* | *1.0* | *1.0* | *1.0* | *1.0* | *1.0* | *1.0* | *1.0* | *1.0* |
| *Malaysia* | *1.6* | *1.5* | *1.5* | *1.5* | *1.6* | *1.5* | *1.5* | *1.5* |
| *Thailand* | *0.6* | *0.7* | *0.8* | *0.8* | *0.6* | *0.7* | *0.8* | *0.8* |
| *Other countries* | *0.4* | *0.4* | *0.4* | *0.4* | *0.4* | *0.4* | *0.4* | *0.4* |
| **Unit values (*a ton*)** | 940 | 740 | 660 | 760 | 960 | 750 | 780 | 960 |
| **Market prices (*a ton*)[2]** | 930 | 750 | 690 | 760 | 960 | 760 | 810 | 990 |

Sources: Data on exports from UN Food and Agricultural Organization, *1986 FAO Trade Yearbook* (Rome), and include only exports of rubber-producing countries; Commodities Division, IMF Research Department for market prices.
[1] Data on exports are estimates of Commodities Division, IMF Research Department.
[2] Malaysian RSS1, f.o.b. Malaysian/Singapore ports.

ever, no buffer stock *purchases* will take place. The Buffer Stock Manager (BSM) is authorized to implement at his discretion a modest sales program in order to cover contingencies, such as the cost of servicing and maintaining the buffer stock without disrupting the market. The monthly cost of servicing and maintaining the outstanding buffer stock is estimated at M$ 3 million, equivalent to about 2,000 tons of rubber. The Natural Rubber Council is to review and decide whether to continue or to revise this sales program before the end of April 1988. Apart from this sales program, under the rules of the old agreement that require market sales of buffer stock when prices move above the "must sell" level of M/S 242 cents a kilogram, the BSM sold a large quantity of buffer stock in January 1988, when the market indicator price averaged M/S 245 cents a kilogram. The price fell below the "must sell" level in early February.

## Cotton

The average price of cotton in 1987 was 56 percent higher than in 1986 in terms of U.S. dollars and 42 percent higher[72] in terms of SDRs. The sharp increase in price began in September 1986 with reports that weather conditions in Texas might lead to a very low harvest in the 1986/87 crop year (August/July), which would contribute to greatly reduced U.S. production.

[72] Unless specified otherwise, "cotton prices" refer to medium-staple cotton. Price quotations for medium-staple cotton refer to the Liverpool Index "A," 1³⁄₃₂ inch staple, average of the cheapest five of ten styles, c.i.f., Liverpool. There was virtually no change in the price of long-staple cotton because of an adequate crop in Egypt, the principal supplier of long-staple cotton. The price differential between these two types of cotton in September 1987 was around 85 U.S. cents a pound compared with over 100 cents in 1985–86. The price of long-staple cotton, however, increased in December 1987, and the differential widened to over 125 cents a pound.

71

The price of cotton rose progressively over the following 12 months as these expectations were confirmed and higher-than-anticipated increases in cotton consumption were reported. As a consequence, by the third quarter of 1987, the price of cotton, at an average of 84 U.S. cents a pound, was more than double its level one year earlier. Because of expectations of a considerably larger 1987/88 crop, however, in the final quarter of 1987 there was a reduction in the cotton price to about 75 cents a pound.

In mid-1986, before the sharp price increase, the dollar price of cotton was at its lowest level since 1972 and was only one half the level prevailing in the period 1980–84. This low price was associated with huge stocks, resulting from exceptionally large harvests in two successive years (Table 54). In 1984/85 there was a record world crop with production over 30 percent higher than in the previous year on account of increased acreage and exceptionally high yields. The 1985/86 world crop, although considerably below the 1984/85 crop, was well above the level of world consumption. World stocks at the end of the 1985/86 season were nearly 10 million tons, equivalent to about 60 percent of world consumption.

World cotton production declined by nearly 11 percent in 1986/87. The area planted to cotton declined significantly in many countries owing to the effect of lower prices on the profitability of cotton production. The largest decrease was in the United States where the output fell by 28 percent from 2.9 million tons in 1985/86 to 2.1 million tons in 1986/87. This decline was a result of heavy participation in the U.S. Government's Acreage Reduction Program (ARP), under which planted area declined by nearly 17 percent to 3.4 million hectares. At the same time, owing largely to weather conditions, estimated yield a hectare in the United States also declined from a record 706 kilograms in 1985/86 to 618 kilograms a hectare in 1986/87. Planted acreage in China fell by nearly 16 percent; this was attributable partly to competition from other cash crops, such as groundnuts, vegetables, and maize, and partly to changes in government policy that placed increased emphasis on grain production. Special incentives for cotton, which had been offered in earlier years, were withdrawn and limits were placed on procurement. In contrast to the sharp drop in output in the United States and China, output in the U.S.S.R. fell only marginally. Acreage planted to cotton increased from 3.3 million hectares to 3.5 million hectares, but this was offset by a decline in yield owing to inadequate moisture in some major producing areas. A number of other countries showed marked decreases in output; in Brazil output declined by nearly 25 percent because of lower yields; in Mexico, output declined following a marked decline in acreage; and in India,

output fell following inadequate monsoons. The main exception to declining output in 1986/87 was Pakistan, where output set a new record of 1.3 million tons, owing largely to record yields owing to excellent weather conditions in most areas and increasing application of better plant protection measures. In Greece, too, there was a record harvest, largely as a result of a sharp increase in yields.

The growth in cotton consumption over the last two seasons is notable for its size and duration. According to latest estimates consumption is estimated to have increased by 6 percent in 1986/87 following an increase in the previous year of 8 percent. These are unprecedented increases and basically reflect three factors: first, a basic shift in consumer preferences toward natural fibers seems to have gathered momentum in the last two to three years, particularly in the United States and other industrial countries; second, consumption was stimulated by a period of exceptionally low cotton prices, especially 1985–86; and third, incomes have been rising in most consuming markets, and this increase has been reflected in an expansion in the total textile market. Aggregate world consumption of all fibers rose 7.6 percent to 35.6 million metric tons in 1986. Cotton's market share of the world fiber market rose from 48 percent during 1985 to 50 percent in 1986.

The main gain in consumption was concentrated in the United States, where consumption increased by nearly 16 percent, reflecting a sharp increase in the cotton use by U.S. mills. Cotton's share of apparel products made in the United States was estimated at 41 percent in 1986, up from the record 40 percent of the previous year and from about 39 percent in the immediately preceding years. China continued to be the largest cotton consuming nation in the world, with total use estimated at about 4.3 million tons—practically unchanged from the previous year. During 1986/87, yarn production in China totaled over 4.1 million tons; cotton accounted for about 86 percent of the fibers used compared with 82 percent in 1985/86. Nonmill use of cotton in China is estimated to have been only 0.8 million tons compared with the unusually high 1.2 million tons used for padding in 1985/86. Consumption also rose noticeably in Brazil, India, Japan, and Pakistan, and by a small amount in the U.S.S.R.

Reflecting the excess of consumption over production, world stocks by the end of 1986/87 were down to 7.3 million tons, equivalent to just over 40 percent of annual consumption from an all-time high of 9.9 million tons at the beginning of the crop year. The decline in stocks occurred mainly in China and in the United States. In China, mill use picked up sharply, and, as in the previous season, the government encouraged the use of low-quality cotton in order to

**Table 54. Cotton: World Commodity Balance, 1981/82–87/88**

(In millions of tons)

| | August/July Crop Years | | | | | | |
|---|---|---|---|---|---|---|---|
| | 1981/82 | 1982/83 | 1983/84 | 1984/85 | 1985/86[1] | 1986/87[2] | 1987/88[2] |
| **Production[3]** | **15.4** | **14.9** | **14.6** | **19.1** | **17.3** | **15.4** | **16.6** |
| China | 3.0 | 3.6 | 4.6 | 6.3 | 4.2 | 3.6 | 3.8 |
| United States | 3.4 | 2.6 | 1.7 | 2.8 | 2.9 | 2.1 | 2.8 |
| U.S.S.R. | 2.8 | 2.7 | 2.5 | 2.5 | 2.7 | 2.6 | 2.5 |
| Other countries | 6.2 | 6.0 | 5.8 | 7.5 | 7.5 | 7.1 | 7.5 |
| **Consumption[3]** | **14.4** | **14.8** | **15.2** | **15.5** | **16.8** | **17.8** | **17.8** |
| China | 3.6 | 3.6 | 3.6 | 3.7 | 4.3 | 4.3 | 4.1 |
| United States | 1.2 | 1.2 | 1.3 | 1.2 | 1.4 | 1.6 | 1.6 |
| U.S.S.R. | 1.9 | 2.0 | 2.0 | 2.0 | 2.1 | 2.1 | 2.2 |
| Other countries | 7.7 | 8.0 | 8.3 | 8.6 | 9.0 | 9.8 | 9.9 |
| **Closing stocks[3,4]** | **5.4** | **5.8** | **5.4** | **9.2** | **9.8** | **7.3** | **6.4** |
| China | 0.4 | 0.6 | 1.5 | 3.9 | 3.1 | 1.7 | 1.1 |
| United States | 1.4 | 1.7 | 0.6 | 0.9 | 2.0 | 1.1 | 0.8 |
| U.S.S.R. | 0.6 | 0.6 | 0.5 | 0.5 | 0.6 | 0.5 | 0.5 |
| Other countries | 3.0 | 2.9 | 2.8 | 3.9 | 4.1 | 4.0 | 4.0 |

Source: International Cotton Advisory Committee, *Cotton: World Statistics* (Washington), various issues.

[1] International Cotton Advisory Committee estimate.
[2] International Cotton Advisory Committee forecast.
[3] All staples.
[4] May not agree with production and consumption data because of difference in coverage.

ensure that storage space would be available for the higher grades. Over the last two seasons, stocks in China have declined from an estimated 3.1 million tons to 1.7 million tons. In the United States, stocks declined by nearly 50 percent as a result of the low 1986/87 crop and increases in both domestic demand and exports. Stocks fell in most other exporting countries, except for Pakistan and a number of importing countries, including the Republic of Korea and Japan.

World cotton production in 1987/88 is projected to be about 16.6 million tons, an increase of nearly 8 percent over the previous year. Harvested area is expected to surpass the 1985/86 level of 32.5 million hectares because of higher cotton prices and increased government emphasis on cotton cultivation in many countries. Yields worldwide are expected to rise to an average of 523 kilograms a hectare, or 3 percent higher than in 1986/87. The increase in output is likely to be concentrated in China and the United States, but larger crops are also indicated for Brazil, India, and Mexico. Early forecasts were for even higher production but the generally unfavorable weather, especially in China, have reduced expectations. Harvested area in the Soviet Union is expected to rise slightly from last year's 3.48 million hectares, while yields could fall to about 700 kilograms a hectare on account of heavy rain, hail, and cool weather in some parts of the normally dry cotton areas of Uzbekistan. In India, the monsoon has been erratic; much of Central India (especially Gujarat) did not receive enough rain to plant. Given the large increases in cotton prices, especially when compared with the prices of other crops such as wheat, corn, and soybeans, the area planted to cotton in the Southern Hemisphere has increased by a substantial margin.

World cotton consumption for 1987/88, forecast at 17.8 million tons, is expected to be almost identical to the level in the previous season. One reason for this is that consumption in China is expected to drop by about 0.2 million tons because special allocations for non-mill use have been discontinued. Cotton consumption in the U.S.S.R. is expected to reach a record 2.2 million tons during the 1987/88 season. Estimates of world production and consumption point to lower cotton stocks at the end of this marketing season. Stocks seem likely to fall by nearly 1.0 million tons from an estimated 7.3 million at the end of the 1986/87 crop year to 6.4 million tons at the end of the 1987/88 crop year. World cotton stocks had increased from around 5.4 million tons at the beginning of the 1982/83 season to 9.8 million tons at the beginning of the 1986/87 season. If stocks decline to the levels now anticipated, they will amount to only 36 percent of anticipated consumption during 1987/88. This will be the lowest ratio of world stocks to use in six years. The tightening of the world supply-stock situation suggests that prices are likely to maintain their current levels. There may be some slackening in the first half of the season, but the average for the season is expected to be high.

The volume of world cotton exports is estimated to have increased in 1987 by over a million tons to a record 5.2 million tons (Table 55). Most of this increase was the result of a sharp increase in exports from the

United States, which increased from 660,000 tons in 1986 to 1.5 million tons in 1987. This increase in exports is largely attributable to an improvement in price competitiveness following the adoption of a new cotton program in 1986. U.S. exports, which are still below the peak reached in 1984, could increase substantially. Exports from China are estimated to have declined from 0.6 in 1986 to 0.5 million tons in 1987 reflecting partly the decline in production in 1986/87. Exports from Sudan also increased sharply, while there was a modest increase in exports from Brazil and India. In contrast, there were considerable declines in exports from Mexico, Paraguay, and some African countries; there was also a small decline in exports in dollars from the U.S.S.R. Preliminary estimates indicate that world export earnings increased by nearly 65 percent in 1987, reflecting both the sharp increase in export volumes and in unit values. Earnings of industrial countries are estimated to have increased dramatically by over $1.9 billion largely on account of an increase in U.S. exports. Export earnings of developing countries are estimated to have increased by 50 percent. World trade in cotton is forecast to remain quite buoyant during 1988. There may be some slackening in volume terms but prices are expected to remain firm with export earnings likely to match those achieved in 1987.

## Wool

The price of wool has fluctuated considerably in recent years. The dollar price of fine wool fell by 17 percent from 1984 to 1986 and then increased by 53 percent in 1987.[73] The price increase from the trough in the third quarter of 1986 to the final quarter of 1987 was 87 percent.

The decline in prices in 1985 and 1986 reflected in part a decline of the currency of the dominant exporter—Australia—vis-à-vis the U.S. dollar. The Australian dollar depreciated by 20 percent against the U.S. dollar in 1985 and by over 4 percent in 1986. In terms of Australian dollars, the market price actually increased by 14 percent in 1985 and declined only marginally in 1986. Part of the upturn is also explained by expected currency movements as many buyers who had delayed purchases in anticipation of further depreciations in the Australian dollar were forced eventually to make purchases to replenish their depleted stocks. These purchases contributed to the sharp rise in prices during the first half of 1987.

World production of wool in the 1986/87 season (July/June in many countries) is estimated to have increased by 2 percent with respect to the previous season after remaining unchanged in the 1985/86 season. For 1987/88 a further increase of about 2 percent is expected. With a considerable improvement in weather conditions in a number of countries, world sheep numbers, which had remained virtually unchanged for three seasons, increased by 11.5 million or 1 percent during 1985/86 to reach a record 1,120 million head by the commencement of the 1986/87 season. Since returns from wool production are expected to remain high relative to those from other agricultural activities, a further overall buildup in flock levels is envisaged in the coming seasons.

In Australia, the leading sheep rearing country, favorable weather for a succession of seasons across most wool producing areas, together with a shift into sheep rearing from less profitable agricultural enterprises and a shift from production of sheepmeat to wool, has led to a recovery in the population of sheep reared for their wool from the low levels recorded in the early 1980s. Following a 12 percent increase between March 1983 and March 1985, sheep numbers rose further during the next two seasons by 7 percent to reach 160 million by March 1987, their highest level in 15 years. In response to improved profitability and the reduced risk of sheep enterprises vis-à-vis agricultural field crops, further flock growth is projected during 1987/88, taking numbers possibly to the 164 million mark by the end of the season. Australia, however, is believed to be approaching the stage where the capacity to feed additional sheep is limited so that some slowdown in the rate of increase in the flock size seems inevitable. In New Zealand, the largest exporter of the coarser-type wools used mainly in carpets, further reductions in numbers are expected with the result that wool production during 1987/88 is expected to decline by 3 percent to 350,000 tons—its lowest level in almost a decade. Sheep numbers are expected to increase somewhat in the U.S.S.R. and China.

Wool consumption data are rather fragmentary, with only 11 countries reporting regularly. These data indicate that wool consumption increased by about 2 percent in 1985 and by 1 percent in 1986. During 1986 the challenge from competing fibers—both man-made and non-wool natural fibers—became increasingly severe, but wool, helped by exchange rate movements that ensured that it was attractively priced in major wool consuming countries, improved its market share for the third successive season. Wool's share in overall fiber consumption at the carding stage in the 11 major wool-textile manufacturing countries providing consumption data, edged up to 30.5 percent from the preceding year's 30 percent. In both years wool usage

---

[73] Price quotations for fine wool refer to the United Kingdom, Dominion, 64's clean, dry combed basis.

## Table 55. Cotton: Export Earnings, 1984–87

| | 1984 | 1985 | 1986 | 1987[1] | 1984 | 1985 | 1986 | 1987[1] |
|---|---|---|---|---|---|---|---|---|
| | (Values in SDRs) | | | | (Values in U.S. dollars) | | | |
| **Earnings** (*in billions*) | 6.9 | 6.0 | 4.5 | 6.7 | 7.0 | 6.1 | 5.2 | 8.6 |
| Industrial countries | 2.6 | 1.9 | 1.0 | 2.3 | 2.6 | 1.9 | 1.1 | 3.0 |
| Developing countries | 3.3 | 3.1 | 2.5 | 3.5 | 3.4 | 3.1 | 3.0 | 4.5 |
| Non-Fund members | 1.0 | 1.0 | 1.0 | 0.9 | 1.0 | 1.1 | 1.1 | 1.1 |
| **Volumes** (*in millions of tons*) | 4.3 | 4.3 | 4.7 | 5.2 | 4.3 | 4.3 | 4.7 | 5.2 |
| Industrial countries | 1.6 | 1.3 | 1.0 | 1.8 | 1.6 | 1.3 | 1.0 | 1.8 |
| *United States* | *1.5* | *1.1* | *0.7* | *1.5* | *1.5* | *1.1* | *0.7* | *1.5* |
| *Other countries* | *0.1* | *0.2* | *0.3* | *0.3* | *0.1* | *0.2* | *0.3* | *0.3* |
| Developing countries | 2.1 | 2.3 | 3.0 | 2.7 | 2.1 | 2.3 | 3.0 | 2.7 |
| *China* | *0.2* | *0.4* | *0.6* | *0.5* | *0.2* | *0.4* | *0.6* | *0.5* |
| *Egypt* | *0.2* | *0.1* | *0.1* | *0.1* | *0.2* | *0.1* | *0.1* | *0.1* |
| *Other countries* | *1.7* | *1.8* | *2.3* | *2.1* | *1.7* | *1.8* | *2.3* | *2.1* |
| Non-Fund members | 0.6 | 0.7 | 0.7 | 0.7 | 0.6 | 0.7 | 0.7 | 0.7 |
| *U.S.S.R.* | *0.6* | *0.6* | *0.7* | *0.7* | *0.6* | *0.6* | *0.7* | *0.7* |
| **Unit values** (*a ton*) | 1,600 | 1,410 | 955 | 1,280 | 1,640 | 1,430 | 1,120 | 1,660 |
| Industrial countries | 1,590 | 1,460 | 100 | 1,300 | 1,630 | 1,480 | 1,170 | 1,680 |
| Developing countries | 1,630 | 1,350 | 840 | 1,280 | 1,670 | 1,370 | 990 | 1,660 |
| Non-Fund members | 1,520 | 1,500 | 1,360 | 1,250 | 1,560 | 1,520 | 1,600 | 1,620 |
| **Market prices** (*a ton*) | | | | | | | | |
| Medium[2] | 1,740 | 1,300 | 900 | 1,280 | 1,780 | 1,320 | 1,060 | 1,650 |
| Long Staple[3] | 3,520 | 3,560 | 2,980 | 2,830 | 3,610 | 3,620 | 3,490 | 3,660 |

Sources: UN Food and Agriculture Organization, *1986 FAO Trade Yearbook* (Rome) for exports; Commodities Division, IMF Research Department for market prices.

[1] Data on exports are estimates of Commodities Division, IMF Research Department.
[2] Liverpool Index A, c.i.f. Liverpool.
[3] Egyptian, c.i.f. Liverpool.

in the U.S.S.R. and China increased sharply. In 1986, usage increased by 4.5 percent to reach a record 1.72 million tons of clean wool with nearly 70 percent of this increase being accounted for by China. Import demand from Japan, the third largest wool consumer in the world, also increased very sharply following the rapid appreciation of the yen. Over the 12 months to June 1987, Japan accounted for 18 percent of Australia's wool export earnings followed by the U.S.S.R. and China (each 12 percent).

Raw wool exports from the five major surplus producing countries of the Southern Hemisphere (Argentina, Australia, New Zealand, South Africa, and Uruguay), which had reached a 13-year high in 1985/86, accelerated in the first three quarters of 1986/87. The combined total export volume for these five countries, which together account for over 85 percent of the world's raw wool exports, increased by 9 percent to over 630,000 tons of raw fiber in the nine months to March, compared with the corresponding period of 1985/86. Export earnings increased even more sharply owing to higher prices; Australia's earnings from wool exports in the year to June 1987 rose by over 25 percent.

The excess of consumption demand relative to production that developed as the 1986/87 season progressed enabled wool marketing authorities in the main wool growing and exporting countries of the Southern

Hemisphere to dispose of a large part of stocks previously accumulated in the course of their market support operations. Stocks carried forward into 1987/88 are estimated at 88,000 tons of clean wool, about one half the level one year earlier and the lowest recorded since the early 1970s. At current levels of consumption, this represents only one month's requirements by the main importing countries. Stocks in the main producing countries are now negligible for many of the main categories of wool so that further demand will have to be met almost exclusively from new clip supplies. The largest reduction in carryover stocks was in Australia, where the depreciation of the Australian dollar against the currencies of most major wool using countries and increased purchases by the three major consumers, helped to keep Australian wools in demand. Thus, by the end of July 1987, the size of the Australian stockpile, the major component of world stocks, had been reduced from the 1986/87 opening level of nearly 80,000 tons to a five-year low of 38,000 tons. At the same time, there were only 4,000 tons left in the New Zealand stockpile as against 15,000 tons a year earlier.

## Jute

The price of jute in recent years has fluctuated over an even wider range than is customary for this commodity. In late 1984 and early 1985 the price in U.S. dollars rose to a record level—in excess of $800 a ton.[74] By the fourth quarter of 1986 the price had fallen to only $234 a ton, the lowest level since 1964. From the fourth quarter of 1986 to the fourth quarter of 1987 the dollar price increased by almost 50 percent—to $359 a ton, although the increase in SDR terms was much less (38 percent).

The cause of these wide fluctuations has been large year-to-year changes in production coupled with a very low short-term price elasticity of demand. The major factor triggering these fluctuations was the exceptionally low 1983/84 crops in Bangladesh and India, which were caused by drought in the planting season and severe flooding in the harvest season. The 1984/85 world crop, although 8 percent higher than that of the previous year, was still 10 percent below the average for the period 1978/79–80/81. Thus, following an increase of over 70 percent in 1984, prices rose by a further 10 percent in 1985 to an all-time high. High prices encouraged larger plantings and the 1985/86 world crop was a record 6.4 million tons. This in turn led to a sharp fall in prices in the second quarter of 1986.

Although the record crop in 1985/86 led to the replenishment of depleted stocks and to an increase in exports, supplies remained well in excess of requirements. Stocks at the beginning of the 1986/87 season in the five major producing countries, Bangladesh, Burma, India, Nepal, and Thailand, amounted to a record 1.6 million tons, more than three times the level at the beginning of the previous season. In 1986/87 there was a sharp drop in world production of jute, but owing to the large stock carryover from the previous season, the supply was ample throughout the season. World production of jute dropped by about 40 percent in 1986/87 to some 3.8 million tons owing mainly to reduced plantings in response to depressed prices of jute relative to those of alternative crops. Production in India, the largest supplier, fell to about 1.3 million tons and the crop in China was estimated to have declined to 1.0 million tons in 1986/87 compared with the peak level of 1.7 million tons in the previous year. Output in Bangladesh also dropped by nearly 38 percent from a peak level of 1.5 million tons in the previous season.

World exports of jute have reflected to some extent the movements in production and prices. Following the price rise in 1984, world exports fell to a record low of 390,000 metric tons. There was an increase in 1985 of 5 percent, and in 1986 world exports rose further to 484,000 tons, an increase of 18 percent over the previous year. This was, however, still below the average over 1980–82 of 550,000 tons and reflects an underlying trend of substitution away from jute and toward synthetics (primarily polypropylene). The competition with synthetics is particularly acute in industrial countries, whose share of world jute imports fell from 50 percent in the early 1980s to under 37 percent in 1985. This share recovered to 39 percent during 1986 following an improvement in the competitive position of jute relative to polypropylene. Although the sharp drop in the price of crude oil in 1986 was accompanied by an equally sharp fall in the price of several petroleum products, given the buoyant demand for polypropylene, its prices fell by less than 3 percent. During the same period jute prices fell by nearly 50 percent. Although jute prices rose in 1987, those of polypropylene advanced even more rapidly so that jute's competitive position has been maintained.

The increase in jute prices followed adverse weather conditions in a number of areas in the second quarter of 1987 and flooding in Bangladesh in August, with prices rising sharply from May to August. Given the low average prices prevailing in the 1986/87 season, however, farmers are expected to have shifted away from jute to alternative crops. As a result, the 1987/88 crop is likely to be even smaller than the 1986/87 crop. Despite the adverse weather, given the high level of stocks, a further substantial rise in prices in the short run is unlikely. As existing stocks are gradually reduced, however, expectations of lower output will start to exercise an upward influence on prices. The decision by the Government of Bangladesh to maintain buffer stocks in 1987/88 to balance supply and demand for jute in the local and world markets is also likely to contribute to stabilization.

## Sisal

The price of sisal declined by about 2 percent in 1986 following a decline of over 10 percent in 1985.[75] The earlier decline was the result of a fall in demand and a considerable accumulation of stocks in early 1985. Preliminary estimates for 1986 indicate a reduction in output of some 4 percent after it had recovered from its 1983 low to 430,000 tons by 1985. The recovery was entirely attributable to a sharp increase in the production of Brazilian sisal, which more than offset lower fiber production in all other major producing countries.

In 1987 further reductions in production are estimated for almost all producing countries. The lower

---

[74] Price quotations refer to raw Bangladesh jute, BWD, f.o.b. Chittagong or Chalna.

[75] The price refers to East African sisal, ungraded, c.i.f. European ports.

production is largely the result of unremunerative prices that led to lower replantings, but, in some cases, shortages of production inputs and shipping facilities were also contributing factors. Brazilian output for domestic spinning or export declined with continuing efforts to limit supplies in line with the downward trend in foreign demand and requirements of the local mills. Only in Tanzania is output, after declining over several seasons, estimated to have recovered somewhat, as a result of a rehabilitation program implemented during recent years. In order to reduce dependence on the international market, governments of producing countries continued to promote domestic consumption of sisal products, mainly bags, cordage, twines for nonagricultural uses, and paper pulp. Despite the large carryover stocks, these efforts, combined with an expected fall in output, suggest that prices are likely to remain steady in 1988.

## Hides

After falling by 13 percent in 1985 to an average of 51 U.S. cents a pound, the price of hides rebounded by 25 percent in 1986 to a record 64 cents a pound.[76] Although there was a substantial increase in supply of hides from the United States, partly as a result of the dairy termination program,[77] world supply increased only slightly. Increased slaughterings in Australia, the EC, the United States, and the U.S.S.R. exceeded by

a small margin reduced slaughtering in Brazil and Eastern Europe. The U.S.S.R. became self sufficient in the production of hides and exported a small amount to Italy and Eastern Europe. This added to the supply available from higher EC slaughter, and along with the stagnation of the European leather industry in the face of Far Eastern competition, led to a decline in the price of hides in most European countries in 1986.

Weak demand in Europe was outweighed by higher demand from Japan, the Republic of Korea, and Taiwan Province of China. The demand for hides is derived from the demand for footwear and leather goods. Assisted by favorable exchange rates and low labor cost, Korea and Taiwan Province of China were able to increase substantially their global market share of these products at the expense of European producers in 1986. Japanese leather output is mostly consumed domestically, and Japanese demand for both leather and hides rose in response to higher disposable income.

The price of United States' hides remained fairly stable in the final quarter of 1986 and the first quarter of 1987 at about 65 cents a pound, but then increased sharply in April (by 18 percent) and remained high, averaging 85 cents a pound in the third quarter of 1987.

Although the global supply of hides is estimated to have been virtually unchanged in 1987, the supply in the United States contracted sharply, and the surge in prices in April reflected continued strong export demand (assisted by the depreciation of the U.S. dollar) and the anticipated completion of the dairy termination program by the end of the second quarter of the year. A lower global supply of hides owing to herd rebuilding in countries other than the U.S.S.R. suggests that prices should remain firm in 1988 if, as expected, demand remains reasonably strong.

---

[76] Price quotations refer to the U.S. wholesale price for hides of packer's heavy native steers, over 53 pounds, f.o.b. shipping point Chicago.

[77] See the discussion on beef in Section II.

# V

# Minerals and Metals

Prices of many minerals and metals rebounded sharply in 1987 (Chart 7). From the fourth quarter of 1986 to the fourth quarter of 1987, the price of copper in terms of SDRs increased by 67 percent, that of nickel by 60 percent, aluminum by 44 percent, and lead by 20 percent (Table 56). When measured in terms of U.S. dollars, these price increases were even greater. The large price rises were associated with exceptionally low stock levels: by 1987 stocks of these metals had been reduced to such low levels that any supply interruption or unexpected strength in consumption was quickly reflected in higher prices. By comparison, the changes in the prices of iron ore, tin, and zinc were small, while a substantial drop—nearly 20 percent in SDRs—occurred in the price of phosphate rock.

The low stock situation that prevailed in 1987 in the markets for most metals and minerals developed in response to the depressed demand and price situation of the early and mid-1980s. Activity in metals-using sectors in the major industrial countries declined progressively each year in the early 1980s. An index of production aggregated for these sectors in the seven major industrial countries shows a decline of 2.6 percent, 2.5 percent, and 2.3 percent for 1980, 1981, and 1982, respectively (Table 57). These declines were more than matched by decreases in the consumption of metals over this period. Although by 1981 world production of metals also began to decline and declined by a large amount in 1982, world production continued to exceed world consumption, leading to an increase of stocks of nearly 50 percent over the three-year period. As a consequence of these developments, in 1982 the index of prices of minerals and metals had fallen 12 percent below its level in 1980 in terms of SDRs and was 25 percent lower in dollars.

Following the buildup of metals stocks from 1980 through 1982, there was a steady reduction from 1983 through 1987. Changes in production policies, lower desired inventory levels, and economic expansion leading to increases in metals consumption all contributed to this turnaround. Because of the extended period of low prices, many companies closed unprofitable operations and dramatically reduced costs at others. As a result, beginning about 1983 and lasting into 1987, there was a fairly continuous period of mine closures. In addition to making reductions in wages of their employees, many mining companies dramatically cut the size of their labor force, including significant reductions in the number of layers of management. The streamlining of operations served to reduce costs worldwide. Consumers of metals, on their part, adapted to the stock buildup and falling prices of the early 1980s by pursuing minimum inventory policies for metals and purchasing materials only when needed for immediate use. Following the declines in 1980–82, world consumption of metals increased by 3.5 percent in 1983 and by nearly 6 percent in 1984. In 1983 there were particularly large increases in many industrial countries in the output of the metals using sectors, including increases in automobile production and in housing starts. In 1984 exceptionally large increases

**Chart 7. Prices of Minerals and Metals, 1980–87**

(In SDRs; indices: 1980 = 100)

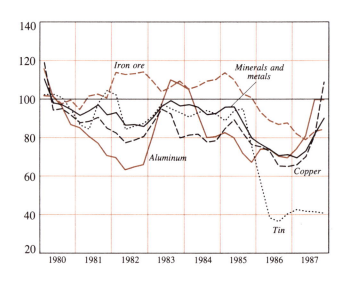

**Table 56. Prices of Minerals and Metals, 1979–88**

| Years | Index of Prices of Minerals and Metals[1] | Copper[2] | Aluminum[3] | Tin[4] | Nickel[5] | Zinc[6] | Lead[7] | Iron Ore[8] | Steel[9] | Phosphate Rock[10] |
|---|---|---|---|---|---|---|---|---|---|---|
| | *(1980 = 100)* | | *(In SDR 0.01 a pound)* | | | | | | *(In SDRs a ton)* | |
| 1979 | 92.0 | 69.3 | 56.3 | 542 | 210 | 26.0 | 42.2 | 18.1 | 285 | 25.5 |
| 1980 | 100.0 | 76.2 | 61.9 | 585 | 227 | 26.5 | 31.6 | 20.9 | 295 | 35.9 |
| 1981 | 93.6 | 67.0 | 48.6 | 545 | 229 | 32.5 | 27.9 | 20.9 | 304 | 42.0 |
| 1982 | 88.1 | 60.9 | 40.7 | 527 | 199 | 30.6 | 22.4 | 23.7 | 320 | 38.4 |
| 1983 | 95.6 | 67.6 | 61.0 | 551 | 198 | 32.4 | 18.0 | 22.4 | 294 | 34.5 |
| 1984 | 94.4 | 60.9 | 55.4 | 541 | 210 | 40.8 | 19.6 | 22.5 | 307 | 37.3 |
| 1985 | 89.9 | 63.3 | 46.5 | 515 | 219 | 35.0 | 17.5 | 22.3 | 273 | 33.4 |
| 1986 | 73.1 | 53.0 | 44.5 | 251 | 150 | 29.2 | 15.7 | 18.7 | 264 | 29.2 |
| 1987 | 78.7 | 62.1 | 54.9 | 244 | 171 | 28.0 | 20.9 | 17.2 | 292 | 24.0 |
| 1986 I | 76.6 | 57.3 | 45.8 | 332 | 163 | 25.2 | 14.8 | 19.5 | 258 | 29.8 |
| II | 73.9 | 55.5 | 45.7 | 225 | 159 | 28.3 | 15.2 | 18.6 | 277 | 29.6 |
| III | 70.7 | 49.7 | 43.5 | 213 | 144 | 31.3 | 14.8 | 18.2 | 260 | 28.9 |
| IV | 71.2 | 49.5 | 42.9 | 237 | 136 | 31.4 | 17.9 | 18.4 | 263 | 28.9 |
| 1987 I | 69.5 | 50.2 | 45.8 | 250 | 132 | 26.8 | 16.9 | 17.2 | 251 | 24.6 |
| II | 73.2 | 53.4 | 50.0 | 245 | 149 | 28.9 | 21.9 | 16.5 | 280 | 24.0 |
| III | 82.2 | 62.3 | 61.7 | 243 | 182 | 28.3 | 23.3 | 17.4 | 319 | 24.3 |
| IV | 90.0 | 82.8 | 61.6 | 238 | 217 | 28.0 | 21.4 | 17.7 | 320 | 23.1 |
| 1988 I | 98.9 | 81.2 | 73.7 | 232 | 356 | 30.2 | 21.8 | 17.5 | 336 | 22.7 |
| | *(1980 = 100)* | | *(In U.S. cents a pound)* | | | | | | *(In US dollars a ton)* | |
| 1979 | 91.3 | 89.5 | 72.7 | 701 | 271 | 33.6 | 54.6 | 23.4 | 368 | 33.0 |
| 1980 | 100.0 | 99.1 | 80.5 | 761 | 296 | 34.5 | 41.1 | 27.2 | 384 | 46.7 |
| 1981 | 84.8 | 79.1 | 57.3 | 643 | 270 | 38.4 | 32.9 | 24.6 | 358 | 49.5 |
| 1982 | 74.8 | 67.2 | 45.0 | 582 | 219 | 33.8 | 24.8 | 26.2 | 354 | 42.4 |
| 1983 | 78.5 | 72.2 | 65.2 | 589 | 212 | 34.7 | 19.3 | 24.0 | 315 | 36.9 |
| 1984 | 74.4 | 62.5 | 56.8 | 555 | 216 | 41.8 | 20.0 | 23.1 | 314 | 38.3 |
| 1985 | 70.0 | 64.3 | 47.2 | 523 | 222 | 35.5 | 17.7 | 22.7 | 277 | 33.9 |
| 1986 | 65.9 | 62.1 | 52.1 | 294 | 176 | 34.2 | 18.4 | 21.9 | 310 | 34.3 |
| 1987 | 78.4 | 80.8 | 71.0 | 316 | 221 | 36.2 | 27.1 | 22.2 | 379 | 31.0 |
| 1986 I | 66.2 | 64.5 | 51.5 | 374 | 184 | 28.4 | 16.6 | 22.0 | 290 | 33.5 |
| II | 66.0 | 64.5 | 53.1 | 261 | 185 | 32.8 | 17.6 | 21.6 | 322 | 34.4 |
| III | 65.4 | 59.8 | 52.3 | 256 | 173 | 37.7 | 17.8 | 21.9 | 313 | 34.8 |
| IV | 66.0 | 59.7 | 51.8 | 286 | 164 | 37.9 | 21.5 | 22.1 | 317 | 34.8 |
| 1987 I | 67.3 | 63.3 | 57.8 | 316 | 167 | 33.7 | 21.3 | 21.6 | 317 | 34.8 |
| II | 72.8 | 69.2 | 64.8 | 317 | 193 | 37.4 | 28.4 | 21.4 | 363 | 31.0 |
| III | 80.6 | 79.5 | 78.8 | 310 | 233 | 36.1 | 29.8 | 22.2 | 407 | 31.0 |
| IV | 92.9 | 111.2 | 82.6 | 320 | 292 | 37.5 | 28.7 | 23.7 | 430 | 31.0 |
| 1988 I | 103.9 | 111.1 | 100.8 | 318 | 487 | 41.3 | 29.8 | 24.0 | 460 | 31.0 |

Source: Commodities Division, IMF Research Department.

[1] The weights in the index are as follows: copper, 26 percent; aluminum, 20 percent; iron ore, 19 percent; tin, 10 percent; nickel, 8 percent; zinc, 6 percent; lead, 5 percent; and phosphate rock, 6 percent.
[2] London Metal Exchange (LME) price, c.i.f. U.K. ports.
[3] LME price, c.i.f. European ports.
[4] LME price, c.i.f. European ports.
[5] LME price, c.i.f. Northwest European ports.
[6] LME price, c.i.f. U.K. ports.
[7] LME price, c.i.f. U.K. ports.
[8] Brazilian ore, c.i.f. German ports.
[9] Cold rolled coil, price for export, f.o.b. European Coal and Steel Community mills.
[10] Moroccan rock, f.a.s. Casablanca.

in industrial production and in domestic fixed investment were recorded in these countries. Despite this activity, the overhang of large stocks and the persistence of excess production capacity meant that prices of minerals and metals increased by only a small amount in 1983–84. With the lower rates of economic growth in 1985–86 and despite much reduced stock levels, prices of most minerals and metals fell below even the 1982 trough.

The weakness in the prices of minerals and metals

**Table 57.  Movements in Prices of Minerals and Metals and Related Economic Indicators, 1980–87**

(Annual percentage changes)

|  | 1980 | 1981 | 1982 | 1983 | 1984 | 1985 | 1986 | 1987 |
|---|---|---|---|---|---|---|---|---|
| Prices of minerals and metals[1] |  |  |  |  |  |  |  |  |
| In SDRs | 8.7 | − 6.4 | − 5.9 | 8.5 | − 1.3 | − 4.8 | − 18.7 | 7.7 |
| In U.S. dollars | 9.5 | − 15.2 | − 11.8 | 4.9 | − 5.2 | − 5.9 | − 5.9 | 19.0 |
| Real[2] | − 0.5 | − 11.8 | − 10.0 | 8.1 | − 2.4 | − 6.5 | − 20.5 | 5.9 |
| Unit value of manufactured exports |  |  |  |  |  |  |  |  |
| In SDRs | 9.6 | 6.0 | 4.5 | 0.4 | 1.2 | 2.1 | 2.1 | 1.7 |
| In U.S. dollars | 10.4 | − 3.9 | − 2.1 | − 2.8 | − 3.0 | 1.1 | 18.0 | 12.0 |
| GNP deflator in seven industrial countries |  |  |  |  |  |  |  |  |
| In SDRs | 8.8 | 11.9 | 6.5 | 5.1 | 4.0 | 3.1 | 2.1 | 0.3 |
| In U.S. dollars | 9.6 | 1.4 | − 0.3 | 1.8 | − 0.2 | 2.2 | 18.0 | 10.6 |
| Economic activity in seven industrial countries |  |  |  |  |  |  |  |  |
| Real GNP | 1.2 | 1.7 | − 0.5 | 2.8 | 5.2 | 3.2 | 2.8 | 3.1 |
| Industrial production | − 0.2 | 0.6 | − 3.8 | 3.8 | 8.5 | 2.8 | 1.0 | 3.3 |
| Domestic fixed investment | − 2.2 | − 0.2 | − 5.2 | 3.9 | 9.6 | 4.5 | 2.8 | 3.3 |
| Housing starts | − 10.5 | − 9.8 | − 2.4 | 26.4 | − 0.9 | − 1.3 | 4.9 | − 0.9 |
| Automobile production | − 17.0 | − 7.4 | 1.0 | 5.7 | − 1.7 | 5.1 | 3.7 | − 0.2 |
| Index of production in metals-using sectors[3] | − 2.6 | − 2.5 | − 2.3 | 7.1 | 4.8 | 3.2 | 2.3 | 1.0 |
| World consumption of metals[4] |  |  |  |  |  |  |  |  |
| Index of consumption | − 3.6 | − 1.9 | − 3.5 | 3.5 | 5.8 | − 1.0 | 3.7 | 1.9 |
| World supply of minerals and metals[4] |  |  |  |  |  |  |  |  |
| Index of production | 1.3 | − 0.9 | − 6.5 | 1.2 | 5.4 | 1.1 | − 0.2 | 1.9 |
| Index of supply[5] | − 1.8 | − 0.3 | − 3.4 | 5.1 | 4.8 | − 0.8 | − 1.1 | − 0.5 |
| Index of closing stocks | 5.0 | 16.6 | 20.0 | − 1.2 | − 11.7 | − 7.1 | − 13.3 | − 16.0 |

Sources: Commodities Division and Current Studies Division, IMF Research Department.

[1] Refers to IMF world index of prices of minerals and metals. These percentages differ from those reported in the *World Economic Outlook* which refer to the index of commodities *exported by developing countries*.

[2] Index of dollar prices of minerals and metals deflated by the index of dollar unit values of manufactured exports.

[3] Production in metals-using sectors of the seven industrial countries weighted in accordance with metals consumption in each sector.

[4] Overall indices constructed using the same weights for the indices of individual commodities as in overall (world) price index. The commodity coverage of the indices of consumption and stocks is less comprehensive (includes only metals) than the coverage of the indices of production and supply (includes iron ore and phosphate rock).

[5] Supply is defined as production plus *beginning*-of-year stocks.

in the mid-1980s, notwithstanding large reductions in stocks, can be explained by the perception that excess productive capacity existed and that additional supplies would be readily available. Toward the end of the first quarter of 1987, however, this perception was tested when relatively minor supply disruptions led to increased prices for both copper and aluminum. As consumers bid for additional supplies—which came from already low stocks rather than from additional production—the fundamentally tight situation became evident. The tightness in the near-term market for these two metals was evidenced by the fact that for most of 1987 spot prices were significantly above the futures prices. The psychology in many of the metals markets quickly shifted from one of perceived excess capacity and desired inventory decumulation to one of market tightness and desired inventory buildup. The

situation was accentuated by stronger-than-expected growth in consumption of metals in 1987 in the United States, in Japan, and in the newly industrializing countries of Asia, although the overall rate of growth of world consumption was only moderate.

At the end of 1987, reported commercial stocks measured in terms of weeks of consumption were extremely low (Table 58). Copper stocks were even lower than in the period of tight supplies during 1973–74 when copper prices rose from roughly 50 cents a pound to 130 cents a pound and then fell to 60 cents. Expressed in terms of weeks of consumption, reported commercial stocks of copper at the end of 1987 were roughly 30 percent below the low level at the end of 1973. Similarly, aluminum stocks during 1987 were at a level comparable to the low level at the end of 1979. Aluminum prices increased from 64 cents per pound

## Table 58. Reported Closing World Commercial Stocks of Selected Metals, 1973–87

(Weeks of consumption)[1]

|      | Copper | Aluminum | Tin  | Nickel | Zinc | Lead |
|------|--------|----------|------|--------|------|------|
| 1973 | 4.0    | 7.5      | 3.5  | . . .  | 6.1  | 6.4  |
| 1974 | 6.5    | 7.5      | 3.3  | . . .  | 6.2  | 5.3  |
| 1975 | 12.2   | 14.3     | 4.3  | 15.4   | 10.6 | 6.4  |
| 1976 | 11.1   | 8.6      | 3.3  | 13.9   | 9.0  | 4.8  |
| 1977 | 11.3   | 9.0      | 3.4  | 16.4   | 9.4  | 4.4  |
| 1978 | 8.4    | 7.0      | 2.1  | 10.6   | 5.6  | 3.6  |
| 1979 | 5.8    | 4.9      | 1.9  | 5.3    | 6.5  | 4.1  |
| 1980 | 5.7    | 7.1      | 3.1  | 14.4   | 6.0  | 4.9  |
| 1981 | 6.2    | 11.7     | 4.7  | 17.1   | 7.1  | 4.8  |
| 1982 | 9.4    | 11.7     | 13.7 | 16.1   | 6.6  | 5.3  |
| 1983 | 9.7    | 7.6      | 15.1 | 13.8   | 5.1  | 5.1  |
| 1984 | 6.3    | 9.1      | 11.1 | 9.7    | 4.7  | 3.9  |
| 1985 | 5.6    | 7.9      | 16.8 | 8.6    | 4.4  | 4.3  |
| 1986 | 4.5    | 6.2      | 12.8 | 8.5    | 4.5  | 3.7  |
| 1987 | 2.7    | 4.6      | 9.3  | 7.0    | 4.6  | 2.7  |

Sources: Based on data on stocks in *World Metal Statistics* (London: World Bureau of Metal Statistics), various issues, 1975–87.

[1] Calculated in relation to consumption in year closing.

in December 1978 to 97 cents a pound February 1980 and then progressively fell to 65 cents by December 1980. Stocks of zinc and lead at the end of 1987 were also at low levels, below those in either 1973–74 or 1979.

The rebounding of metals prices in 1987 should be seen as a response to the closure of some of the excess capacity that had been overhanging the market and a means for stock correction rather than as a signal of longer-term higher prices. The factors that were of concern on the demand side throughout the 1980s, namely "downsizing," particularly of automobiles, and "miniaturization," particularly with reference to electronics, continued to be relevant. Technological changes resulting in the use of a lower quantity of metals per unit of output and the use of plastics and other materials as substitutes for metals did not abate. Consequently, while the economic environment continues to be one of only modest overall economic growth, the growth in metals consumption is likely to continue to be even lower.

The supply side adjustments made in the industry in response to the lower prices of the early and mid-1980s can be expected to have a significant impact on the price outlook for minerals and metals. With the closure of high-cost facilities and the initiation of new investment in only low-cost projects, many mining companies have made adjustments in their operations that could enable them to continue to operate at the low prices prevailing in 1986. Having positioned themselves to survive at 1986 prices, these companies earned substantial profits in the higher price environ-

ment of 1987. It would appear that the trough in prices for most minerals and metals was indeed reached in 1986 as a considerable part of the excess capacity that was evident in the early 1980s has remained closed and the reopening of these facilities would require major new investment. Barring a recession, therefore, it is unlikely that prices will fall again to 1986 levels in the near future. Prices are likely to fall from late-1987 levels, however, as the production response to these prices materializes.

## Copper

Following an extended period of depressed prices from 1982 through 1986, copper prices increased dramatically in 1987. In the fourth quarter of 1987 the dollar price averaged 111 cents a pound, nearly twice the price for the comparable quarter a year earlier.[78] During December 1987 the price of copper rose as high as 145 cents a pound, although the price fell back to average 111 cents a pound in the first quarter of 1988.

Despite the strong growth in world copper consumption in 1986, of about 5 percent, and a continued voluntary reduction in inventories that brought copper stocks to very low levels, the price of copper began to increase only about the middle of 1987. While stocks at the end of 1986 were at levels comparable to those during previous periods of shortage, such as 1973 and 1980 (Table 58), prices did not respond because the market apparently considered the new low levels as adequate. Copper prices had been virtually unchanged since 1984 and most consumers of copper did not feel the need to lock in supplies at low prices. The change in mid-1987 was triggered by strikes in Canada and Peru, production problems in Chile, and transportation problems in Zambia. Spot prices began to increase sharply, and as futures market prices remained well below spot prices, incentives were clearly directed toward rapidly bringing additional supplies on to the market. The added supplies, however, were modest and could not keep pace with the growth in demand. After the lengthy period of low copper prices and mine closures, producers were reluctant to reopen properties because of uncertainty regarding the overall economic outlook and the expense and lengthy gestation period involved. Nevertheless, with copper prices at the end of 1987 over two times the estimated average operating cost of production for many companies, eventual production increases are likely to cause prices to decline.

[78] Price quotations refer to prices on the London Metal Exchange (LME), cash for delivery on the following business day, higher grade cathodes, minimum purity 99.9 percent, c.i.f. U.K. ports.

**Table 59.   Copper: World Commodity Balance, 1981–87**

(In thousands of tons)

| | 1981 | 1982 | 1983 | 1984 | 1985 | 1986 | 1987[1] |
|---|---|---|---|---|---|---|---|
| **Mine production**[2] | **8,160** | **8,040** | **8,110** | **8,270** | **8,390** | **8,460** | **8,690** |
| Canada | 690 | 610 | 650 | 720 | 740 | 770 | 780 |
| Chile | 1,080 | 1,240 | 1,260 | 1,290 | 1,360 | 1,400 | 1,390 |
| United States | 1,540 | 1,150 | 1,040 | 1,100 | 1,100 | 1,150 | 1,250 |
| Zaïre | 510 | 500 | 500 | 500 | 500 | 500 | 500 |
| Zambia | 590 | 530 | 590 | 580 | 510 | 490 | 480 |
| U.S.S.R. | 1,000 | 1,010 | 1,020 | 1,020 | 1,030 | 1,030 | 1,030 |
| China | 180 | 190 | 180 | 190 | 200 | 210 | 210 |
| Other countries | 2,570 | 2,810 | 2,870 | 2,870 | 2,940 | 2,910 | 3,050 |
| **Refined production**[2] | **9,560** | **9,430** | **9,660** | **9,540** | **9,700** | **9,840** | **10,000** |
| Chile | 780 | 850 | 830 | 880 | 880 | 940 | 960 |
| Japan | 1,050 | 1,080 | 1,090 | 940 | 940 | 940 | 990 |
| United States | 2,000 | 1,690 | 1,580 | 1,490 | 1,440 | 1,480 | 1,550 |
| Canada | 480 | 340 | 460 | 500 | 500 | 490 | 480 |
| Zaïre | 150 | 170 | 230 | 220 | 230 | 220 | 220 |
| Zambia | 560 | 590 | 570 | 520 | 510 | 490 | 520 |
| China | 320 | 330 | 340 | 360 | 360 | 360 | 360 |
| U.S.S.R. | 1,320 | 1,350 | 1,400 | 1,380 | 1,400 | 1,400 | 1,400 |
| Other countries | 2,900 | 3,030 | 3,160 | 3,250 | 3,440 | 3,520 | 3,520 |
| **Refined consumption** | **9,530** | **9,030** | **9,140** | **9,920** | **9,640** | **10,080** | **10,290** |
| Germany, Fed. Rep. of | 750 | 730 | 740 | 790 | 750 | 770 | 770 |
| Japan | 1,250 | 1,240 | 1,220 | 1,370 | 1,230 | 1,220 | 1,250 |
| Other Asia | 380 | 360 | 460 | 540 | 560 | 690 | 730 |
| United States | 2,030 | 1,660 | 1,810 | 2,120 | 1,910 | 2,090 | 2,190 |
| China | 390 | 400 | 400 | 410 | 450 | 470 | 470 |
| U.S.S.R. | 1,320 | 1,320 | 1,320 | 1,280 | 1,310 | 1,300 | 1,300 |
| Other countries | 3,410 | 3,320 | 3,190 | 3,410 | 3,430 | 3,540 | 3,580 |
| **Market balance**[3] | **30** | **400** | **520** | **−380** | **60** | **−240** | **−290** |
| **Closing stocks of refined copper**[2,4] | **1,130** | **1,640** | **1,710** | **1,190** | **1,030** | **870** | **540** |
| United States | 520 | 760 | 730 | 590 | 360 | 320 | 160 |
| COMEX | 170 | 250 | 370 | 250 | 110 | 80 | 30 |
| Other U.S. stocks | 350 | 510 | 360 | 340 | 250 | 240 | 130 |
| Other countries | 620 | 880 | 980 | 600 | 670 | 550 | 380 |
| London Metal Exchange | 130 | 250 | 440 | 120 | 190 | 170 | 90 |
| Other country stocks | 490 | 630 | 540 | 480 | 480 | 380 | 290 |
| Stocks/consumption ratio (number of weeks)[5] | 6.2 | 9.4 | 9.7 | 6.3 | 5.6 | 4.5 | 2.7 |

Sources: *World Metal Statistics* (London: World Bureau of Metal Statistics), various issues in 1987, and *CRU Metal Monitor: Copper* (London: Commodities Research Unit Ltd.), December 1987.

[1] Estimated by Commodities Division, IMF Research Department.
[2] Excludes China and Council for Mutual Economic Assistance (CMEA) countries.
[3] World production minus world consumption.
[4] May not agree with production and consumption data because of differences in coverage.
[5] Total commercial stocks reported in terms of weeks of world consumption.

A 5 percent increase in world refined copper consumption in 1986 followed a four-year period over which the total increase was only 1 percent (Table 59). The increase in 1986 occurred primarily because of rapid growth of consumption in the United States, China, and in the newly industrializing countries of Asia. Copper consumption in the United States has continued to exhibit a high degree of variability, increasing by 9 percent in 1986 after declining by 10 percent in 1985.[79] One of the major factors influencing the strength of U.S. copper consumption in 1986 was housing construction. The number of housing starts

percent in 1986. These variations can only partly be explained by movements in production in the copper-consuming sectors. The decline in consumption in 1982 was over twice the decline in output of copper consuming sectors. In 1983, with activity in the copper consuming sectors increasing by an average of almost 20 percent, reflecting in large part an increase in housing construction and automotive sales, copper consumption increased by only 9 percent. In 1984, however, consumption increased by 17 percent in response to an activity increase of only 10 percent in the copper consuming sectors. The decline in consumption of 10 percent in 1985 was associated with a 2.5 percent increase in activity, whereas in 1986 an increase in overall economic activity in the copper-consuming sectors of only 1 percent was associated with a 9 percent increase in consumption.

[79] After falling by 18 percent in 1982, U.S. copper consumption grew by 9 percent in 1983 and by another 17 percent in 1984, only to decline by 10 percent in 1985, and then rise by approximately 9

increased by almost 4 percent during 1986. Capital investment in infrastructure and modernization of existing plants led to rapid growth in metal consumption in China in 1986. An 18 percent increase in industrial production in China in 1985 contributed to an increase of 10 percent in copper consumption in the year. In 1986 copper consumption in China increased by 4 percent, in part reflecting a very large increase of 8 percent estimated for its gross national product. In 1986 copper consumption grew by about 23 percent in the newly industrializing countries of Asia. This dramatic increase was the result in part of a significant rise in consumption in both the Republic of Korea and Taiwan Province of China. Copper consumption in the Republic of Korea increased by 25 percent because of an export boom. In Taiwan Province of China, following a sharp reduction in 1985, consumption rose by over 50 percent, although most of this increase represented a return to the 1984 level of copper consumption. In Japan, however, consumption declined by 1 percent in 1986, largely because of the impact of the strong yen on export sales of final products containing copper; this effect was partly offset by higher domestic demand, as the number of housing starts in Japan increased by almost 11 percent in 1986. In this period copper consumption in the U.S.S.R. was relatively stable; consumption increased by 2 percent in 1985 before declining by 1 percent in 1986.

In 1987 world copper consumption increased by a further 2 percent. U.S. copper consumption is estimated to have increased by almost 5 percent in 1987 because of a surge in activity in the manufacturing and business equipment sectors. Commercial construction and renovation activity, particularly in the third quarter, took up some of the slack in demand resulting from reduced housing starts. Increased activity in the investment sector was aided by moderate interest rates and depreciation of the dollar. The depreciation of the U.S. dollar enabled copper fabricators to regain domestic markets and be more competitive in export markets. Japanese consumption of copper is estimated to have increased by 2 percent in 1987, as the increase in domestic demand outweighed a weakening in export markets that was caused by a sharp appreciation in the yen. Housing starts in Japan in 1987 are estimated to be more than 20 percent higher than in 1986, or nearly double the 1986 rate of increase. Industrial activity, although weak overall, was strong in the sectors producing consumer goods. Copper consumption is estimated to have grown by approximately 3 percent in the rest of Asia, largely as a result of the strong export performance of the newly industrializing countries. European consumption growth was about 2 percent, with the strong consumption growth in France and Italy more than offsetting the weak growth in the Federal Republic of Germany and the United Kingdom.

Despite the lengthy period of low prices from 1982 through 1986, world mine production of copper rose, albeit at low rates. An increase of 3 percent in 1987 followed an increase of 1 percent in 1986. Growth in production in 1986 tended to occur in those countries in which there was a continuation of cost-cutting measures that had started in the early 1980s in response to low prices. These measures included the closure of high-cost mines, reduction in wages and overhead costs, and the introduction of low-cost methods of expanding production, such as leech and solvent extraction and electro-winning technology. In 1986 mine production increases of 4 percent in both Canada and the United States and of 3 percent in Chile more than offset decreases of 8 percent in Australia, 6 percent in South Africa, and 4 percent in Zambia. Zäire's production remained unchanged. The estimated increase of 3 percent in world mine production during 1987 was in large part attributable to mine expansions, such as those occurring in Chile (Chuquicamata, El Indio, and El Soldado) and Mexico (Cananea and La Caridad). In addition, the new Ok Tedi mine in Papua New Guinea and the reopening of the Bingham Canyon mine in the United States also contributed to the increased production during the year.

In 1986 the expansions that occurred in mine production were generally reflected in refined production as well. U.S. refined production, which grew by 3 percent, had been enhanced by an additional secondary recovery, and in Chile refined production grew by 7 percent. Mine production in Zäire and Zambia, however, suffered from stagnation or decline, which was reflected in the roughly 4 percent drop in refined production in both countries during 1986. In 1987 the upturn continued; refined production is estimated to have increased by approximately 2 percent. This was attributable to strong production growth in Australia (11 percent), Japan (5 percent), the United States (5 percent), and Zambia (6 percent). Higher prices and a depreciated dollar contributed to the increase in U.S. production. The rise in Zambian production was a result mainly of the improved availability of equipment which had been a serious constraint on production.

Low rates of increase in world production have combined with somewhat higher rates of world consumption since 1983 to reduce world copper inventories. In terms of weeks of world consumption, reported commercial stocks declined from 9.7 weeks at the end of 1983 to 2.7 weeks by the end of 1987. In 1987, therefore, the strong consumption demand, supply difficulties, and low overall stock levels reinforced each other to maintain a very tight copper market, particularly in the second half of the year.

**Table 60.   Copper: Export Earnings, 1984–87**

| | 1984 | 1985 | 1986[1] | 1987[1] | 1984 | 1985 | 1986[1] | 1987[1] |
|---|---|---|---|---|---|---|---|---|
| | *(Values in SDRs)* | | | | *(Values in U.S. dollars)* | | | |
| **Copper Ore** | | | | | | | | |
| **Earnings** (*in billions*) | **1.5** | **1.8** | **1.6** | **1.9** | **1.6** | **1.8** | **1.9** | **2.4** |
| Industrial countries | 0.5 | 0.6 | 0.6 | 0.7 | 0.5 | 0.6 | 0.7 | 0.9 |
| Developing countries | 1.0 | 1.2 | 1.0 | 1.2 | 1.1 | 1.2 | 1.2 | 1.5 |
| **Volumes** (*in thousands of tons*)[2] | **1,390** | **1,560** | **1,590** | **1,690** | **1,390** | **1,560** | **1,590** | **1,690** |
| Industrial countries | 520 | 580 | 650 | 680 | 520 | 580 | 650 | 680 |
| Developing countries | 870 | 980 | 940 | 1,010 | 870 | 980 | 940 | 1,010 |
| **Unit values** (*a ton*) | **1,120** | **1,130** | **1,000** | **1,100** | **1,150** | **1,150** | **1,170** | **1,430** |
| Industrial countries | 1,020 | 1,060 | 900 | 990 | 1,050 | 1,070 | 1,050 | 1,270 |
| Developing countries | 1,180 | 1,170 | 1,070 | 1,180 | 1,220 | 1,190 | 1,260 | 1,530 |
| **Refined Copper** | | | | | | | | |
| **Earnings** (*in billions*) | **4.4** | **4.4** | **3.9** | **4.7** | **4.5** | **4.5** | **4.6** | **6.1** |
| Industrial countries | 1.4 | 1.3 | 1.2 | 1.5 | 1.5 | 1.3 | 1.4 | 1.9 |
| Developing countries | 2.6 | 2.7 | 2.3 | 2.8 | 2.6 | 2.8 | 2.7 | 3.7 |
| U.S.S.R. and Eastern European countries | 0.4 | 0.4 | 0.4 | 0.4 | 0.4 | 0.4 | 0.5 | 0.5 |
| **Volumes** (*in thousands of tons*) | **3,280** | **3,280** | **3,320** | **3,640** | **3,280** | **3,280** | **3,320** | **3,640** |
| Industrial countries | 1,040 | 940 | 1,000 | 1,110 | 1,040 | 940 | 1,000 | 1,110 |
| Developing countries | 1,940 | 2,040 | 2,030 | 2,240 | 1,940 | 2,040 | 2,030 | 2,240 |
| *Chile* | *830* | *890* | *900* | *910* | *830* | *890* | *900* | *910* |
| *Peru* | *180* | *180* | *190* | *190* | *180* | *180* | *190* | *190* |
| *Zäire* | *220* | *230* | *220* | *220* | *220* | *230* | *220* | *220* |
| *Zambia* | *530* | *500* | *470* | *500* | *530* | *510* | *470* | *500* |
| *Others* | *180* | *240* | *230* | *390* | *180* | *240* | *230* | *390* |
| U.S.S.R. and Eastern European countries | 300 | 300 | 290 | 290 | 300 | 300 | 290 | 290 |
| **Unit values** (*a ton*) | **1,350** | **1,370** | **1,180** | **1,300** | **1,380** | **1,390** | **1,390** | **1,680** |
| Industrial countries | 1,380 | 1,410 | 1,210 | 1,320 | 1,420 | 1,430 | 1,420 | 1,710 |
| Developing countries | 1,330 | 1,340 | 1,130 | 1,250 | 1,360 | 1,360 | 1,330 | 1,650 |
| U.S.S.R. and Eastern European countries | 1,340 | 1,400 | 1,280 | 1,430 | 1,380 | 1,420 | 1,500 | 1,850 |
| **Market prices** (*a ton*)[3] | **1,340** | **1,400** | **1,170** | **1,380** | **1,380** | **1,420** | **1,370** | **1,780** |

Sources: UN Conference on Trade and Development (UNCTAD), *Yearbook of International Commodity Statistics, 1986* for exports; Commodities Division, IMF Research Department for market prices.

[1] Data on exports are estimates of Commodities Division, IMF Research Department.
[2] Copper content.
[3] London Metal Exchange, spot delivery, higher grade cathodes, c.i.f. U.K. ports.

Over the near term, the attempt to rebuild stocks and ease supply constraints production will be balanced by scheduled expansions in the Bingham mine in the United States and at the Ok Tedi mine in Papua New Guinea. Expansions at other mines in Canada and Mexico are also anticipated. As expected, the high prices that occurred toward the end of 1987 have had little depressing effect on consumption since the demand for copper is quite inelastic in the short term. The only recent evidence of an impact of high prices on consumption was a modest shifting away from copper as roofing material in Europe. These prices have not yet resulted in a large increase in production as producers will be reluctant to increase production unless they expect prices to remain high. The current high prices are not expected to last much longer, but

neither are they expected to return to the level of 60 cents a pound.

Earnings from exports of copper rose significantly in 1987 with increases in both unit values and volumes (Table 60). Earnings from exports of copper ore increased from 1.9 billion in 1986 to 2.4 billion dollars in 1987. While most of this growth is a result of a rise in unit values, the volume of exports is estimated to have increased by 6 percent, with developing countries responsible for most of the expansion. Refined copper exports, which are more important in international trade, are estimated to have risen in value from 4.6 billion U.S. dollars in 1986 to 6.1 billion in 1987. While most of the rise is attributable to higher unit values, export volumes also increased by almost 10 percent. The recovery in earnings from exports of copper ore and refined copper in 1987 in terms of SDRs, although lower than in terms of dollars, was nevertheless substantial: 19 percent for ore and 20 percent for refined copper. As in 1986, however, the increase in exports from developing countries was again limited by production and export difficulties, particularly in Chile, Peru, and Zambia. CODELCO, the largest producer in Chile, reported problems owing to weather and a lack of shipping capacity. Strikes and shutdowns also limited exports from Peru. Transportation problems played a key role in limiting Zambian exports.

## Aluminum

The price of aluminum increased sharply during 1987, rising from an average of 52 cents a pound in the fourth quarter of 1986 to 83 cents a pound in the fourth quarter of 1987.[80] The price in the latter part of 1987 and early 1988 was highly variable, rising to 97 cents in mid-October just prior to the stock market crash, then falling to 75 cents in November and rising again to an average of 101 cents in the first quarter of 1988.

The major factor behind the large increase in the price level was a drawdown in stocks. Reported commercial stocks of aluminum declined from the equivalent of roughly nine weeks of consumption at the end of 1984 to below five weeks at the end of 1987 (Table 61). The stock decline was largely the result of the closing of aluminum production capacity in Japan, the United States, and Europe in response to an extended period of low prices—in the 50 cent a pound range—at a time when world consumption continued to grow. World consumption rose by 2 percent in 1985, by over 3½ percent in 1986, and is estimated to have risen by roughly 3 percent in 1987. During 1987, with stocks already at low levels, stronger-than-expected demand led to a dramatic increase in prices as consumers attempted to bid for limited supplies.

In 1987 consumption in the major aluminum consuming countries, apart from the Federal Republic of Germany, grew at a significantly higher rate than the underlying rate of growth of production in the aluminum consuming sectors of these economies. Aluminum consumption is estimated to have risen by nearly 10 percent in Japan and by 7 percent in both the United States and Italy. Although overall manufacturing production in Japan did not show much growth in 1987, policies to stimulate domestic demand contributed to

strong demand for consumer goods and a very large increase in housing starts. Housing starts in 1987 were over 20 percent higher than in 1986. Growth in these sectors, which are important components of overall domestic demand, may have also stimulated capital spending by companies serving the domestic market. In the United States, overall manufacturing production and durable goods production each increased by roughly 4 percent, and consumer goods production increased by 3 percent. Housing starts, however, declined by almost 10 percent, and automobile production declined by about 6 percent. The 5 percent increase in consumption of aluminum was to some extent probably the result of an attempt by consumers to restock inventories through double ordering or other means, which increased demand only temporarily and which may not have been reflected in reported inventories. Increased aluminum consumption in Italy was associated with strong growth in the production of consumer goods and automobiles. An 8 percent drop in aluminum consumption in the Federal Republic of Germany can be explained by weak industrial growth and also by an 11 percent decline in housing starts in 1987.

In 1987 world production of bauxite grew by 3.6 percent, following a 2.6 percent increase in 1986. The largest increases were recorded by Brazil and Jamaica.[81] Bauxite production in Brazil increased by about 10 percent in each year. In Jamaica the 22 percent rise in bauxite production in 1987, following a 13 percent increase in 1986, reversed the declining trend in production experienced over the previous ten years. The increase in Jamaica was within the framework of a plan to restore bauxite products to 9 million tons and was facilitated by sharply lower energy costs associated with the decline in oil prices.

During the 1980s the production of aluminum has tended to become more concentrated in the bauxite producing countries, in particular in Australia, Brazil, Indonesia, and Venezuela. An increase in vertical integration from bauxite to aluminum production has produced substantial savings resulting from reduced transportation costs and use of cheaper local sources of labor and electric power. This trend has meant that the share of world production accounted for by the United States, Japan, and Europe has declined, although the share of Canada in world production has increased.

After growing by 33 percent in 1986, aluminum production in Brazil remained unchanged 1987 because

---

[80] Price quotations refer to aluminum sold in the LME, cash for delivery on the following business day, 99.5 percent minimum aluminum content, in the form of T-bars or ingots, c.i.f. European ports.

[81] The production of bauxite is more concentrated than that of the other major base metals because bauxite tends to occur in a relatively small number of large high grade deposits. Two thirds of world production occurs in four countries: Australia, Brazil, Guinea, and Jamaica.

## Table 61.  Aluminum: World Commodity Balance, 1981–87

(In millions of tons)

| | 1981 | 1982 | 1983 | 1984 | 1985 | 1986 | 1987[1] |
|---|---|---|---|---|---|---|---|
| **Bauxite** | | | | | | | |
| **Mine production** | **88.5** | **77.9** | **79.5** | **92.5** | **88.9** | **91.2** | **94.5** |
| Australia | 25.4 | 23.6 | 24.4 | 31.5 | 31.8 | 32.4 | 32.8 |
| Brazil | 4.7 | 4.2 | 5.2 | 6.4 | 5.8 | 6.5 | 7.1 |
| Guinea | 12.8 | 11.8 | 13.0 | 14.7 | 14.0 | 14.7 | 15.0 |
| Jamaica | 11.6 | 8.2 | 7.7 | 8.7 | 6.2 | 7.0 | 8.5 |
| Suriname | 4.1 | 3.1 | 2.8 | 3.5 | 3.7 | 3.7 | 3.7 |
| U.S.S.R. | 6.4 | 6.4 | 6.3 | 6.2 | 6.4 | 6.3 | 6.3 |
| Yugoslavia | 3.3 | 3.7 | 3.5 | 3.4 | 3.5 | 3.5 | 3.3 |
| Other countries | 20.2 | 16.9 | 16.6 | 18.1 | 17.5 | 17.1 | 17.8 |
| **Production of alumina** | **26.7** | **22.2** | **23.3** | **27.1** | **25.5** | **26.1** | **27.3** |
| **Aluminum** | | | | | | | |
| **Primary production** | **15.7** | **14.0** | **14.3** | **15.9** | **15.5** | **15.5** | **16.2** |
| Australia | 0.4 | 0.4 | 0.5 | 0.8 | 0.9 | 0.9 | 1.0 |
| Brazil | 0.3 | 0.3 | 0.4 | 0.5 | 0.6 | 0.8 | 0.8 |
| Canada | 1.1 | 1.1 | 1.1 | 1.2 | 1.3 | 1.4 | 1.6 |
| Germany, Fed. Rep. of | 0.7 | 0.7 | 0.7 | 0.8 | 0.7 | 0.8 | 0.8 |
| Norway | 0.6 | 0.7 | 0.7 | 0.8 | 0.7 | 0.7 | 0.8 |
| U.S.S.R. | 2.4 | 2.4 | 2.4 | 2.3 | 2.3 | 2.3 | 2.4 |
| United States | 4.5 | 3.3 | 3.4 | 4.1 | 3.5 | 3.0 | 3.2 |
| Other countries | 5.7 | 5.1 | 5.1 | 5.4 | 5.5 | 5.6 | 5.6 |
| **Primary consumption** | **14.5** | **14.1** | **15.4** | **15.8** | **16.1** | **16.7** | **17.2** |
| China | 0.6 | 0.6 | 0.6 | 0.6 | 0.7 | 0.8 | 0.8 |
| France | 0.5 | 0.6 | 0.6 | 0.6 | 0.6 | 0.6 | 0.6 |
| Germany, Fed. Rep. of | 1.0 | 1.0 | 1.1 | 1.2 | 1.2 | 1.2 | 1.1 |
| Japan | 1.6 | 1.6 | 1.8 | 1.7 | 1.8 | 1.8 | 2.0 |
| U.S.S.R. | 1.9 | 1.9 | 1.9 | 1.8 | 1.8 | 1.9 | 1.9 |
| United States | 4.1 | 3.6 | 4.2 | 4.5 | 4.3 | 4.3 | 4.5 |
| Other countries | 4.8 | 4.8 | 5.2 | 5.4 | 5.7 | 6.1 | 6.3 |
| **Market balance**[2] | **1.2** | **−0.1** | **−1.1** | **0.1** | **−0.6** | **−1.2** | **−1.0** |
| **Ending stocks**[3] | **3.4** | **3.2** | **2.2** | **2.8** | **2.5** | **2.0** | **1.5** |
| Metal exchanges | 0.3 | 0.3 | 0.2 | 0.2 | 0.3 | 0.1 | 0.1 |
| Producers | 3.1 | 2.9 | 2.0 | 2.6 | 2.2 | 1.9 | 1.4 |
| Stocks/consumption ratio (number of weeks)[4] | 11.7 | 11.7 | 7.6 | 9.1 | 7.9 | 6.2 | 4.6 |

Source: *World Metal Statistics* (London: World Bureau of Metal Statistics), various issues in 1987.

[1] Estimated by Commodities Division, IMF Research Department.
[2] World production minus world consumption.
[3] May not agree with production and consumption data because of differences in coverage.
[4] Reported commercial stocks expressed as weeks of world consumption.

of a drought that affected the hydroelectric power supply to smelters and resulted in an increase in rates charged for electric power. In Canada the reactivation of idle capacity and the opening of new capacity resulted in a 16 percent increase in aluminum production in 1987. Similar factors were responsible for a 11 percent increase in Australian production during 1987. In the United States the reactivation of previously idled capacity was the major factor behind a production increase of almost 7 percent during the year.

Despite the increase in world production of aluminum in 1987, amounting to nearly 5 percent, the low level of aluminum stocks, combined with the unexpected strong demand in both Japan and the United

States, created a tight market situation throughout the entire year. In addition, concern about a possible strike in Canada increased pressure on consumers to build inventories. This market tightness is expected to ease as additional supplies enter the market, and prices are expected to decline by late 1988.

Although there is a trend toward local processing of bauxite into alumina and aluminum, a large portion of bauxite still enters international trade. This is a reflection of the fact that many of the refineries are still located in industrial countries that do not have bauxite deposits. The major trade flows for bauxite are from Jamaica to mainly the United States and from Guinea to a large number of industrial countries. Australia

## Table 62. Aluminum: Export Earnings, 1984–87

| | 1984 | 1985 | 1986[1] | 1987[1] | 1984 | 1985 | 1986[1] | 1987[1] |
|---|---|---|---|---|---|---|---|---|
| | (Values in SDRs) | | | | (Values in U.S. dollars) | | | |
| **Bauxite** | | | | | | | | |
| **Earnings** (*in billions*) | **1.0** | **0.9** | **0.8** | **0.8** | **1.0** | **0.9** | **0.9** | **1.0** |
| Industrial countries | 0.1 | 0.1 | 0.1 | 0.1 | 0.1 | 0.1 | 0.1 | 0.1 |
| Developing countries | 0.9 | 0.8 | 0.7 | 0.7 | 0.9 | 0.8 | 0.8 | 0.9 |
| **Volumes** (*in millions of tons*)[2] | **34.9** | **32.8** | **34.3** | **35.5** | **34.9** | **32.8** | **34.3** | **35.5** |
| Industrial countries | 5.9 | 5.8 | 6.6 | 6.3 | 5.9 | 5.8 | 6.6 | 6.3 |
| Developing countries | 29.0 | 27.0 | 27.7 | 29.2 | 29.0 | 27.0 | 27.7 | 29.2 |
| *Guinea* | *12.4* | *13.0* | *13.6* | *13.9* | *12.4* | *13.0* | *13.6* | *13.9* |
| *Jamaica* | *4.4* | *2.6* | *2.9* | *3.5* | *4.4* | *2.6* | *2.9* | *3.5* |
| *Others* | *12.2* | *11.4* | *11.2* | *11.8* | *12.2* | *11.4* | *11.2* | *11.8* |
| **Unit values** (*a ton*) | **28.5** | **27.9** | **23.6** | **22.0** | **29.2** | **28.4** | **27.7** | **28.5** |
| Industrial countries | 18.2 | 16.9 | 15.5 | 14.7 | 18.7 | 17.2 | 18.2 | 19.0 |
| Developing countries | 30.6 | 30.3 | 25.5 | 23.6 | 31.4 | 30.8 | 30.0 | 30.5 |
| **Unwrought aluminum** | | | | | | | | |
| **Earnings** (*in billions*) | **7.8** | **7.4** | **7.3** | **9.3** | **8.0** | **7.5** | **8.5** | **12.0** |
| Industrial countries | 5.1 | 4.8 | 4.7 | 5.9 | 5.2 | 4.8 | 5.5 | 7.6 |
| Developing countries | 1.7 | 1.8 | 1.7 | 2.2 | 1.8 | 1.9 | 2.0 | 2.9 |
| U.S.S.R. and Eastern European countries | 1.0 | 0.8 | 1.7 | 1.1 | 1.0 | 0.8 | 1.0 | 1.5 |
| **Volumes** (*in millions of tons*) | **5.8** | **6.5** | **6.8** | **7.1** | **5.8** | **6.5** | **6.8** | **7.1** |
| Industrial countries | 3.6 | 4.1 | 4.2 | 4.3 | 3.6 | 4.1 | 4.2 | 4.3 |
| Developing countries | 1.3 | 1.6 | 1.6 | 1.8 | 1.3 | 1.6 | 1.6 | 1.8 |
| U.S.S.R. and Eastern European countries | 0.9 | 0.8 | 1.0 | 1.0 | 0.9 | 0.8 | 1.0 | 1.0 |
| **Unit values** (*a ton*) | **1,330** | **1,120** | **1,070** | **1,310** | **1,370** | **1,140** | **1,250** | **1,690** |
| Industrial countries | 1,390 | 1,160 | 1,110 | 1,380 | 1,430 | 1,180 | 1,310 | 1,780 |
| Developing countries | 1,310 | 1,130 | 1,030 | 1,280 | 1,350 | 1,140 | 1,210 | 1,650 |
| U.S.S.R. and Eastern European countries | 1,110 | 940 | 930 | 1,080 | 1,140 | 950 | 1,100 | 1,400 |
| **Market prices** (*a ton*)[3] | **1,220** | **1,030** | **980** | **1,210** | **1,250** | **1,040** | **1,150** | **1,570** |

Sources: UN Conference on Trade and Development (UNCTAD), *Yearbook of International Commodity Statistics, 1985* for exports; Commodities Division, IMF Research Department for market prices.
[1] Data on exports are estimates of Commodities Division, IMF Research Department.
[2] Actual weight.
[3] London Metal Exchange, spot delivery, 99.5 percent aluminum, in the form of T-bars or ingots, c.i.f. European ports.

and Brazil are also major exporters. Global earnings from exports of bauxite increased by 11 percent in terms of dollars in 1987, but remained unchanged in terms of SDRs (Table 62).

The significant growth in exports of aluminum since the early 1980s by Australia, Brazil, Indonesia, and Venezuela reflects the trend toward greater local processing. This trend is also evidenced by the increasing importance of imports of aluminum by a number of industrial countries. Japan has virtually shut down its aluminum smelting industry, and aluminum imports into Japan have almost tripled over the last ten years. Aluminum imports have more than doubled in the United States during the same period. Global dollar earnings from exports of aluminum in 1987 are estimated to have increased by over 40 percent, while the corresponding increase in terms of SDRs was nearly 30 percent.

## Iron Ore

In 1987 iron ore prices increased marginally in terms of dollars, but fell by 8 percent in terms of SDRs.[82] Despite an estimated increase in both world consumption and trade, the world iron ore industry continued to suffer from overcapacity, uncertainty regarding the impact of new projects, and generally declining demand for steel in the industrial countries.

The major determinant of the demand for iron ore has been the market for crude steel. Although world production of crude steel has been at roughly the same level for about a decade, production in the industrial countries has declined steadily from 395 million tons in 1977 (nearly 60 percent of world production) to 342

[82] Price quotations refer to "spot" deliveries (c.i.f. at German ports) of Brazilian ore (with 65 percent iron content).

**Table 63.   Iron Ore: World Commodity Balance Together with Production of Pig Iron and Steel, 1981–87**

(In millions of tons)

|  | 1981 | 1982 | 1983 | 1984 | 1985 | 1986 | 1987[1] |
|---|---|---|---|---|---|---|---|
| **Production of iron ore** | **887** | **813** | **776** | **869** | **905** | **908** | **919** |
| Australia | 85 | 88 | 71 | 89 | 96 | 92 | 87 |
| Brazil | 98 | 93 | 92 | 112 | 128 | 132 | 136 |
| China | 105 | 107 | 114 | 122 | 132 | 138 | 138 |
| United States | 76 | 37 | 39 | 52 | 50 | 40 | 41 |
| U.S.S.R. | 242 | 244 | 245 | 247 | 248 | 250 | 250 |
| Other countries | 281 | 244 | 215 | 247 | 251 | 256 | 265 |
| **Apparent consumption of iron ore**[2] | **886** | **823** | **777** | **871** | **905** | **905** | **917** |
| Brazil | 17 | 20 | 22 | 24 | 36 | 40 | 41 |
| China | 107 | 109 | 118 | 128 | 142 | 152 | 152 |
| Germany, Fed. Rep. of | 46 | 40 | 37 | 44 | 46 | 42 | 41 |
| Japan | 124 | 122 | 110 | 126 | 125 | 116 | 114 |
| United States | 99 | 49 | 48 | 64 | 60 | 52 | 55 |
| U.S.S.R. | 198 | 201 | 202 | 201 | 204 | 203 | 203 |
| Other countries | 295 | 280 | 240 | 284 | 292 | 300 | 311 |
| **Production of pig iron** | **534** | **477** | **461** | **491** | **494** | **502** | **508** |
| Of which: industrial countries | 265 | 221 | 218 | 239 | 241 | 222 | 226 |
| **Production of crude steel** | **711** | **646** | **663** | **710** | **720** | **725** | **736** |
| Of which: industrial countries | 387 | 321 | 327 | 358 | 355 | 331 | 339 |

Source: *Statistics on Iron Ore*, UN Conference on Trade and Development (UNCTAD), September 9, 1987.

[1] Estimated by Commodities Division, IMF Research Department.

[2] Production minus exports plus imports.

million tons by 1986 (less than 50 percent of world production). Production in the developing countries doubled during the same period, from approximately 46 million tons in 1977 (7 percent of world production) to 90 million tons in 1986 (13 percent of world production). In 1986 the industrial countries produced 25 percent of world iron ore output compared with 34 percent in 1977 and consumed only 38 percent of world iron ore output compared to 49 percent in 1977. In line with this trend, in 1986 and 1987 developing countries—in particular Brazil, India, and Venezuela—increased production of iron ore, while production of iron ore declined in such industrial countries as Australia, Canada, France, and the United States (Table 63).

In the industrialized countries in 1986 only two thirds of steel capacity was utilized, one of the lowest rates of utilization in the last ten years. Crude steel production in these countries declined by 7 percent in 1986, and total apparent steel consumption fell by 3 percent, despite the fact that GDP growth in industrial countries was roughly 3 percent during 1986. In 1987, however, world steel production is estimated to have increased by roughly 2 percent. In Japan, crude steel production fell by almost 7 percent in 1986 and by an estimated 1 percent in 1987. Part of this decline is related to the sharp appreciation of the yen, which affected industrial activity in general, as evidenced by a 0.3 percent decline of industrial production during

1986 and an increase of only 1.3 percent estimated for 1987. In the Federal Republic of Germany, steel production declined by 8 percent in 1986 and by an estimated 4 percent for 1987. Overall growth in industrial production in Germany in 1986 and 1987 was low, registering only 1.2 percent in 1986 and an estimated decline of 0.8 percent in 1987. Roughly similar performance was evidenced in the manufacture of consumer goods, automobiles, and investment goods. After registering a 20 percent decline in 1985, housing starts in Germany declined by 3 percent in 1986 and by 11 percent in 1987. In the United States, crude steel production declined by 8 percent in 1986, while apparent iron ore consumption declined by 14 percent. The decline in the 1986 steel production in the United States was related to low growth (only 1 percent) in industrial production. The production of investment goods actually declined by 1.9 percent, and automobile production declined by 6.1 percent. For 1987, however, preliminary estimates indicate that both steel production and iron ore consumption increased by over 5 percent in the United States. Strong growth in steel production in 1987 was associated with an increase of over 3 percent in the production of manufactured goods and a 3 percent increase in production of consumer goods.

In the developing countries, apparent iron ore consumption increased by 11 percent in 1986 and is estimated to have increased by roughly 3 percent in 1987. Much of this increase occurred in the countries which have experienced large expansions in their steel production, notably Brazil, China, India, the Republic of Korea, and Venezuela. During the last ten years, Brazil has approximately doubled its steel production; Venezuela has almost quadrupled its production; India has increased steel production by roughly 50 percent; and Korea has increased steel production by a factor of 7. China has emerged a major iron ore importing country. In accordance with plans to dramatically expand its steel production, China has increasingly used imported high-grade ores rather than relying entirely on its own large reserves of low-grade ore.

Iron ore production in the developing countries rose by about 5 percent in 1986 and is estimated to have increased by 3.5 percent in 1987. The largest increases were in Brazil, India, and Venezuela. The start-up of the Carajas project in Brazil, has contributed to an almost 50 percent surge in Brazilian iron ore production since 1983. This project produces low-cost iron ore and is expected to have a sustained production of 35 million tons, or roughly 3 percent of world production. Although China is the largest producer of iron ore in Asia, because of the poor quality of its ore, it is not a major exporter; India, on the other hand, plays an important role as an export supplier, particularly to iron ore importing countries in Asia. Australia, the world's second largest iron ore supplier produced 92 million tons, or 10 percent of world production in 1986. Although Australia has the potential to develop several additional high-quality deposits, market conditions for iron ore may not warrant significant expansion in the near term. Australia's production has remained at roughly the same level during the last ten years. Although the capacity expansion by low-cost producers in developing countries has coincided with capacity reductions by higher-cost producers in the industrial countries, such as the United States, there remains a capacity overhang of about 20 percent in the world iron ore industry.

World trade in iron ore has been stagnant with the volume of exports in 1987 equal to the level in 1981 and 10 percent below the volume recorded in the peak year of 1974. Exports from the industrial countries have been on a declining trend. The volume of exports from these countries in 1986 was 14 percent below the volume in 1977. Exports by the developing countries, however, grew by 19 percent during the period from 1977 to 1986. Much of the increased trade has resulted from shipments from Brazil to Japan and the newly industrializing countries of Asia.

The excess capacity situation has dominated price determination in the market for iron ore. Although the dollar price of steel increased by 45 percent from the first quarter of 1987 to the first quarter of 1988, it is not clear that much of that increase will filter down to iron ore producers. With new capacity coming on stream and a continued need for rationalization by many of the high-cost producers, iron ore prices are not likely to recover substantially during the next few years.

Consistent with developments with respect to unit values and volumes, dollar export earnings from iron ore remained virtually unchanged from 1984 to 1987, while earnings expressed in terms of SDRs have declined by over 20 percent (Table 64). As a consequence of the change in market shares, earnings of developing countries have performed better in this period than earnings of industrial countries.

## Tin

The tin market in 1986 and 1987 continued to be dominated by repercussions of the collapse in October of 1985 of price-support operations by the International Tin Council (ITC). The price fell from $5.62 a pound, just prior to the collapse, to about $2.55 a pound in July 1986, nine months later.[83] Once it became clear, however, that the large stocks acquired by creditor banks following the cessation of ITC support operations were not being sold off rapidly, the tin price first stabilized, and then, toward the end of 1986, began to rise. The price was relatively stable in 1987, averaging about $3.16 a pound.

At the end of 1985, world commercial stocks of tin amounted to 73,000 tons, of which over 50,000 tons represented stocks that had been held by the buffer stock manager of the ITC. In addition, the U.S. strategic stockpile contained 188,000 tons of tin. The stocks of tin, even without taking account of the U.S. stockpile holdings, represented roughly one third of annual world consumption. In 1986, world refined production fell by 2 percent and in 1987 by a further 4 percent (Table 65). While this decline in production was small in relation to the decline in the market price, it did contribute to a reduction in stocks over this period, particularly as world production was below world consumption by 15 percent in 1987. Thus, despite augmented supplies as a result of sales of 8,000 tons from the U.S. strategic stockpile in 1986, commercial stocks were reduced to little more than 40,000 tons at the end of 1987.

Apart from the reduction in stocks, an important factor contributing to the stability of tin prices in 1987

---

[83] Price quotations refer to prices on the LME, cash for delivery on the following business day, minimum purity 99.75 percent, c.i.f. European ports.

**Table 64.   Iron Ore: Export Earnings, 1984–87**

| | 1984 | 1985 | 1986[1] | 1987[1] | 1984 | 1985 | 1986[1] | 1987[1] |
|---|---|---|---|---|---|---|---|---|
| | *(Values in SDRs)* | | | | *(Values in U.S. dollars)* | | | |
| **Earnings** (*in billions*) | 6.8 | 6.9 | 5.9 | 5.3 | 7.0 | 7.0 | 6.9 | 6.8 |
| Industrial countries | 2.9 | 2.9 | 2.3 | 2.0 | 3.0 | 3.0 | 2.7 | 2.5 |
| Developing countries | 3.0 | 3.1 | 2.6 | 2.5 | 3.0 | 3.1 | 3.1 | 3.2 |
| Non-Fund members | 0.9 | 0.9 | 1.0 | 0.8 | 1.0 | 0.9 | 1.1 | 1.1 |
| **Volumes** (*in millions of tons*) | 369 | 371 | 366 | 370 | 369 | 371 | 366 | 370 |
| Industrial countries | 151 | 152 | 143 | 135 | 151 | 152 | 143 | 135 |
| *Australia* | *85* | *85* | *80* | *73* | *85* | *85* | *80* | *73* |
| *Canada* | *31* | *32* | *31* | *33* | *31* | *32* | *31* | *33* |
| *Others* | *35* | *35* | *32* | *30* | *35* | *35* | *32* | *30* |
| Developing countries | 172 | 175 | 176 | 188 | 172 | 175 | 176 | 188 |
| *Brazil* | *88* | *92* | *92* | *91* | *88* | *92* | *92* | *91* |
| *India* | *26* | *29* | *32* | *34* | *26* | *29* | *32* | *34* |
| *Others* | *58* | *54* | *52* | *63* | *58* | *54* | *52* | *63* |
| U.S.S.R. and Eastern European countries | 46 | 44 | 47 | 47 | 46 | 44 | 47 | 47 |
| **Unit values** (*a ton*) | 18 | 19 | 16 | 14 | 19 | 19 | 19 | 19 |
| Industrial countries | 19 | 19 | 16 | 14 | 20 | 20 | 19 | 19 |
| Developing countries | 17 | 18 | 15 | 13 | 18 | 18 | 18 | 17 |
| U.S.S.R. and Eastern European countries | 20 | 20 | 20 | 18 | 21 | 21 | 24 | 23 |
| **Market prices** (*a ton*)[2] | 22.5 | 22.3 | 18.7 | 17.2 | 23.1 | 22.7 | 21.9 | 22.2 |

Sources: UN Conference on Trade and Development (UNCTAD), Fourth Preparatory Meeting on Iron Ore, "Statistical Issues, Statistics on Iron Ore," TD/B/IPC/Iron Ore/21 (September 9, 1987) for exports; Commodities Division, IMF Research Department for market prices.

[1] Data on exports are estimates of Commodities Division, IMF Research Department.

[2] Brazilian ore prices, c.i.f. German ports.

was the ability of the Association of Tin Producing Countries (ATPC)—Australia, Bolivia, Indonesia, Malaysia, Nigeria, Thailand, and Zäire—to devise a set of country quotas which limited total member exports to 96,000 tons for the 12-month period beginning April 1987. This tonnage was in line with the level of actual exports by these countries in 1986 and represented about 60 percent of world exports. In addition, during 1987, the major holders of tin inventories managed their stock disposal policies so as to protect tin prices.

The market's ability to absorb the stock overhang has, nevertheless, been limited by a lack of growth in tin demand. Estimated consumption in 1987 was unchanged from the previous year. The lack of demand response to lower tin prices was the result of uncertainty surrounding the future direction of prices over the medium and long term, as well as lags in adjustment in the short terms. The tin price facing consumers in 1986 and 1987 may not have fully reflected the decline in spot prices since many tin plate producers were still working off higher price inventories and did not immediately reduce prices to reflect the new market conditions. In addition, before tin consumers make a long-term investment decision on whether to use tin plate rather than aluminum or plastic as a packaging material, they may want more certainty regarding long-term tin prices relative to those of its substitutes.

The tin price decline has had a major impact on the production of certain tin producers. In particular, Bolivian production declined by 27 percent in 1986 and by a further 45 percent in 1987. The decline in Bolivia was expected since it is a high-cost producer suffering from declining ore grades and a lack of investment for several years. This decline was also attributable in part to a restructuring of the state-owned mining company, COMIBOL. Malaysian output fell by 21 percent in 1986 because the effect of lower prices made certain operations unprofitable.[84] Aided by the 31 percent devaluation of its currency in September of 1986, by a temporary reduction in costs by mining richer ore grades, and the beneficial effect of lower oil prices, Indonesian mine production, however, is estimated to have increased by 12 percent in 1987. After increasing by 62 percent in 1983, 54 percent in 1984, and 35 percent in 1985, Brazilian tin mine production was relatively constant in 1986 and 1987, declining by 7 percent in 1986 and increasing by an estimated 4 percent in 1987. Brazil's low production cost has permitted it to increase its market share from a negligible 3 percent in 1981 to 14 percent in 1987. China increased production by approximately 22 percent in 1986. This increase was, however, absorbed

---

[84] The number of active mines in Malaysia which had fallen from 710 in 1981 to 444 in September 1985, plummeted to 185 by October 1986.

**Table 65.   Tin: World Commodity Balance, 1981–87**

(In thousands of tons)

| | 1981 | 1982 | 1983 | 1984 | 1985 | 1986 | 1987[1] |
|---|---|---|---|---|---|---|---|
| **Mine production** | **239** | **225** | **210** | **205** | **197** | **186** | **185** |
| Bolivia | 30 | 27 | 25 | 19 | 15 | 11 | 6 |
| Brazil | 8 | 8 | 13 | 20 | 27 | 25 | 26 |
| China | 16 | 16 | 17 | 18 | 18 | 22 | 22 |
| Indonesia | 35 | 34 | 27 | 23 | 22 | 25 | 28 |
| Malaysia | 60 | 52 | 41 | 41 | 37 | 29 | 32 |
| Thailand | 32 | 26 | 20 | 22 | 17 | 21 | 18 |
| U.S.S.R. | 16 | 16 | 17 | 17 | 16 | 16 | 16 |
| Other countries | 42 | 44 | 50 | 47 | 45 | 37 | 37 |
| **Refined production** | **244** | **229** | **207** | **206** | **210** | **206** | **197** |
| Bolivia | 20 | 19 | 14 | 16 | 12 | 8 | 3 |
| Brazil | 8 | 9 | 13 | 19 | 25 | 25 | 27 |
| China | 16 | 17 | 17 | 17 | 19 | 20 | 20 |
| Indonesia | 33 | 30 | 28 | 23 | 20 | 22 | 26 |
| Malaysia | 70 | 63 | 53 | 43 | 46 | 44 | 45 |
| Thailand | 33 | 26 | 19 | 20 | 18 | 22 | 16 |
| U.S.S.R. | 16 | 17 | 18 | 19 | 18 | 18 | 18 |
| Other countries | 48 | 48 | 45 | 49 | 52 | 47 | 42 |
| **Consumption** | **226** | **216** | **216** | **231** | **225** | **232** | **233** |
| China | 13 | 13 | 29 | 30 | 30 | 30 | 30 |
| Germany, Fed. Rep. of | 15 | 14 | 14 | 16 | 16 | 17 | 18 |
| Japan | 31 | 29 | 30 | 33 | 32 | 33 | 33 |
| United States | 54 | 46 | 46 | 49 | 52 | 50 | 48 |
| U.S.S.R. | 26 | 27 | 29 | 30 | 30 | 30 | 30 |
| Other countries | 87 | 87 | 66 | 73 | 66 | 72 | 73 |
| **Market balance**[2] | **18** | **13** | **−9** | **−25** | **−15** | **−26** | **−36** |
| **Commercial stocks**[3] | **25** | **57** | **63** | **49** | **73**[4] | **57** | **42** |
| Stocks/consumption ratio (number of weeks)[5] | 5.9 | 13.7 | 15.1 | 11.1 | 16.8 | 12.8 | 9.4 |
| ITC stocks | 2 | 53 | 55 | 62 | 0[6] | 0 | 0 |
| U.S. strategic stocks | 200 | 194 | 191 | 193 | 188 | 180 | 176 |

Sources: *World Metal Statistics* (London: World Bureau of Metal Statistics), various issues in 1987, and *CRU Metal Monitor: Tin* (London: Commodities Research Unit Ltd.), December 1987.

[1] Estimates of Commodities Division, IMF Research Department.

[2] World production minus world consumption.

[3] Total commercial stocks reported at end of period.

[4] Some of the stocks held by ITC prior to the collapse of its market operations in October 1985 may not be included at the end of 1985 in the series of commercial stocks.

[5] Commercial stocks measured as weeks of consumption.

[6] ITC creditors acquired the ITC stocks following collapse of ITC market operations.

domestically by stock building or additional consumption, and exports from China declined during the year. While the decline in the stock overhang has brought the tin market into better balance, the modest improvement in tin prices in 1987 could generate additional production and exports from ATPC members or from non-ATPC members. The ATPC quota system has been effective to date because the quotas agreed for the period April 1987 to March 1988 were at or beyond capacity export levels for all of the countries except Malaysia, which is the world's largest tin exporter and may have acted as a swing producer in an effort to stabilize prices.[85] In the case of Bolivia, exports are

[85] ATPC export quotas for 1987/88 were as follows: Malaysia 28,526 tons, Indonesia 24,516 tons, Thailand 19,000 tons, Bolivia 13,761 tons, Australia 7,000 tons, Nigeria 1,461 tons, and Zäire 1,736 tons.

expected to be far below its allocated quota. Preliminary indications, however, indicate that in 1987 China may have exported roughly twice the amount of tin it exported in 1986. A new quota scheme starting in March 1988 raised the overall ATPC quota to 101,900 tons and contains higher quotas for Malaysia and Indonesia.

Tin prices are expected to rise modestly in 1988 as slow growth in consumption permits further reductions in stocks. As prices continue to put pressure on higher cost suppliers to cut back production, lower cost producers should be able to increase market shares.

Earnings from exports of tin metal in 1986 and 1987 were little more than half the level in 1985 in terms of dollars and less than one half in terms of SDRs (Table 66). Because of a substantial increase in volume, earnings from exports of tin-in-concentrates fell by a

**Table 66.  Tin: Export Earnings, 1984–87**

| | 1984 | 1985 | 1986 | 1987[1] | 1984 | 1985 | 1986 | 1987[1] |
|---|---|---|---|---|---|---|---|---|
| | *(Values in SDRs)* | | | | *(Values in U.S. dollars)* | | | |
| **Tin-in-concentrates** | | | | | | | | |
| **Earnings** (*in billions*) | **0.3** | **0.3** | **0.2** | **0.2** | **0.3** | **0.3** | **0.3** | **0.3** |
| Industrial countries | 0.1 | 0.1 | 0.1 | 0.1 | 0.1 | 0.1 | 0.1 | 0.1 |
| Developing countries | 0.2 | 0.2 | 0.1 | 0.1 | 0.2 | 0.2 | 0.2 | 0.2 |
| **Volumes** (*in thousands of tons*) | **33** | **31** | **44** | **45** | **33** | **31** | **44** | **45** |
| Industrial countries | 8 | 7 | 12 | 13 | 8 | 7 | 12 | 13 |
| Developing countries | 25 | 24 | 32 | 32 | 25 | 24 | 32 | 32 |
| **Unit values** (*a ton*) | **9,790** | **8,950** | **4,930** | **4,740** | **10,030** | **9,080** | **5,780** | **6,130** |
| Industrial countries | 11,240 | 11,560 | 5,630 | 5,410 | 11,520 | 11,730 | 6,610 | 6,990 |
| Developing countries | 9,470 | 8,360 | 4,730 | 4,540 | 9,710 | 8,490 | 5,550 | 5,860 |
| **Tin metal** | | | | | | | | |
| **Earnings** (*in billions*) | **1.7** | **1.8** | **0.8** | **0.8** | **1.7** | **1.9** | **0.9** | **1.0** |
| Industrial countries | 0.3 | 0.2 | 0.1 | 0.1 | 0.3 | 0.2 | 0.1 | 0.1 |
| Developing countries | 1.4 | 1.6 | 0.7 | 0.7 | 1.4 | 1.7 | 0.8 | 0.9 |
| **Volumes** (*in thousands of tons*) | **145** | **168** | **152** | **152** | **145** | **168** | **152** | **152** |
| Industrial countries | 28 | 22 | 29 | 29 | 28 | 22 | 29 | 29 |
| Developing countries | 117 | 146 | 123 | 123 | 117 | 146 | 123 | 123 |
| **Unit values** (*a ton*) | **11,490** | **11,100** | **5,230** | **5,090** | **11,780** | **11,270** | **6,130** | **6,580** |
| Industrial countries | 8,540 | 10,030 | 3,960 | 3,860 | 10,550 | 10,220 | 4,650 | 5,000 |
| Developing countries | 11,890 | 11,220 | 5,510 | 5,450 | 12,070 | 11,430 | 6,490 | 6,960 |
| **Market prices** (*a ton*)[2] | **11,930** | **11,360** | **5,530** | **5,380** | **12,230** | **11,530** | **6,490** | **6,960** |

Sources: UN Conference on Trade and Development (UNCTAD), *Yearbook of International Commodity Statistics, 1985* for exports; Commodities Division, IMF Research Department for market prices.

[1] Estimates of Commodities Division, IMF Research Department.

[2] LME standard grade, spot delivery, c.i.f. European ports through October 1985; *Metals Week*, New York dealer price thereafter.

much smaller amount in this period, but these concentrates still represent only about one quarter of total exports of tin.

## Nickel

The price of nickel increased sharply in 1987, rising from an average of 164 U.S. cents a pound in the fourth quarter of 1986 to 292 cents a pound in the fourth quarter of 1987.[86] In March 1988, the price averaged a record 703 cents a pound.

From 1981 through 1986 the market for nickel was characterized by over-capacity in industrial countries and continuous reductions in operating costs, which generally were passed along to consumers of nickel through lower prices. In 1986 world nickel production, already below world consumption, declined by roughly 2 percent. World nickel consumption was unchanged from the previous year. A 20 percent decline in the dollar price of nickel in 1986 can be explained by the

large increase, of almost 50 percent, in exports of nickel by the Soviet Union.

In 1987 an 8 percent increase in primary nickel consumption combined with an increase of only 2 percent in primary nickel production and tight scrap nickel supplies to decrease inventories by 11 percent (Table 67). Demand for stainless steel and nonferrous alloys grew rapidly in 1987 and, at least in the United States, the availability of stainless steel scrap was limited. At the beginning of the year, it was expected that Japanese stainless steel producers would suffer both from the strength of the yen and limited imports of stainless steel into the United States. Strong demand for stainless steel in the Republic of Korea, Singapore, and Taiwan Province of China, however, contributed to an increase of 4 percent in Japanese production of stainless steel. In the United States, the voluntary restraint agreement limiting imports, together with the fall in the value of the dollar, enabled U.S. stainless steel producers to benefit from an increase in domestic demand.

Technical production problems in Canada and the U.S.S.R., two major nickel producing countries, resulted in a very tight nickel market in 1987, particularly in the second half of the year. The market response

[86] Price quotations refer to prices on the LME, cash for delivery on the following business day, minimum 99.8 percent purity, in the form of cathodes, pellets, or briquettes, c.i.f. northwest European ports.

**Table 67. Nickel: World Commodity Balance, 1981–87**

(In thousands of tons)

| | 1981 | 1982 | 1983 | 1984 | 1985 | 1986 | 1987[1] |
|---|---|---|---|---|---|---|---|
| **Mine production** | **723** | **629** | **663** | **747** | **787** | **792** | **807** |
| Australia | 74 | 88 | 77 | 77 | 86 | 78 | 71 |
| Canada | 167 | 93 | 125 | 174 | 170 | 181 | 196 |
| U.S.S.R. | 150 | 170 | 172 | 172 | 172 | 170 | 170 |
| Other countries | 332 | 278 | 289 | 324 | 359 | 363 | 370 |
| **Refined production** | **704** | **629** | **686** | **746** | **765** | **753** | **776** |
| Australia | 43 | 46 | 42 | 39 | 41 | 42 | 45 |
| Canada | 111 | 74 | 96 | 121 | 119 | 124 | 135 |
| Japan | 94 | 87 | 82 | 89 | 95 | 96 | 94 |
| Norway | 43 | 26 | 29 | 36 | 38 | 38 | 40 |
| U.S.S.R. | 170 | 190 | 192 | 193 | 190 | 188 | 190 |
| Other countries | 243 | 206 | 245 | 268 | 282 | 265 | 272 |
| **Consumption** | **662** | **649** | **687** | **788** | **783** | **784** | **846** |
| Germany, Fed. Rep. of | 62 | 58 | 63 | 78 | 75 | 77 | 80 |
| Japan | 105 | 107 | 115 | 146 | 136 | 127 | 140 |
| United States | 140 | 125 | 137 | 141 | 143 | 125 | 132 |
| U.S.S.R. | 130 | 138 | 145 | 147 | 150 | 146 | 146 |
| Other countries | 225 | 221 | 227 | 276 | 279 | 309 | 348 |
| **Market balance**[2] | **42** | **−20** | **−1** | **−42** | **−18** | **−31** | **−70** |
| **Stocks**[3,4] | **218** | **201** | **183** | **147** | **129** | **128** | **114** |
| Stocks/consumption ratio (number of weeks)[5] | 17.1 | 16.1 | 13.8 | 9.7 | 8.6 | 8.5 | 7.0 |

Sources: *World Metal Statistics* (London: World Bureau of Metal Statistics), various issues in 1987, and *CRU Metal Monitor: Nickel/Chrome/Molybdenum* (London: Commodities Research Unit Ltd.), December 1987.

[1] Estimated by Commodities Division, IMF Research Department.
[2] World production minus world consumption.
[3] Total commercial stocks measured at end of period.
[4] May not agree with production and consumption data because of differences in coverage.
[5] Commercial stocks measured as weeks of consumption.

to the news of these difficulties resulted in consumers attempting to build inventories in anticipation of higher prices. Against this background, a reduction in nickel exports from the Dominican Republic beginning in December of 1987 brought succcessive and large month-to-month increases in prices through March 1988.

Unless the exceptionally rapid expansion in stainless steel production or supply problems continue, it is likely that nickel prices will drop sharply. With capacity utilization of roughly 80 percent, additional supplies should come on the market as long as prices remain above $3.00. Producers will be reluctant, however, to reopen properties closed in the early and mid-1980s unless they feel that high prices will be sustained for a considerable period.

## Zinc

In comparison with the prices for aluminum, copper, and nickel, the price of zinc in 1987 was relatively stable. The market for zinc remains influenced by potential oversupply as a result of excess capacity that has not been closed. Expected production rationali-

zation, especially in Europe, has been slow to occur. As a result, the price of zinc has been less affected by the low stock situation and supply disruptions that occurred in 1987 than were the prices of many other metals.

The price of zinc during the first quarter of 1987 fell from 36 U.S. cents a pound to 33 cents, but toward mid-year strengthened to nearly 40 cents a pound on account of a four-month strike affecting a major Canadian producer (COMINCO).[87] The market response was limited because many consumers had sufficient stocks which enabled them to hold off purchases pending the settlement of the strike. There were, however, further shipment delays later in the year, with the result that following a decrease of prices in the third quarter, prices increased again to over 41 cents a pound by the first quarter of 1988.

In 1986 strong growth in zinc consumption in Europe and the United States contributed to an increase in world zinc consumption of 2.4 percent (Table 68). In

---

[87] Price quotations refer to prices on the LME, cash for delivery on the following business day, zinc produced by distillation or electrolysis, minimum purity 98 percent (standard), c.i.f. U.K. ports.

**Table 68.   Zinc: World Commodity Balance, 1981–87**

(In thousands of metric tons)

| | 1981 | 1982 | 1983 | 1984 | 1985 | 1986 | 1987[1] |
|---|---|---|---|---|---|---|---|
| **Mine production** | **6,110** | **6,480** | **6,540** | **6,760** | **6,920** | **6,850** | **7,270** |
| Australia | 520 | 670 | 700 | 660 | 740 | 690 | 820 |
| Canada | 1,100 | 1,190 | 1,070 | 1,210 | 1,170 | 1,290 | 1,550 |
| U.S.S.R. | 1,010 | 1,020 | 1,020 | 980 | 1,000 | 970 | 970 |
| Other countries | 3,480 | 3,600 | 3,750 | 3,910 | 4,010 | 3,900 | 3,930 |
| **Slab production** | **6,170** | **5,980** | **6,320** | **6,600** | **6,750** | **6,640** | **6,920** |
| Australia | 300 | 300 | 300 | 310 | 290 | 310 | 300 |
| Canada | 620 | 510 | 620 | 680 | 690 | 570 | 580 |
| France | 260 | 240 | 250 | 260 | 250 | 260 | 270 |
| Germany, Fed. Rep. of | 370 | 330 | 360 | 360 | 370 | 370 | 390 |
| Italy | 180 | 160 | 160 | 170 | 210 | 230 | 240 |
| Japan | 670 | 660 | 700 | 750 | 740 | 710 | 680 |
| United States | 370 | 300 | 300 | 330 | 310 | 320 | 340 |
| U.S.S.R. | 1,060 | 1,050 | 1,060 | 1,050 | 1,050 | 1,030 | 1,030 |
| Other countries | 2,340 | 2,430 | 2,570 | 2,690 | 2,840 | 2,840 | 3,090 |
| **Consumption** | **6,000** | **5,920** | **6,270** | **6,440** | **6,510** | **6,670** | **6,740** |
| China | 220 | 260 | 290 | 330 | 350 | 360 | 360 |
| France | 270 | 260 | 270 | 280 | 250 | 260 | 240 |
| Germany, Fed. Rep. of | 370 | 370 | 400 | 430 | 410 | 430 | 430 |
| Italy | 220 | 200 | 210 | 210 | 220 | 230 | 230 |
| Japan | 700 | 700 | 770 | 780 | 780 | 750 | 770 |
| United States | 830 | 800 | 930 | 960 | 940 | 1,000 | 1,000 |
| U.S.S.R. | 1,040 | 1,050 | 1,050 | 1,050 | 1,000 | 990 | 990 |
| Other countries | 2,350 | 2,280 | 2,350 | 2,400 | 2,560 | 2,650 | 2,720 |
| **Market balance[2]** | **170** | **50** | **50** | **160** | **240** | **−30** | **180** |
| **Stocks[3,4]** | **820** | **760** | **620** | **580** | **560** | **570** | **550** |
| Stocks/consumption ratio (number of weeks)[5] | 7.1 | 6.6 | 5.1 | 4.7 | 4.4 | 4.5 | 4.2 |

Sources: *World Metal Statistics* (London: World Bureau of Metal Statistics), various issues in 1987, and *CRU Metal Monitor: Zinc* (London: Commodities Research Unit Ltd.), December 1987.

[1] Estimated by Commodities Division, IMF Research Department.
[2] World production minus world consumption.
[3] Total commercial stocks measured at end of period.
[4] May not agree with production and consumption data because of differences in coverage.
[5] Commercial stocks measured as weeks of consumption.

1987, however, the increase in world consumption fell to 1 percent. There are also indications that increases in consumption reported elsewhere may have been overstated because of a buildup of unreported consumer stocks. Nevertheless, there was strong consumption growth in a number of developing countries, in particular the newly industrializing countries of Asia, and this growth more than offset the declines in Europe and the United States.

World mine production of zinc is estimated to have increased by over 6 percent in 1987 following a 1 percent decrease in 1986. This increase was mainly attributable to 20 percent growth in Canadian production, despite the strike action. Canadian slab zinc production in 1987, as in 1986, was adversely affected by strike action, however, and remained more than 15 percent below the level of production in 1985. Japanese production of slab zinc also fell sharply in 1986 and 1987. Nevertheless, although world production of slab zinc in 1986 was nearly 2 percent below the level of 1985, in 1987 a 4 percent increase in production was recorded, because large increases in European countries, in the Republic of Korea, and the United States more than offset the reductions in Canada and Japan.

In the near future, unless there are further supply disruptions or stronger-than-expected consumption growth, the pressure of excess capacity should lead to a fall in the price of zinc as the market goes into surplus and stocks increase to normal levels. Zinc prices are expected to decline from the 41 cent level recorded in the first quarter of 1988.

## Lead

During 1987 the price of lead rose to its highest levels since 1981. The price increased by one third from the first to the second quarter of the year, and

## Table 69. Lead: World Commodity Balance, 1981–87

(In thousands of tons)

| | 1981 | 1982 | 1983 | 1984 | 1985 | 1986 | 1987[1] |
|---|---|---|---|---|---|---|---|
| **Mine production** | 3,450 | 3,560 | 3,470 | 3,400 | 3,540 | 3,390 | 3,390 |
| **Refined production** | 5,370 | 5,290 | 5,290 | 5,480 | 5,640 | 5,460 | 5,510 |
| Canada | 240 | 240 | 240 | 250 | 240 | 260 | 230 |
| China | 170 | 170 | 200 | 200 | 210 | 220 | 220 |
| France | 230 | 210 | 200 | 210 | 220 | 230 | 230 |
| Germany, Fed. Rep. of | 350 | 350 | 350 | 360 | 360 | 370 | 370 |
| Japan | 320 | 300 | 320 | 360 | 370 | 360 | 340 |
| United Kingdom | 330 | 310 | 320 | 340 | 330 | 330 | 330 |
| United States | 1,070 | 1,030 | 960 | 1,010 | 1,070 | 910 | 940 |
| U.S.S.R. | 800 | 800 | 800 | 800 | 810 | 790 | 790 |
| Other countries | 1,860 | 1,880 | 1,900 | 1,950 | 2,030 | 1,990 | 2,060 |
| **Consumption** | 5,260 | 5,250 | 5,230 | 5,480 | 5,430 | 5,490 | 5,560 |
| China | 220 | 220 | 220 | 220 | 220 | 230 | 230 |
| France | 210 | 200 | 200 | 210 | 210 | 210 | 200 |
| Germany, Fed. Rep. of | 330 | 330 | 320 | 360 | 340 | 360 | 350 |
| Italy | 260 | 240 | 230 | 230 | 230 | 230 | 240 |
| Japan | 380 | 350 | 360 | 390 | 400 | 390 | 370 |
| United Kingdom | 270 | 270 | 290 | 290 | 270 | 280 | 280 |
| United States | 1,130 | 1,110 | 1,130 | 1,190 | 1,120 | 1,120 | 1,200 |
| U.S.S.R. | 800 | 810 | 810 | 790 | 780 | 760 | 760 |
| Other countries | 1,660 | 1,720 | 1,670 | 1,800 | 1,860 | 1,910 | 1,930 |
| **Market balance[2]** | 110 | 40 | 60 | 0 | 210 | −30 | −50 |
| **Commercial stocks[3,4]** | 490 | 540 | 510 | 410 | 450 | 390 | 320 |
| Stocks/consumption ratio (number of weeks)[5] | 4.8 | 5.3 | 5.1 | 3.9 | 4.3 | 3.7 | 3.0 |

Sources: *World Metal Statistics* (London: World Bureau of Metal Statistics), various issues in 1987, and *CRU Metal Monitor: Lead* (London: Commodities Research Unit Ltd.), December 1987.

[1] Estimated by Commodities Division, IMF Research Department.
[2] World production minus world consumption.
[3] Total commercial stocks measured at end-of-period.
[4] May not agree with production and consumption data because of differences in coverage.
[5] Commercial stocks measured as weeks of consumption.

remained at about nearly 30 U.S. cents a pound through the first quarter of 1988.[88] The improvement in the price of lead in 1987 was largely a reflection of earlier adjustments in the industry to the low price that had prevailed since 1982. In 1986 world mine production of lead declined by 4 percent, and refined lead production declined by 3 percent, while refined lead consumption increased by 1 percent (Table 69). This was the first year since 1979, in which the overall refined lead market was in deficit.

The growth in consumption in 1986 was in large part a result of strong demand for batteries. The proportion of lead output used in the production of batteries has increased from roughly 50 percent at the beginning of 1980 to 60 percent because of reduced demand for lead in other uses, such as petroleum additives, pigments, cables, and alloys. The growth in demand for lead in batteries of roughly 2 percent a year has,

however, helped keep the market stable. Part of the growth in battery demand was attributable to a general increase in automobile production, particularly in the newly industrializing nations, such as Brazil and the Republic of Korea.

The decline in mine production of lead in 1986 to a level similar to that in the late 1960s, was the result of the temporary and permanent mine closures mainly in Australia and the United States. Lower production of refined lead was attributable mainly to the closure of a major smelter in the United States that resulted in a 15 percent reduction in production and also to a 2 percent reduction in production in the U.S.S.R. Commercial lead stocks declined from 450,000 tons at the end of 1985 to 390,000 by the end of 1986, or from 4.3 weeks to 3.7 weeks of world consumption.

The rationalization of excess lead production capacity that occurred in 1986 and earlier years helped to tighten the market in 1987 with refined world consumption exceeding world production. With excess production no longer depressing prices, temporary work stoppages for maintenance and repair and on

___
[88] Price quotations refer to prices on the LME, cash for delivery on the following business day, refined pig, minimum purity 99.97 percent, c.i.f. U. K. ports.

account of strikes created temporarily tight supply situations. The price increase in the second quarter of the year was triggered by a strike in Canada. Although the restructuring of the industry has led to the closure of much excess capacity, as higher prices provide an incentive to expand production, the run-down in stocks should be reversed. Lead prices are expected to weaken from levels experienced at the end of 1987, but to still remain significantly above their 1986 level.

In the period from 1982 to 1985 world trade in lead remained fairly stable. In 1986, however, exports as a percentage of consumption declined mainly because of a reduction, in response to low prices, in production and exports in Australia and Spain. The volume of world trade in lead is estimated to have increased in 1987 as a result of the increase in world consumption and the improved export performance of Australia and Spain.

## Phosphate Rock

In spite of a continuation of low prices for food commodities that resulted in continued weak demand for fertilizer, and consequently for phosphate rock and other mineral ingredients used in fertilizer production, world production of phosphate rock in 1987 increased by 6 percent to 150 million tons. Phosphate rock production in the United States, the world's largest producer and consumer of phosphatic fertilizers, rose by 5 percent to 41 million tons, although it is estimated that U.S. mines continued to operate at only 60 percent of capacity. Production in Morocco rose by 4 percent to 22 million tons.

Weak demand and increased phosphate rock production led to price declines. Morocco lowered its official export price for phosphate rock for calendar year 1987 to $31.00 a ton from $34.80.[89] The unit value of phosphate rock exported by the United States fell to $21 a ton in 1987 from $27 a ton in 1986 (Table 70). The prices of some finished products, however, increased in 1987 as a result of supply adjustments associated with consolidation of operations and plant closures, particularly in the United States. Dollar prices for diammonium phosphate (DAP) and triple superphosphate (TSP) increased by 13 percent and 14 percent, respectively.

The volume of world exports of phosphate rock in 1987 grew by less than 1 percent to over 45 million tons. World exports of phosphoric acid and other phosphatic products (TSP, DAP, and monoammonium phosphate (MAP)) measured in terms of their nutrient value increased by 13 percent to 11 million tons. The volume of U.S. exports of phosphate rock in 1987 increased by 14 percent and exports of phosphate products increased by 13 percent from the low levels recorded in 1986 for both rock and products. The volume of these exports in 1987, however, remained below the levels of 1984 and 1985. Morocco's exports of rock declined by 4 percent in 1987, but exports of products increased by more than 25 percent. The shift toward greater exports of phosphate products relative to exports of phospate rock in recent years has reflected lower primary feedstock costs in countries producing phosphate rock and the comparative cost advantage of transporting finished fertilizers.

Until fertilizer demand recovers, there is little prospect for large increases in the price of phosphate rock. Morocco is expected to begin production of DAP in mid-1988, and this increased capacity should check any tendency for an upward movement in the price of this product.

---

[89] Moroccan rock, 70 percent BPL (bone phosphate of lime), f.a.s. Casablanca.

**Table 70. Phosphate Rock and Products: World Production, Exports, and Market Prices, 1980–87**

| | 1980 | 1981 | 1982 | 1983 | 1984 | 1985 | 1986 | 1987 |
|---|---|---|---|---|---|---|---|---|
| **Production of rock** | | | | | | | | |
| (*in millions of tons*) | **139.0** | **138.0** | **128.0** | **138.9** | **153.8** | **148.4** | **141.8** | **149.8** |
| Morocco | 18.8 | 19.7 | 17.8 | 20.1 | 21.2 | 20.7 | 21.2 | 22.0 |
| United States | 54.4 | 53.6 | 37.4 | 42.6 | 49.2 | 50.8 | 38.7 | 40.8 |
| Other countries | 65.8 | 64.7 | 72.8 | 76.2 | 83.4 | 76.9 | 81.9 | 87.0 |
| **Exports** | | | | | | | | |
| **Rock (*in millions** | | | | | | | | |
| **of tons*)** | **52.3** | **45.8** | **43.7** | **46.4** | **48.1** | **47.1** | **45.0** | **45.3** |
| Morocco | 16.5 | 15.6 | 14.0 | 14.7 | 15.0 | 14.8 | 13.7 | 13.1 |
| United States | 13.9 | 9.9 | 9.2 | 11.3 | 10.5 | 10.3 | 7.8 | 8.9 |
| Other countries | 21.9 | 20.3 | 20.5 | 20.4 | 22.6 | 22.0 | 23.5 | 23.3 |
| **Phosphate products[1]** | | | | | | | | |
| **(*in millions of** | | | | | | | | |
| **tons of nutrients*)** | **7.6** | **7.0** | **7.2** | **8.0** | **10.1** | **10.2** | **9.6** | **10.8** |
| Morocco | 0.5 | 0.7 | 0.9 | 1.2 | 1.3 | 1.3 | 1.4 | 1.8 |
| United States | 4.2 | 3.6 | 3.3 | 3.5 | 4.8 | 4.9 | 3.8 | 4.3 |
| Other countries | 2.9 | 2.7 | 3.0 | 3.3 | 4.0 | 4.0 | 4.4 | 4.7 |
| **Market prices (*in SDRs*)** | | | | | | | | |
| Phosphate rock (*a ton*) | | | | | | | | |
| Morocco | 35.9 | 42.0 | 38.4 | 34.5 | 37.4 | 33.4 | 29.3 | 24.0 |
| United States[2] | ... | ... | ... | ... | 27.5 | 28.5 | 23.0 | 16.5 |
| World fertilizer | | | | | | | | |
| price index[3] | | | | | | | | |
| (1980 = 100) | 100.0 | 104.6 | 99.2 | 96.3 | 103.8 | 94.0 | 79.6 | 72.0 |
| World food price | | | | | | | | |
| index[4] | | | | | | | | |
| (1980 = 100) | 100.0 | 106.9 | 96.8 | 108.8 | 112.5 | 96.1 | 73.1 | 67.9 |
| **Market prices** | | | | | | | | |
| **(*in U.S. dollars*)** | | | | | | | | |
| Phosphate rock (*a ton*) | | | | | | | | |
| Morocco | 46.7 | 49.5 | 42.4 | 36.9 | 38.3 | 33.9 | 34.4 | 31.0 |
| United States[2] | ... | ... | ... | ... | 28.2 | 28.9 | 27.0 | 21.4 |
| World fertilizer | | | | | | | | |
| price index[3] | | | | | | | | |
| (1980 = 100) | 100.0 | 94.7 | 84.1 | 79.1 | 81.7 | 73.3 | 71.7 | 71.5 |
| World food price | | | | | | | | |
| index[4] | | | | | | | | |
| (1980 = 100) | 100.0 | 96.8 | 82.1 | 89.3 | 88.6 | 74.9 | 65.9 | 67.4 |

Sources: U.S. Bureau of Mines for U.S. production; International Fertilizer Industry Associated Ltd. for other production; Fertilizer Economic Studies Limited (FERTECON) for exports; Commodities Division, IMF Research Department for market prices.

[1] Phosphoric acid, TSP, MAR, and DAP.

[2] Average export unit value.

[3] Weighted by relative values from 1983–85, based on export volumes and spot prices: phosphate rock, 35.6 percent; phosphoric acid, 20.5; DAP, 33.5; and TSP, 10.4.

[4] IMF index of prices of food commodities.